D1499077

BUGSY'S BABY

BUGSY'S BABY

The Secret Life of Mob Queen Virginia Hill

Andy Edmonds

A BIRCH LANE PRESS BOOK
Published by Carol Publishing Group

To Popeye
Who was always there
when I needed her

A Birch Lane Press Book
Published by Carol Publishing Group
Birch Lane Press is a registered trademark of Carol Communications, Inc.
Editorial Offices: 600 Madison Avenue, New York, N.Y. 10022
Sales and Distribution Offices: 120 Enterprise Avenue, Secaucus, N.J. 07094
In Canada: Canadian Manda Group, P.O. Box 920, Station U, Toronto, Ontario M8Z
    5P9
Queries regarding rights and permissions should be addressed to Carol Publishing
Group, 600 Madison Avenue, New York, N.Y. 10022

Manufactured in the United States of America

ISBN 1-55972-164-2

Preface

When she told Warren Beatty's Bugsy Siegel to "run outside and jerk yourself a soda," Annette Bening's Virginia Hill captivated movie audiences across America and around the world. Here, most believed, was a brash, brassy, and tough woman who knew how to handle her man and had the world at her feet. What most people do not know, however, is that the real Virginia Hill was far more cunningly ruthless, icy, sexy, fascinating, and tragic than the screen character could even begin to suggest.

In addition to the movie *Bugsy*, Hill has been mentioned in, or has been the subject of, several books and hundreds of newspaper and magazine articles has been the basis for countless fictional characters. Yet many myths, misconceptions, and falsehoods continue to be perpetuated and repeatedly quoted as fact, among them how she actually obtained her powerful position in the underworld, how she kept it, and how she really died. It is fair to say that Hill herself was responsible for most of the fabrications. She was a convincing liar who rarely told the truth about anything and often seemed to have actually believed the tales she spun and repeated.

Virginia Hill was a paradox. She was loved and hated by the wealthy socialites, degraded but feared by those who could not get close to her, courted by the underworld and then ignored by it. Although Hill loved to see her picture in the newspaper and secretly devoured every magazine article written about her, she often attacked reporters in hysterical outbursts of rage. She screamed that she wanted to be left alone but staged repeated suicide attempts to get attention. She posed as a lady of refinement and dignity but could be a vulgar alcoholic who shimmied barefoot in public bars and used language salty enough to make most truck drivers blush.

She repeatedly proved her loyalty to allies in the underworld; fencing stolen property, laundering money without stealing any for herself, keeping confidences, even lying on the witness stand during the 1951 Estes Kefauver congressional hearings on organized crime. She put her life on the line numerous times. In the end, she was publicly ridiculed, her face splashed at the top of an IRS "Most Wanted" poster, stripped of her money and possessions, and booted out of the country. Those in the underworld she called her friends, the people for whom she lied and lost everything, abruptly denounced her, declared her Mafia *persona non grata*, and eventually silenced her.

She called "Bugsy" Siegel the soul of her existence, "Baby Blue Eyes," the only man she ever loved. Together they wrote flowery poetry, built the flashy Flamingo Hotel in Las Vegas, and talked of growing old as a couple. But when she learned of an assassination plot that targeted him, Hill packed her bags and ran to Paris, leaving Siegel to die alone in the house they shared. There are even some who staunchly believe she was in on the hit.

For nearly three decades she consorted with and plotted against some of the most notorious underworld figures of New York, Chicago, Los Angeles, and Las Vegas: New York bosses Meyer Lansky, Charles "Lucky" Luciano, and part-time lover Joey Adonis; Chicago crime lords Charles Fischetti and Jack Dragna, who came to the West Coast to rule Los Angeles, fueling a simmering gang war between New York and the Capone mob; and L.A. bookie Mickey Cohen, gambling lord Tony "Strella" Cornero, and Ben "Bugsy" Siegel.

Poorly educated and possessing a gratingly shrill and squeaky voice, she certainly rose above her station. The most respected and high-ranking politicians often considered it an honor to dine with her. Hill even claimed that several Washington senators paid her handsomely for a night's frolic under the sheets. The Hollywood crowd made a point of being seen with her, especially when she teamed up with Bugsy Siegel, turning her and the Bug into Tinseltown royalty. When bored with them all, she would wave them away with a brush of her hand, loudly toss out a snide remark, or abruptly stand up and walk away. Her minions always came back until it was no longer fashionable to do so.

One of the most difficult jobs in writing this book was sorting through a mass of information, separating fact from fantasy while trying to present a portrait of Virginia Hill that has not been seen before. My reportorial networking in Los Angeles and Chicago led me to a key source of information—Virginia Hill's diary. The diary turned up in Chicago, hidden away in the original brown butcher paper in which Hill had wrapped it and mailed it to a safe deposit box more than twenty-five years ago. The book is nearly complete, spanning the period from Hill's first association with Siegel to approximately six months after his assassination. The diary proved what only a few suspected: This seemingly illiterate, wisecracking southern waif was one of the most calculating, treacherous, and manipulating women ever born. The diary pulls everything into sharp focus and explains how she managed to hold the deadliest of men in the palm of her hand.

The diary also exposes the truth about her curious death in Austria. Though officially declared a suicide, those who knew her suspected otherwise. The diary reveals the shocking truth behind her relationship with top mobsters and offers strong evidence that she died at the hands of the mob. The diary clearly indicates that Hill had calculated a shakedown that led to her death.

In addition to the diary, I also had the good fortune of finding several people who knew Hill personally and could offer firsthand accounts of her activities rather than hearsay stories that would have been impossible to verify. I also had at my disposal historical documents that offer detailed accounts of underworld operations in Chicago and Los Angeles from 1930 through 1959, the period in which Hill had risen through the Mafia hierarchy. The documents shed new light on the corruption as well as the control of hoodlums of that era—not only those who became notorious for their criminal activity but crooked and venal politicians and city officials as well. The documents clearly illustrate how the time was right for a Virginia Hill to exist.

A valuable source of information continues to be personal contacts both "above" and "below" the law in Los Angeles and Chicago. Some of these people had helped in one of my previous books, *Hot Toddy*, which exposed the mob infiltration of Hollywood in the 1930s and offered convincing evidence that the so-called accidental death of actress Thelma Todd was a "Big Julie" contract hit ordered by Lucky Luciano. Several spoke to me on the promise that, in exchange for information, their names would be kept confidential. I considered that a trust, kept my word then, and will continue to do so now. (My basic belief is that when someone in the underworld volunteers to answer personal questions but asks for no credit, his story is of great value simply because he gets absolutely nothing out of it. It's a safe assumption that he has no ulterior motive in giving up several hours of free time. But someone who asks for credit could be suspect because it can be implied he is talking just to see his name in print.) Since the publication of *Hot Toddy* in 1989, other new sources have come forward, verified the conclusions of that book, and volunteered new information for this one.

In addition to interviewing sources in Los Angeles, New York, Las Vegas, and Chicago who knew the key players—Virginia Hill, Joey Adonis, Ben Siegel, Al Capone, Lucky Luciano, Joe Epstein, Jack Dragna, and Johnny Roselli—I took great care to comb through city and county documents, newspapers, and police records. This was perhaps the most tedious aspect of putting the book together, but by doing so, I was able to verify the stories and the conclusions drawn by many of the people I had interviewed. By the time I was ready to write, I clearly had enough information for several books and tried to train the focus of this one on "new" information about Virginia Hill and why and how she achieved her phenomenal power.

I also made it a point to explore files and sources that had not been tapped by other writers or historians. I searched for, and found, so-called lost files from the Los Angeles Police Department and government documents (both local and federal) that shed light on the dealings of the gangsters and Hill's role in their operations. I tried to limit my interviews to people who had firsthand information but had not given numerous interviews. I have found that in past research these people have altered their stories to fit the writer's interpretations, often so much so that the truth has been twisted or completely lost. I believe I have uncovered fresh anecdotes as well as information that is as untainted as possible.

Parts of history will be rewritten in this book, sometimes completely contradicting previous notions. Most of what follows has been confirmed by what writers often call the "two-source rule." When information was given, it was independently verified without prompting or it was not considered valid. What could not be substantiated is attributed when it is mentioned.

To understand Hill and her rise through the ranks of the mob, it is necessary to also understand the men she knew and how they achieved power in the times in which they lived. A portion of this book lays out the history of the Chicago and New York mobs and the cities in which they operated. I believe that to fully understand the how and the why of Virginia Hill, and to draw as complete and accurate a picture of Hill and her era as possible, one must get a working knowledge of these men and their operations.

Virginia Hill has left behind a bizarre legacy. One side of her nature is colored by everything corrupt and despicable—lust, greed, murder, and power; the other is a blend of compassion, love of life, and loyalty to family and friends. Hill ran the gamut of life—soaring to the loftiest of social and powerful positions, only to die broke, abandoned, and desperate. She was envied and despised, loved and hated, used and abused. The underworld treated her as a subservient woman. Only a few considered her an equal. But all underestimated her.

Hill was in the right place at the right time. A Virginia Hill could not exist today because the mob, as she knew it, has since lost much of its stranglehold on the country. No woman will ever share her place in gangland history. Virginia Hill was, and will remain, a legend.

Acknowledgments

From the time I first heard of Virginia Hill to the moment the last page of this book was written, many people have come forward and offered their help, their stories, and personal recollections, opening doors and pointing me in the right direction. Some have asked to remain completely anonymous; others granted interviews and provided information under the condition they be identified in the text only as "a friend of _____" with no name given; others gave no stipulation. I thank them all, including:

Robert Gottlieb of the William Morris Agency, who struck the match that ignited the fire; Jen Stulgis and Robert Fuesel of the Chicago Crime Commission, who provided a wealth of information; the staffs of the Chicago Historical Society and Newberry Library; the staffs of the UCLA Main Research Library, Glendale Public Library, Los Angeles Main Library, USC Research Library; Bill Kinney of the *Marietta* (Georgia) *Daily Journal*; Mary and Ray Ingersoll; actress Rose Marie; Steve Rodrigues; Ward Farrell of the Las Vegas Flamingo Hilton Hotel; Dr. Lorraine Blakeman; Susan Javis of the Las Vegas Gambling Research Center; Frank Wright of the Nevada Historical Society; former Los Angeles Police Department officer Danny Galindo; Louise Sheffield, retired from the Department of Justice; author John Gilmore; Holly Jones; the City of Los

Angeles Mayor's Office; the Los Angeles District Attorney's Office; Skip Brezinski; Nancy Davis, Academy of Motion Picture Arts and Sciences; the staff of the Hollywood Park racetrack; Charlie Parsons and Martin Schwartz of the Federal Bureau of Investigation; J. Kevin O'Brien of the Freedom of Information Privacy Acts Division of the FBI; Marguerite Collins, Pete Noyes, Jerry Kaufman, Jack Pignataro, "KJ" Stimpson, Harry Brescelli, and Tony Stipone, and the thirteen men and women both "above" and "below" the law who spoke to me, obtained "unobtainable" files, and guided me anonymously but opened a major door.

Thanks to Ira "Bud's for You" Fellner for "Second Base."

And special thanks to my mom and dad for "the leg work."

BUGSY'S BABY

1

WANTED. For Federal Income Tax Evasion.

"Virginia Hill Hauser—Alias Virginia D'Algy, Dalgy, Watson, Juan Dietah, Dagby, Reid, Onie Brown, Betty Hood, Ona V. Hill, O. V. Hall, Mrs. W. Hall, Mrs. Norma Hall, Mrs. Onie V. Reid, Mrs. H. Harper, Mrs. Hunn, Mrs. Jamison, Mrs. J. H. Herman, Mrs. Ona Virginia Herman, Mrs. V. Herman, Mrs. J. H. Hoff.

Description: White; female; age 39; height 5' 4"; 130 pounds; complexion fair; hair auburn; eyes gray.

Nationality American; born Lipscomb, Alabama, August 26, 1916. Last known address in United States was Spokane, Washington.

Virginia Hill Hauser was indicted on June 23, 1954, by a federal Grand Jury at Los Angeles, California, for federal income tax evasion. At the time of her indictment she was reportedly residing in Klosters, Switzerland. She is presently married to an Austrian-born ski instructor, Hans Hauser, and has a five-year-old son, Peter Jackson Hauser. Virginia Hill Hauser was formerly a paramour and associate of gangsters and racketeers.

Please furnish any information which may assist in locating this individual to the Director, Intelligence Division, Internal Revenue Service, Washington 25, D.C., or the Assistant Regional Commissioner, Intelligence, which is nearest your city.

Issued December 1, 1955 by: J. Perry August, Director, Intelligence Division."

And so read the "Wanted" poster that was printed by the tens of thousands and prominently displayed in every post office, city hall, police department, and government office from California to New York. Less than five years earlier, Hill had been the darling of the media, with her flippant and arrogant lies before the Senate Kefauver hearings on organized crime, the woman who had flashed furs and diamonds and casually dropped the name of every top-ranking hood in America. In addition to her own spicy testimony, Hill's name had been mentioned on the stand by gangsters at least fifteen times and called everything from a "nice gal" to "southern white trash" by these nefarious men who claimed they operated clothing stores or sold office supplies. She was front-page news, sizzling copy for newspapers all over the world and every national magazine.

Virginia Hill was the epitome of a gangster's moll—gun toting, wisecracking, glamorous and sexy, and most of all, rich. Her name was familiar in nearly every household in America; women hated her, men fantasized about her, and the government vowed to destroy her.

When the IRS issued its Wanted poster, it made sure Virginia Hill would become the country's favorite pinup girl. It declared her number three on its "Most Wanted" list. In a matter of months the two on the list ahead of her (both men) had been apprehended, leaving a bitter and angry Hill as America's number-one tax evader, a position that brought national ridicule and isolation to a woman who said she was just "doing her job" and "helping her friends."

The government claimed she owed more than $80,000 in back taxes. Hill claimed she owed nothing; in fact, the government, she insisted, owed her tax refunds for 1944 and 1945. She was wanted on both civil and federal tax and fraud charges and faced five years in jail and a $10,000 penalty on top of the back taxes owed. Treasury agents called Hill "the female Al Capone" and joked about knocking her down the same way federal agents took care of Capone two decades before.

Virginia finally fled the country with nothing more than the little she carried on her back and the wealth of damaging information she carried in her head. The latter, she believed, would compensate for the former.

Within government circles Hill's name became synonymous with a string of jokes and double entendres. They joked about "hill climbing," "mounting Virginia's hill," and "going over the hill" and hummed "Carry Me Back to Old Virginny" when they schemed about finding a loophole in the law to extradite her back to the United States. (Income-tax evasion was not and is not an extraditable offense.) Agents swapped stories, some truthful, others malicious lies, about her numerous affairs with gangsters and politicians and outdid one another in details of her sexual prowess.

Hill also faced far worse than the clutches of the feds. The men she had consorted and slept with, trusted, and lied for, were now out to get her. The mob's number-one moll had become the country's number-one lawbreaker, and to the underworld, any publicity was bad publicity. They knew Virginia had a vindictive nature and a smart mouth when pressed, and those close to her realized it was only a matter of time before she would break—and talk.

Her hunch that the mob would pay for her silence must have paid off, because Hill and her ski instructor–husband, Herman Johann "Hans" Hauser, seemed to have an inexhaustible cash supply. They traveled across Europe in expensive cars, lived in luxury hotels and apartments, draped themselves in jewelry. But try as they might, they were never quite absorbed into European society. The constant crush of reporters always ignited Hill's violent temper, which, in turn, drove away the more dignified and wealthy socialites.

Hill vowed revenge. She wrote a close associate in Chicago that she would "destroy those fucking jerks who ruined me" and that she would "have the last say" and "make all them know what they done." Hill had always been known to keep her promises.

Twelve years later, she was found dead near a footpath by a brook in Koppl, a small village near Salzburg, Austria. Her death was at first ruled a heart attack; then the local coroner changed the cause of death to suicide—an overdose of pills, a poisoning. There was supposedly a note left near the body, allegedly written by Virginia, claiming that she was "tired of life." Case closed, the cause of death accepted as fact by the general public.

Though her life appeared to many to be in ruins, at the end the alleged suicide seemed unlikely for a woman who had been privy to the secret dealings of the New York, Chicago, Los Angeles, and Las Vegas underworld; information the U.S. government would certainly have made generous concessions to obtain and which the gangsters would stop at nothing to suppress.

Virginia Hill was a tough and cunning woman, a fighter, a master at timing who knew how to seize an opportunity to her best advantage. She was apparently bargaining with the underworld, offering to sell, and threatening to expose, highly incriminating information that had at least one top mobster very concerned. It was common knowledge in both the Mafia and law enforcement circles that Hill had in her possession the tools to destroy the East Coast mob and send the Chicago outfit tumbling like a house of cards. Hill would not have committed suicide while she still had several cards left to play. Suicide seemed the least credible end to a colorful career that took forty-nine years to shape and build.

Virginia Hill was born at a turbulent time in an uncertain America, a country whose citizens had begun to accept hoodlums as community leaders, where thugs seized control of city streets and elected politicians on all levels answered to gang lords, and where the haves and have-nots were quite often separated by the barrel of a gun. For the ambitious it was a matter of being in the right place at the right time and knowing how to seize each opportunity. Virginia Hill was a self-made woman who knew how to do just that.

Certainly it seemed that Virginia's early life offered no indication of the nefarious and glamorous future that lay ahead. Born Onie Virginia Hill on August 26, 1916, she was the seventh of ten children of W. M. "Mack" Hill, a poor Lipscomb, Alabama, horse and mule trader and livery-stable operator. Locals considered Mack a sharp businessman, when sober, inasmuch as he knew how to set up and play out a fast con, selling livestock for more than fair value and often skimming the profits for himself. Virginia, who detested him, said he rarely used the extra money to help feed the family; instead, he squandered it away on bourbon, women, and low-life bar friends. Mack viciously beat his children and his wife, Margaret, when he was either drunk or hung over. And he was usually one or the other.

To try and ease some of the financial burden from her husband, Margaret Hill went to work, picking up odd jobs and factory employment whenever and wherever she could and allowing her husband to raise the children and to fend for themselves. Her motives were strictly financial, and those who knew her said that she did love her family, at least in the beginning.

But Mack's drunken rages continued and escalated, possibly due to the confinement with children in a small house. Mack complained that the four-room ramshackle house was too small for a growing family and blamed his outbursts on their cramped quarters. A short time after Virginia was born, the Hills moved to Bessemer, a little town several miles from Lipscomb. While Mack continued to ply his trade, Margaret Hill operated a boardinghouse. Life for the family only got worse as Mack's periods of sobriety grew shorter and his attacks more virulent.

Virginia claimed she was most often the recipient of her father's drunken attacks. Being rather small, unkempt, and willowy as a child, she seemed the least likely of the clan to fight back. And in the beginning she quietly took the beatings, more or less by accepting them as her due. In fact, her brothers nicknamed her "Tab," after a tabby cat, because of her passive demeanor and helpless, waiflike looks. Her mother, always a proper, old-fashioned woman, had taught Virginia that the man rules the home and that what abuse he may dish out is to be accepted and kept within the confines of the four familial walls.

But sometime around age seven the demure tabby kitten developed claws and lashed back. Virginia no longer accepted the role of her father's personal punching bag. One evening, Mack came home drunk, with fire in his eyes, and headed straight toward Virginia. Virginia grabbed the first thing she saw, an iron skillet still sizzling from sausage grease, and whacked her father across his chest. As he reeled from the attack, Virginia taunted him and defied him to come near her again. Mack stepped back and vented his rage on Margaret with a stream of verbal obscenities and a solid hit across her face.

Margaret took the beating from Mack, but he never struck Virginia again.

Years later, Virginia told an associate in Chicago that the skillet incident marked the first time she ever stood up to anyone. She recalled that she was afraid at first, but once she saw how quickly her father crumbled and how much he seemed to fear her after that, she knew that she would not take such abuse again. Virginia said her biggest fear at that time was that she would lose the love of her father. But once she hit him, she realized she had lost nothing, because, she felt, there was nothing there to lose. At that moment, she had understood that for her men were only to be used, as they had used women, and she could not allow herself to be put in an emotionally vulnerable position. She would never love a man.

Virginia's formal education went no further than eighth grade, but the time she spent in Roberts Grammar School apparently made an impression. One teacher remembered Tab as a "sweet child, not too interested in her studies, but never caused any problems in class." She also said that Tab used to bring in a slice of pie on occasion instead of the usual "apple for the teacher." Tab was well liked, quiet, and seemed preoccupied with dreams of life outside her small town.

She was forced to do whatever she could to help support her brothers—Billy (called "Cotton" because of his shock of white-blond hair), Robert, James, John, Karl, and Charles (nicknamed "Chick")—and sisters: Ruth, Beatrice, and Toots. Virginia was closest to Cotton and Chick, for whom she acted as both best friend and mother and supported in later years.

Margaret finally took the children and walked out on Mack in the mid-1920s, returning to her hometown of Marietta, Georgia. There she was close to a sister and a cousin as well as her mother, Mrs. J. P. Reid, a feisty, independent woman who chopped cotton until she was eighty-six years old. Margaret was determined to make it without the man Virginia would later refer to only as a "drunken fucking bum." Margaret taught Virginia another big lesson in life: Never depend on any man for either financial or emotional support; depend only on yourself. Virginia carried this lesson with her throughout her life.

Mack moved to Acworth which was near Marietta and ran a

livery stable, continued to drink, and saw his wife only on sporadic visits. The two never formally filed for divorce, though
they remained legally separated.

Margaret supported herself at a Marietta hosiery mill run by
Frank Owenby. Virginia also worked while she lived with her
mother—cooking and cleaning while helping to raise her siblings. What brief childhood Virginia had hoped to enjoy disintegrated as she reluctantly took on adult roles and responsibilities while still a youngster barely in her teens. Virginia later
told several friends that she felt abandoned by her father and
that men could never be trusted to stay the course. Without
anyone to turn to, she drew even closer to her brothers Cotton
and Chick.

This was a major turning point in Virginia's troubled young
life. She withdrew from anyone who tried to get close and further solidified her "emotional brick wall" and aloof attitude.
She seemed to adopt a carefree, will-o'-the-wisp demeanor that
both intrigued strangers and kept them at a distance. She
believed that there were no true loyalties in life, that anyone
and everyone would abandon her if given a chance, that the
best way to live was to do as one pleased and form no close
attachments. So far there had been nothing in her life to dispel
those notions.

Though she had only a basic education, she inherited her
father's business instinct and schemed to get food and money
by promising to work (which she rarely did) or sold sexual
favors (which she often did). Even as a young girl, sex to Virginia
was nothing more than a means to achieving her goals—money
and notoriety.

But Tab was not all business and no play. By the time she was
twelve, Virginia was quite buxom, her once-thin lips rounded
out into a sexy pout, her waiflike appearance matured into a sul-
try appeal. The tabby kitten had blossomed into a sex kitten.
And she knew it. Virginia swept through Marietta wearing halter tops and short shorts and flashed her eyes at local boys, who
gleefully followed her everywhere. She said she did her best to
arouse the boys and rarely said no to any boy who asked for sex.
The Virginia Hill who captured and held the most deadly of
men in the palm of her hand and sent the most righteous beg-

ging for sexual favors had begun to emerge. But her fiery temper and sharp tongue were still simmering just beneath the surface.

Bill Kinney of the *Marietta Daily Journal* knew Virginia in her later years. He said locals remember young Hill as a "quiet, sweet school girl" but one who rode horses through town scantily clad (which earned her the nickname "Lady Godiva"), bounced more often than necessary on the diving board at Marietta's Brumby Center swimming pool while the young boys watched, and climbed Kennesaw Mountain barefoot. According to Kinney, Hill said she even once made love on top of Kennesaw Mountain but would never offer more details than that. The story seems consistent with tales of childhood sexual conquests that Hill later spun around Chicago. By the time Virginia was fourteen, she had the physical attributes and the sexual experience of a woman way beyond her years.

What happened next in Virginia's life is a mixture of supposition, fantasy, and confusion. Virginia often told underworld associates that when she was fourteen or fifteen, she married a man named George Rogers, from whom she inherited a great deal of money, supposedly around $50,000. But she refused to elaborate and continually brushed off further questions with a flat and unemotional statement: "He's dead, so let's not go into it." Virginia then later denied ever marrying anyone named Rogers.

There is no state, county, or city record of any early marriage between Virginia Hill and any man in Georgia or Alabama, nor is there a record of an annulment or divorce. Nor did a search of these records reveal any indication that George Rogers filed a will that went into probate and listed Virginia Hill as the recipient of anything, let alone $50,000.

The mystery deepens because there is serious doubt whether the name George Rogers is correct. Virginia Hill repeatedly told reporters that she was "god-awful with names." Virginia's sister Ruth told reporters in 1948 that she remembered Virginia's running off with a George Brown. A later inquiry to a federal investigative agency hired by the FBI in the 1960s had uncovered a record that showed Hill had married a "George Randell" in a quick ceremony performed by a justice of the peace in Alabama. But even this tale is vague, though Randell allegedly played an important part in her life after she left Georgia.

No matter who Randell was, or if he existed, one thing was certain: Teenage Virginia Hill always seemed to have money to pay her own way, to buy perfume and makeup and drugstore sodas. This all took place at the start of the Great Depression, when the squeeze of a deteriorating economy was sharply felt as thousands of people lost jobs and homes and families disintegrated. Virginia was reportedly unaffected by any economic crisis and carried on as if she had a financial backer.

Virginia always prided herself on the fact that she could parlay "a buck into a bundle," as she later put it, just by flashing her smile and enticing the boys into believing they would get their money's worth at the end. Sometimes they did; sometimes they didn't. However she obtained her mysterious financial stake, it was enough to create a facade of wealth and adopt the attitudes of high society that later helped her hobnob with the social elite.

The wild teenager believed her life was stuck in low gear and that she needed to move on. She claimed she found the Marietta boys dull, with outdated and old-fashioned attitudes. Virginia Hill knew she was a big-city girl at heart, with a love for the fast life that she had only read about in books or heard about in hushed gossip. She realized that if she was going to do anything with her life, she had to shake off the shackles of provincial Georgia.

Virginia was torn between her obligations to her family and an ever-increasing desire to hunt "bigger game," Virginia's term for rich men, in a distant, bigger city where she could invent a past life and no one would be the wiser. She considered running away to New York City but was put off by stories of poverty, tough street gangs, and European immigrant ghettos. Hill believed that that city was beyond her conquest and felt she would be swallowed up and lost there, especially in the tough times of the depression.

She looked toward Chicago, a metropolis with a midwestern "country town" attitude in which people were friendly but one that still had everything a big city could offer, and more.

Even with daily news reports of thousands upon thousands of men and women starving and struggling, unlike New York, Chicago had garnered a reputation as being "the city that works." Many of those who wanted to live in Chicago found sporadic jobs in building and construction or were placed on the city payroll through patronage jobs doled out by ward aldermen in exchange for votes. Those unable to find work were fed in the scores of soup kitchens, many of which were used as fronts and money-laundering scams for Al Capone. But the kitchens offered a constant flow of hot meals and good company in exchange for the "proper" vote at election time.

Work was only part of the lure. A country desperate for diversion had descended upon Chicago to spend its spare change at a massive and gaudy world's fair billed as the "Biggest Carnival in the World"—called by Chicagoans "The Century of Progress Exhibition."

In 1933, seventeen-year-old Virginia Hill left the confines of her Marietta, Georgia, town in the hope of finding excitement in the Windy City. She found that excitement, and far more, when she maneuvered herself into the center of two warring factions: Al "Scarface" Capone's gang in Chicago and Charles "Lucky" Luciano's New York mob. For the last several years the two megaMobsters had been building their empires on the corpses of their enemies. They now were poised for a final showdown.

The two mobs were vying for power, and through a combination of luck and drive, Virginia landed in the perfect position to rise through the ranks of both factions by playing one side against the other. She began her climb with the deadliest and the most notorious group of criminals, the gang of Al Capone.

2

Just as the 1930s have proved to be the most profitable decade for Chicago's vice lords, the 1920s stand as the bloodiest in the city's history. Al Capone was the man who called the shots and reaped the rewards. Through his influence over a bought and paid for police department and state legislature, Capone gang rivals had either been murdered, jailed, or intimidated, which cleared a path for Capone's complete and total domination of every industry, union, and business in Chicago and its suburbs. Once the city and suburbs had knuckled under, Big Al set his sights on a loftier goal: domination of the entire country. Capone's dream of nationwide omnipotence began with two coldly calculated maneuvers plotted to further his megalomaniacal ambitions.

Shoot-outs, drive-by shootings, sedans spinning around corners with their machine guns blazing, and bloody corpses in alleys and gutters had all become commonplace in Chicago by the mid-1920s. In November 1924, Capone ordered the assassination of his archrival, North Side gang boss Dion O'Banion, whose death ignited two years of murderous vengeance by O'Banion's gang, now the "Bugs" Moran gang, which in turn touched off a slew of ethnic as well as territorial gang wars: North Side against South Side, produce peddlers fighting butchers, the Loop area against Cicero, and subsequently, Jews against Irish, Irish against Italians.

The gang wars reached their zenith in 1925, when more than five hundred murders were recorded by the Chicago Police Department; most were believed to be gang related, but few were prosecuted. Capone accepted the brunt of the blame for most of the bloodletting, claiming that as unofficial "ruler" of Chicago it was his responsibility to see that "these gangsters stay in line," as he phrased it in a *Chicago Tribune* interview. The gang wars captured national headlines, which affected tourism, building and construction, and business in general. People were afraid to venture out on the streets, shopped only if they had to, and then only in neighborhood stores. For the underworld, that meant trouble. A dollar a citizen kept in his pocket meant a dollar kept out of gangsters' coffers. Capone realized that the city was out of control.

On October 26, 1926, Big Al called for a citywide peace conference and ordered every local gang lord to attend.

The only gangster who defied the call was Hymie Weiss, a member of the North Side Bugs Moran gang, which refused to abide by anything Al Capone or his thugs demanded. Weiss sent back a note to his nemesis with a stream of misspelled expletives and a vow to enter the meeting with guns blazing and hand grenades exploding, killing everyone who showed up. Capone later said that Weiss was a "mad dog . . . that when a dog's got rabies, nobody's safe . . . the dumb thing's just gotta be killed." Weiss was assassinated ten days later, gunned down on the steps of the Holy Name Cathedral. No one in the city ever again said no to Scarface Al's call for peace or any other demand.

Capone's chief accountant, Jake Guzik, a fat, slovenly whoremaster who maintained a string of First Ward brothels, supervised the meeting, along with Maxie Eisen, who collected vigorish from every produce peddler and street merchant within the city limits. Capone steered clear of the meeting; he believed his presence might antagonize other gang leaders and further incite bloodshed. Guzik and Eisen laid out the Capone plan: The city would be divvied up according to the territory each boss currently dominated, but each gang lord would be ordered to stick to his turf and pay a tariff when shipping goods through another gangster's section. As a concession to peace,

Capone even bargained away pieces of his territory to more clearly define the boundaries. There was only one proviso: Any dispute would be brought to Capone, and his decision would be binding.

The meeting broke up with back patting, hand shaking, and a standing ovation for Guzik and Eisen. Each boss felt confident that the warring had ended, prosperity was secure, and the gangs would grow even wealthier. All agreed that Al Capone was a smart negotiator, but some chuckled that he needlessly sold off parts of his kingdom, which could eventually cost him hundreds of thousands of dollars in kickbacks and payoffs.

But Capone's generous offer proved a shrewd maneuver. Gang wars stopped for two months. Capone took the credit. He was quickly recognized by newspapers and lawmakers around the country as the supreme negotiator and leader of Chicago. The power and prestige of the other city gang lords diminished considerably, along with their influence with lawmakers and law enforcement. Though the peace was fragile and eventually shattered, Capone won the war in his city, and to the victor went the spoils.

But his rise to dominance did not go unnoticed by vice lords in other cities, notably New York, where Lucky Luciano, Meyer Lansky, Frank Costello, Joe Adonis, and Ben Siegel had joined together to take over portions of the city's gambling, drug, and prostitution rackets. Of the five, the one who kept an especially close eye on Capone was Luciano, who had a long-standing childhood vendetta against the Chicago gangster.

Luciano and his friends began their criminal activities as part of a Brooklyn street gang called the Five Pointers, to which Capone had initially belonged. Capone and Luciano were instant and avowed mortal enemies, part of a centuries-old hatred that pitted Sicilians, such as Luciano, against Neapolitans like Capone. Luciano often taunted Capone and ridiculed him for both his weight and bloodline. The two frequently had to be separated and often came within inches of murdering one another.

The feud came to a head one evening around 1910. During a frequent gang nighttime prowl the two ended up in a knife fight with a rival gang. One boy was killed; other gang members were sliced up. Luciano pinned the blame on Capone, who took it and was thereafter labeled a "chump" by Luciano, Lansky, Costello, and the gang.

Capone fled to Chicago and was quickly rescued from disgrace by Chicago gangster Johnny Torrio, who sized up the chubby youngster as a conscienceless killer and immediately put him to work as an executioner. "Big Jim" Colisimo, Torrio's uncle, ran the North Side and was considered by nearly everyone to be the crime commander of Chicago. He became Capone's first assignment, the hit ordered by Torrio in a power play. Capone's ruthlessness garnered Torrio's respect and earned him a place as his right-hand gunsel. It was during this time as Torrio's bodyguard that Capone received scars from a knife fight and earned him the nickname Scarface Al. Capone then inherited Torrio's territory when the elder gangster survived a near-fatal assassination attempt and retired.

Though Capone had his own city, respect, and power and was believed to be one of the richest men in the country by 1925, his hatred never strayed far from Luciano. He vowed he would have his revenge, muscle into New York, and humiliate Luciano before ordering his bloody and painful torture and death. Capone even laid out to associates details of how he would do away with Luciano and claimed he would gleefully perform most of the torture himself. He broadcast his threats loudly and frequently, knowing they would reach Luciano.

The other ill will that festered between Capone and the New Yorkers also stemmed from bloodlines. The Mafia had been, and continues to be, a Sicilian-backed organization, with strict initiation rules. Though they can achieve power within the Mafia, non-Italians, more specifically non-Sicilians, could not become "made" and were therefore never considered official Mafia members. Luciano and Costello were made. Capone never could be made, which gnawed at "Big Al" and delighted Luciano. But even without the formal backing of the Mafia, Capone achieved and held as much, if not more, power than his New York archrival. The two were headed for a showdown that would pit Chicago against New York.

Capone went gunning for Luciano. He boasted that if he could establish peace in a city as volatile as Chicago, he could secure the same climate between gangs in the rest of the country. He relayed his grandiose scheme to the newspapers and on radio and repeated his message often enough that everyone, from politicians to the general public, eventually believed him and bought into his plan. A typical interview with Scarface Al appeared in 1929 in the *Chicago Tribune*.

> Put me in charge, let me sit in as the big boss, like I did in Chicago, and find a workable solution. Things are too divided up right now. No one's in charge and everybody trying to be. We're businessmen. Like everyone else we have to have a board of directors. And someone to sit at the head of the table.

Finding peace nationwide would not prove so easy. New York alone had more gangs and "families" vying for control than Chicago. Other large cities—Philadelphia, Detroit, New Orleans, Miami, Kansas City, Cleveland, and Atlantic City— were completely gang controlled. Luciano had even begun to use members of Detroit's Purple Gang as his "enforcers," his personal assassination squad, and expanded his reach to Capone's backyard.

Frank Costello realized something had to be done to steal the thunder from Capone and keep Chicago from usurping power from the New York cartel. He knew that if Capone became the boss and won the support of the public and press, Luciano would be forced into a nationwide gang war. Costello also knew that such a war would be bloody and destructive to the operations of the underworld. There was also a growing fear that an unknown power, such as other ethnic or foreign gangs, could squeeze the Mafia, putting it out of business. Better a known enemy than one that was unknown. Costello called the underworld leaders together in Atlantic City.

Costello had the respect of every top mafioso. He had only one blot on his record: a charge of carrying a gun, for which he served one year in prison. He was a ruthless bootlegger when Prohibition made rum-running highly profitable. He worked his way through the ranks by remaining loyal to Luciano and Joe "the Boss" Masseria, whose "untimely" death cleared the way for Costello's rise to power. He was clever, and he had power.

On May 9, 1929, Capone and his triggerman Frankie Rio arrived in New Jersey and met with gangland representatives from nearly every major city in America, including Max "Boo Boo" Hoff of Pennsylvania; Joe Masseria, the overlord of the East Coast; Leo Lepke; Joe Adonis; Dutch Schultz from New York; Enoch "Nucky" Joynson of Atlantic City; Abe Bernstein of Detroit's notorious Purple Gang; and a dozen other thugs, including Costello. Luciano steered clear of the gathering to avoid a clash with Capone, much the same tactic Capone had used in Chicago.

Though Costello called the meeting together, it was Capone's show from the beginning. He seized control of the meeting and laid out plans to take over as head of the underworld. He divvied up legitimate industry as well as gambling, labor rackets, extortion, and drugs and called for a nationally controlled "assassination squad," armed and ready, at the beck and call of the gang lords.

Prostitutes would be swapped across state lines in the same fashion that "business" merchandise was shipped. There would be open communication between the factions, especially between New York and Chicago, and any major dispute would be settled in conference instead of on the streets. Narcotics trafficking would be expanded into a national network, with the base of operations in South America and Cuba, where labor was cheap and drug manufacturing legal—for a price.

The mobsters agreed to Capone's plan. The Mafia solidified into one body, but details of the hierarchy were yet to be worked out. Capone was once again hailed as a clever businessman and shrewd mediator by the press, to which specific (and generally peace-oriented) details of the meeting had been deliberately leaked. The public was led to believe that the conference was a call to lay down arms and disband the terrorism of the gang world. The true purpose of the meeting—to divide territories, infiltrate legitimate business, organize racketeering and drug importation and dealing—was kept confidential for many years.

Many people who have devoted their life to studying the underworld have all drawn the same conclusion from the peace conference in Atlantic City. They claim that if one could pinpoint a specific time in which the structure of the Mafia metamorphosed from thousands of warring street gangs into several well-organized "families," May 9, 1929, would stand as the turning point.

One week after the conference, Capone and Rio arranged for their own arrest through Pennsylvania mobster Max Hoff. Capone had become a marked man after an incident in a northern Indiana club in which he savagely beat three of his own gunsels who had failed in an assassination plot against him. Luciano had also made threats against Capone and Rio after the peace conference, calling literally for "open hunting season" on the pair. With Luciano's threat as an incentive, their murder would have elevated any hood into a place of honor in the underworld. Johnny Torrio convinced Capone that the safest place to hide out until the heat cooled was in prison, as long as it was a "friendly" one, that is, a jail where the warden was on the mob's payroll.

Rio and Capone, who had never carried a pistol, each put one in his pocket so that the police had grounds to arrest them when they picked them up in a Philadelphia movie house. Capone and Rio were given a one-year sentence in Holmesburg County Jail. It was understood that Hoff could arrange their release if they changed their mind.

The prison term proved one of Capone's smartest maneuvers. Safe from rival gangs, police harassment, and nosy reporters, Capone and his goons were free to organize and plan. Frequent visitors were Capone's brother Ralph, accountant Jake Guzik, and enforcer Frank Nitti, the heir apparent to Capone's empire.

Capone set up a board of directors: Johnny Torrio became senior adviser. Sharing the responsibilities of supervising the various business and financial operations of the gang were Nitti, Guzik, Ralph Capone, Paul "the Waiter" Ricca, Murray "the Camel" Humphrey, and Capone's cousin Charlie Fischetti. Rio was appointed street-gang liaison; Fischetti was assigned enforcement and narcotics; and Nitti was named executive officer. By the time Capone organized his gang, he had more than six hundred men on his payroll, each ready to move forward when someone was either jailed or killed. Even when the boss himself was imprisoned for income-tax evasion in 1931, the Capone combine rolled on and expanded its reach across the country. Capone called his gang "the best-run business in the country." He was probably correct.

As their mob grew in size and power, both Capone and Nitti knew that the dispute between New York and Chicago had to be settled. Open warfare had virtually ceased since the national conference, but the hatred between the groups continued to escalate, with Chicago working in the shadows to muscle in on Luciano's labor-union rackets.

Luciano and Costello also knew that hostilities between the two factions were about to erupt. Charlie Lucky made it clear that he would not abide by anything proposed by Capone and the Mafia would not respect any plans set forth by an outsider. He told Capone that he had better clean up his own house before trying to run everyone else's business. He called Chicago "a god-damn crazy place" and said that "no one's safe on the streets." Luciano said even he wouldn't feel safe there. He also vowed to make good on a threat aimed at keeping Capone's operation out of the East Coast. Charlie Lucky swore to "gun down any Chicago greaseball who sets foot east of Indiana." The gauntlet had been thrown.

The conference also had a significant effect on Charlie Lucky's grab for power, far and above his open hostility toward Capone. The organization and distribution of national power illustrated the need for a similarly unified power base in New York, much as Capone had established in Chicago. While the various families had drawn territorial boundaries and settled differences within their own hierarchy, they still needed to operate as a unit, with a governing body to settle disputes both within and outside the gang. With the threat of Chicago interference in the New York structure, Luciano recognized the need for tough new blood to sit in control. Luciano believed the man who had held that position, Joe Masseria, had become lazy and frittered away his power. He needed to be eliminated.

Joe Masseria was one of the last so-called Mustache Petes, a gangster from the old school of broken English, gentlemanly behavior, and an adherence to a set of old-fashioned, outdated gangland rules. He would not permit the sale of drugs to children, insisted on restraint when fleecing a man who supported his family, and would not allow the murder of women and children. He would permit the killing of cops, but only as a last resort.

Luciano, who respected no such laws, moved quickly to become his heir apparent. He and his gang of Lansky, Siegel, and Adonis blitzed the city and its boroughs with murders, takeovers, and shakedowns to convince the Mafia that Masseria had lost control. (Costello, who was Masseria's right-hand man, operated as an insider, supplying tips to Luciano as to Masseria's moves.) The Mafia made it clear to Luciano that he could end the old gentleman's reign.

That spring, Luciano invited Masseria to a quiet dinner at a shabby Coney Island Italian eatery called Scarpato's. The two talked, laughed, and gossiped about everyone from Capone to Costello. They ate and drank for several hours, then spent the rest of the evening playing cards. As eleven o'clock approached, with Masseria intoxicated on good wine and rich food, Luciano laid his cards on the table. He explained to Masseria that the boss had to step down, that Luciano and his group were going to take over. The two argued good-naturedly for some time; then Lucky politely excused himself to go to the washroom. Within minutes, three gunmen stormed the restaurant and opened fire on Masseria. They left him slumped across the table in a pool of blood. Luciano slowly emerged from the washroom. He, of course, did not see anything. Costello was appointed Luciano's second-in-command.

Several years later, an underworld associate identified the hit men as Albert Anastasia, Joey Adonis, and Benjamin Siegel. The trio epitomized the melding, for a time, of the New York crime families rather than a show of unity or loyalty to Luciano.

Albert Anastasia headed his own family, usually at war with Luciano and Costello. He needed Masseria out of the way to further his own ambitions. Joey Adonis was one of the underbosses for Masseria, but immediately aligned with Luciano after the hit and formed a strong and loyal partnership. Adonis was placed as head of enforcement and assassinations for Costello and Luciano. Ben Siegel's relationship with Costello and Luciano had been rocky at best; both kept their distance from Siegel because of his hair-trigger temper and the fact that he was irrational and usually out of control. Siegel had run with Meyer Lansky since childhood in their Bugs/Meyer mob days and usually did as Lansky recommended. Lansky, though, had gotten along well with the Italian mobsters since they were teenage thugs pulling robberies and murders together in Brooklyn. For this job Siegel was used as a hired gun. The killing did nothing to solidify his relationship with Luciano. Siegel later said he went in on the hit for the fun of it.

The hit became a major turning point for Luciano. Masseria's death established Luciano's New York family: Lucky became the overlord who orchestrated vice (gambling, drugs, prostitution); Costello handled legitimate rackets (labor, manufacturing); and Lansky oversaw influence peddling and enforcement (political payoffs, bribes, assassinations, shakedowns, and kidnappings), with gambling and narcotics racketeering shared by Adonis and Siegel, Adonis serving as the overlord, which never ceased to gnaw at Siegel.

There were more than four hundred men operating under these four; they ranged from attorneys to hit men to hoodlums who offered bribes to goons who collected shakedown money and infiltrated unions to lackeys who skimmed from city-operated businesses. The Luciano family was in place and, on the surface, rolled along like a well-oiled machine.

But there was dissension within the ranks. The problem was Ben Siegel. Not even he questioned Luciano's authority as head of the clan or Costello's role as second-in-command. Luciano associated only with those who would further the family's interests. His every move was calculated for profit. He had no compunction about killing another person—man, woman, or friend. Siegel became an irritation, and Luciano repeatedly spoke of eliminating him. Costello and Lansky always stepped in to convince Charlie Lucky that Siegel was beneficial to their rackets.

Costello had been noted in the mob as a clever manipulator. His underworld conference was typical of the transparent olive-branch tactics he used to bring solidarity to the underworld for his own gain. But while he appeared to be levelheaded, he in fact was not. Costello was as irrational and deadly as Charlie Lucky, with a string of murders and kidnappings to his credit while still in his teens. Costello understood that financial and personal interests could always be furthered through a settlement, but not necessarily a concession. He would resort to bloodletting if it suited him. Costello and Luciano were cut from the same deadly mold; they thought and acted alike on business matters and saw murder as nothing more than part of their business.

Lansky, being Jewish, was never allowed into the inner circle of the Mafia, but because of his childhood association with Luciano and Costello, he became a key man in the Luciano family. He was worldly, seemingly rational, deliberate in his words and actions, but unlike Luciano and Costello, could be persuaded with reason. Lansky also served as the buffer between the family and outsiders who came "to the table" with problems or requests for the family's help. Though he, too, was a killer, Lansky was quiet and had an air of dignity.

Benjamin Siegel was a treacherous and self-serving thug who had no fear of, or respect for, any man, no matter his rank in the Mafia or the public sector. He showed no emotion; he pummeled any man who crossed him or moved too close to his operations. When personally threatened or angered, Siegel traded brass knuckles for a gun. His signature trademark: two shots in the head, one in the heart. Ben Siegel was a maniac, irrational, explosive. Once in a tirade, he could not be calmed or reasoned with until he vented his anger. Once angered, Siegel always resorted to violence, usually resulting in death to his adversary, before he settled down.

Siegel's moods turned on and off quickly. Once, in 1930, Siegel battered, then shot, a hood who tried to cheat him in a backroom poker game in New York. Tony Stipone, who sat in on that deadly game, related the story in a personal interview:

Ben Siegel was nuts. But we all knew it and accepted it. If he liked you, he could be one hell of a nice guy. Do anything for you. Well, I was sitting in on this poker game . . . me, Ben, and two other guys. I won't tell you their names. Anyway, Benny was dealing, I think, and he passed out the hand. When this other guy holds and doesn't take no cards, Benny gets suspicious. Well, the guy was cheatin'. We all knew it. So Benny slams this jerk one right across the nose. Whack. Then he pulls out a gun and shoots him. Two and one [head and heart].

The stiff drops to the floor, and Benny's watching the dead guy twist and jerk on the floor, how dead guys do, telling the two of us to watch the bum dance.

When the guy quit movin', Ben lifts him up and puts the dead guy back in the chair. He deals again. We all ante up. Except the dead guy, who can't, of course. When the dead guy doesn't ante, Benny blasts the guy again, knocking the jerk to the floor. The dead guy! He looks at the guy's hand

and laughs. "Lucky bastard's got a full house. Now that's nutty, don't ya think?"

Siegel was insane; he had been called Bugsy behind his back since he was a kid. He flew into a rage at the slightest provocation, then would suddenly appear calm, with an almost dashing demeanor. Even with these violent mood swings he never ceased to amaze cohorts with the extremes of his insanity.

He could also be a charmer, a generous tipper, and a good sport when a practical joke was played on him. Several people who knew him well had nothing but great things to say about him: that he would put everything on the line if a friend was down on his luck and that he always took care of his friends. To a point.

Siegel also believed he was one of the most handsome men in the country. And he probably was. Though he was married with several children, Bugsy Siegel had a slew of mistresses and whores at his side at all times. His entourage usually included a couple of Broadway show girls, starlets, rich wives, and royalty. A sharp dresser with deep blue eyes and dimples, Ben rarely passed a mirror without stopping, and he made a point of scoping a room for new conquests when out in public.

Ben Siegel always believed he should have been a movie star. When he heard that a Hollywood star had arrived in New York, Siegel was the first at his side, wining, dining, and pumping him for "inside" information on acting and Hollywood gossip. Ben Siegel was a full-fledged movie fan who seemed to lose a considerable degree of self-possession when seated next to a celebrity. He asked for autographs, posed for pictures, and sat alone in dark movie theaters reciting lines with the screen stars. For many in the Mafia, that, too, meant Siegel was "Bugsy."

Women were not above Siegel's wrath, and he had been known to batter several of his girlfriends when they so much as looked at another man. The only woman he never touched in violence was his wife, Esta Krakower, his childhood sweetheart. He lived a life of lies with her, and she never questioned his whereabouts or his business dealings. Siegel used his marriage as a way of keeping other women at arm's length. The scheme worked.

But in less than five years Siegel would meet a woman who

would outsmart him, play him for a sucker, and force him to shatter the bond between key members of the Luciano family. That woman was Virginia Hill, who was about to take her first step into the sinister enclave of the underworld and who would know every one of these gangsters on a personal, and in some cases intimate, basis.

3

To seventeen-year-old Virginia Hill the world of gangsters, murder, and mob wars was something straight out of Hollywood. The Al Capones and Lucky Lucianos were glamorized as good boys gone wrong from poor families who rose above their humble beginnings to become rich, famous, and respected, albeit dead, when the closing credits rolled. The movies portrayed Chicago as a city of thrills where money flowed freely and crime ran wild. With the Century of Progress fair luring tourists from all over the country, Chicago was "the" place to be to escape Depression woes and land a job.

Virginia Hill seized the opportunity. According to FBI reports, Virginia arrived in Chicago sometime in August 1933 with George Randell, who supposedly posed as her brother for the first week or so. There is no record of why he agreed to leave Bessemer, where they stayed in Chicago, or even if Randell returned to Alabama. Their association in Chicago (if there was one) ended abruptly, for the files show no later meeting or any connection between Hill and Randell. Hill did not need him. With her full figure and thick auburn hair she had no problem finding work or male companionship.

Conflicting stories describe the work she found shortly after her arrival. Bill Kinney of the *Marietta Daily Journal* wrote that Hill became a shimmy dancer for twenty dollars a week in a show called *The Elephant and the Flea.* Others said she was a stripteaser. There are also stories of Virginia's working as a shill on the Midway, wriggling around in scant clothing, luring in customers for a carnival barker. A 1958 article in the *American Weekly* claimed that Hill landed a part in a "wild and woolly production" called *Days of '49;* her pay, twenty dollars a week. Another account claims that Hill actually started as a Loop-area manicurist and was "discovered" by Capone mobsters, who found her work at the fair.

Hill herself, in accounts related by associates and in her own testimony before the Kefauver Committee, said she became a waitress at the San Carlo Italian Village. The job was not as flashy as the others. But the version seems plausible. Her work at the San Carlo would provide the perfect opportunity for her to be seen by and associate with gangsters who had overrun the restaurant and the fair.

The Century of Progress Exhibition turned into one of the biggest financial boons in Chicago's history and remains one of the biggest scams ever perpetuated by organized crime. Ironically, it was the underworld peace conference of 1926 that gave impetus to the fair.

Shortly after the peace conference, the city's leaders recognized that tourism had slackened because of the bad publicity about gang wars and vice. Charles Gates Dawes, the U.S. vice president and a resident of Evanston, Illinois, proposed the idea for a "fair to end all fairs." Dawes envisioned a massive carnival that would bring in millions of tourists and get the city back on its feet. The vice president calculated that the fair would take about ten years from conception to completion, coinciding with the hundredth anniversary of the founding of Chicago. It was scheduled to open in 1937, and a board of directors consisting of city leaders mapped out its strategy.

No one foresaw the stock-market crash of 1929 and the Great Depression that followed. Though tourism virtually died out around the country and hundreds of thousands of people had no income, city leaders forged ahead. They even moved up the date to coincide with the next presidential inauguration, in the spring of 1933, when the country would be inspired by Roosevelt's promise of "prosperity being just around the corner."

The fair posed a serious problem for law enforcement, which

had tried to control vice in the city. It meant that millions of tourists would flock to Chicago during the summer months that the fair was running. Tourism always meant a sharp increase in prostitution. Chicago's leaders understood that there was no way to control prostitution—they had been unable to do so even before the fair—but wanted to limit the spread of venereal disease. They insisted that every prostitute register as a masseuse and undergo weekly physical exams. City leaders also knew that in order to succeed they would have to work with Al Capone. He was "invited" to join the fair's board of directors, and Al took full advantage of the situation.

Capone's cousins Charlie and Joe Fischetti set up the prostitution rackets with accountant Jake Guzik, initiating a citywide price scale that ranged from fifty cents to five dollars, depending on the sex acts performed. Soon massage parlors opened all over town, but few people visited them for the services the signs advertised. The parlors raked in hundreds of thousand of dollars in profit. The Capone gang split the profits with police and legislators. Everyone was happy.

Capone did not stop with prostitution. He knew that millions of dollars would flood the city, and his organization was ready to siphon off its share. Though he remained in jail for income-tax evasion, when the fair finally opened, in 1933, his thugs were pocketing their illegal share from building contracts, parking garages, fair-grounds security, hotels, transportation, and park concessions, such as hot-dog and hamburger stands, drinks, hatcheck stands, and even the rickshas that took visitors from one exhibit to another. The Chicago gangsters also took 20 percent off the top of every souvenir hat, cane, spoon, dish, and doll sold to unsuspecting customers. Though police were allowed to harass Capone's men and slow down their operation, it was to no avail. The gangsters skimmed from land leases to restaurants and cabarets and invested their own money in stock options connected with the fair and restaurants. The Capone combine was so firmly entrenched in the fair that it even built its own crowning jewel—the San Carlo Italian Village, which was a collection of classy, dignified dining areas with pricey menus and an Old World atmosphere.

Capone's men used the village as a meeting place; they were safe from outside interference by other gangs and honest cops.

It was here that Frank Nitti laid out plans for westward expansion, Murray Humphreys called rogue street gangs to order, Charlie Fischetti made sure the crime combine operated smoothly, and Jake "Greasy Thumb" Guzik figured out ways to launder ill-gotten profits through legitimate means. At his side was a quiet, stocky man with thick black glasses. His name was Joe Epstein.

Newspapers called him "the man who put shoes on Virginia Hill." Epstein, called Joey Ep, or "Ep," by underworld insiders, was a Chicago native from the West Side of the city. He studied accounting in school and met Jake Guzik under vague circumstances in 1930. Within two years he became Guzik's chief accountant, his second-in-command, in charge of every nickel, dime, and dollar that passed through the Capone organization. Epstein personally supervised Chicago-area gambling, especially horse racing and the wire services, and was considered the underworld "racetrack commissioner." He operated a large suite on Madison Avenue and two offices at 10 North Clark Street, rooms 301 and 1206, under the name of Stern and Horwick. (Edward Stern and Julius Horwick were among some fifteen hundred bookmakers operating from the building.) Epstein and his cronies took in and covered bets from across the country that were usually too large to be handled by local bookies. Hundreds of thousands of dollars passed through his hands every day; at the time, the average weekly pay of Americans came to about ten dollars a week.

Epstein, a bachelor, was a well-read, quiet intellectual, and everyone who knew him considered him a gentleman. He was slow to anger, and as far as anyone knew, he never killed a man or ordered his death. Epstein kept his word and kept to himself. Guzik and Capone trusted him implicitly and never questioned his actions. At first glance, it seems strange that this quiet, bookworm type of man introduced Virginia Hill into the inner circles of the underworld, especially when she was later so closely associated with such flamboyant and handsome characters as Joey Adonis and Bugsy Siegel.

But there was another side to Epstein. He loved to party. On any evening he could be seen at opening-night shows, dining and dancing at Chicago's Chez Paree and Ciro's or sipping wine with friends and show girls at all-night gatherings. It was at one of those private gatherings that he received a formal introduction to Virginia Hill.

Hill had been in Chicago about one year when she first caught Epstein's eye. Epstein had been a frequent diner at the San Carlo Italian Village, where Virginia had worked as a waitress. Epstein later claimed that he was immediately smitten the first time Hill took his order. She wore a tight peasant-type dress that emphasized her bust, a little too much lipstick, and far too much makeup, which, Epstein said, gave Virginia a "bit of a trashy look," but he found it intriguing. He always left her extraordinary tips, usually double the amount of the check. Epstein was noted throughout the underworld as a big tipper.

But what attracted him most to Virginia was that she never reacted to his advances or seemed impressed with his tips other than throwing a thank-you or a wisecrack his way. She made it clear she was not for sale and not on the prowl to hook a rich man into marriage, as were so many of the fair girls. Epstein believed she was an independent woman with a good heart and solid instincts. He made a point of eating at the village to watch Virginia, and he brought his mob friends with him for the same purpose. It was evident that Epstein had plans for this waitress.

Charlie Fischetti and Guzik made passes at Virginia in front of Epstein, but she ignored them as well. In fact, Hill even had a bit of a reputation around the restaurant as an "ice queen." Hill said that before she was formally introduced to Joey Ep, her life in Chicago was rather routine, consisting of work and little in the way of a social life. The only interesting thing that happened was when Mack Hill sent the police after her shortly after she arrived in Chicago. Virginia claimed the police only asked her a few questions, then left. Despite stories to the contrary, Mack Hill never came to Chicago.

While working as a waitress, Virginia made one friend. This woman frequently stopped in to check on business or socialize, and she struck up a conversation with Virginia, whose name had been mentioned frequently by the Capone men. Her name was Mimi Capone, the wife of Ralph "Bottles" Capone, Big Al's brother, who had supervised bootlegging for the family. Mimi had heard Epstein, Guzik, and the rest gossip about Hill and wanted to see Virginia for herself. She reportedly went to meet her with the intention of not liking her. But they became instant friends.

Mimi and Virginia both liked to laugh hard, talk dirty, drink a bit, and flirt. They went nightclubbing on Mimi's tab and crashed "gangster" parties for fun. Virginia thought the parties were rather dull, filled with boring old men and their mistresses or whores, but knew that these were the men she needed to impress if she was going to get anywhere in Chicago. She did her best acting early on and made these thugs believe they were Valentinos by flattering them and rubbing her body against them.

It is not clear exactly whose party Mimi and Virginia crashed or who had been on the guest list the night of June 12, 1934. But Epstein later told friends that he immediately spotted Virginia as she entered the room and teased her about always brushing him off at the San Carlo restaurant. Instead of apologizing, Hill said she really had no reason to accept his advances, for she "was doing okay by brushing him off." Epstein left her the biggest tips in the restaurant, so why, Hill explained, should she "screw up a nice setup like that?" They talked through the night.

She had the attributes Epstein knew he could use in his operation: a woman who was smart but not hungry, could be trusted with both money and inside information, would do as she was told, pocket what she was given, and not spread secrets or gossip about the "family." One of the oddest and most lucrative business-underworld partnerships was born at that party.

Though it was common knowledge that Joe Epstein was Virginia's entré into the mob, it has never before been explained exactly how Joey Ep used Hill for the mob and how she rose through its ranks. This has always been a major void in each previous account of Hill's life. Several people who had been close to Epstein, the Capone organization, and Hill have all given virtually the same account, which is told here for the very first time.

Epstein's main racket was gambling, the wire services, and bookmaking. He covered bets on all sports but specialized in horses, baseball, and boxing. Epstein was constantly on the prowl for ways to move money around from city to city and state to state, to pay off winning wagers and launder profits, without attracting the attention of the law. He needed a money carrier who was not an actual member of the mob, whom police did not yet know but could be accepted by and get close to others connected with the rackets. Virginia was young and willing, and she was put to the test within the month.

Epstein started Hill with small wagers at the track so she could get a feel for the operation. One of her first jobs was to place small ($1,000) bets on specific horse races at the Hawthorne and Washington Park racetracks. The money was considered large enough to entice Hill to skim, if she was so inclined, but small enough so that if she did steal, it would not be missed and Epstein could cover the debt in his books. Both Epstein and Hill understood that if she did skip off with the mob's money she would be finished and possibly killed.

She did as she was told. Hill put $4,000 on a horse to "place" and $2,000 on another horse in the following race to "show." The first horse landed "win," which garnered Hill and the mob $16,000; a win on the second race pulled in $4,000. Hill took the winnings back to Epstein, who promptly gave her a 10 percent cut.

The reasons for the odd bets were twofold: a major bet on place or show pulled in a bigger purse because it would not lower the odds as significantly as a major bet on win. Place and show bets were also safer because the bettor won a return on his investment at least 70 percent of the time.

But the most lucrative aspect of the deal involved money laundering. The bulk of the underworld's money came from illegal sources: shakedowns, narcotics, racketeering. Mobsters could not spend the money openly because they would have to account for it to the government, especially after the trouble Al Capone incurred with the IRS when he collected millions of "unexplainable" dollars. The mob developed scams in which so-called dirty or illegal money would be handed over to various sources and returned as profit or clean money so that the entire amount of clean money could be declared as legitimate income.

Epstein had numerous money-laundering scams, but his most reliable concerned the track. The $4,000 Virginia turned in to the ticket window would be handed back as winnings, along with any profit, when the horse came in. The entire sum would be "cleaned" and accounted for only as racetrack winnings, declared to the government as income, with taxes being paid promptly and the real (illegal) source of the money buried.

The ever-shrewd Epstein was also careful not to bring down the ire of the Internal Revenue Service. After the Capone debacle, the organization made sure that every dime laundered was accounted for, on the books, as legitimate income. Since Hill was, for all intents and purposes, a working member of the Capone organization, she, too, had to step carefully. Epstein ordered Hill to lose every sixth bet, to provide her with losses for deductions and laundering, and to hold her income to a reasonable tax bracket. Epstein's philosophy was that there was no point in raking in big profits if the bulk of it would wind up in Uncle Sam's pocket.

Associates of Epstein recall that Virginia made only one mistake early in her money-laundering days, and she was duly chided for it.

Within a few weeks Virginia became a regular bettor at the racetracks around Chicago and Indiana. She wore big hats, red lipstick, and costume jewelry and tried to hobnob with high rollers and get to know bookies by name. She eventually met a few professional gamblers. Through these contacts she was given inside tips on certain races. Of course, the underworld had its own inside tips and ordered Hill to bet accordingly. The third or fourth time at the window at Washington Park, Virginia was told of a sure win, though the odds had posted the horse as a long shot. Instead of spreading the bet on place and show, as instructed, Virginia dropped the entire amount on win. The horse won, and Hill pocketed some $200,000.

When Virginia turned the money over to Epstein, he was furious. The problem with such a large take, he explained, was that it would stand out if entered as income in the books. The entire amount would have to be laundered, which would take weeks. Worse yet, because Virginia's bet skewed the odds, he would have to pay off a higher return rate to bookies whose bets he had covered on the race as place and show. The win, in effect, would come in as a substantial loss for the Capone gambling racket. She never again questioned orders from Joey Ep.

In spite of the disaster at Washington Park, Ep sensed that Virginia was ready to work higher-stakes rackets. Though she dressed well, Virginia did not yet have a flair for clothes and a sense of style and class needed to fit in with the free spenders who routinely dropped $50,000 or more on a race or a game.

Epstein thought she still dressed like a working girl, and he wanted Virginia to get close to these people in order to coax them into larger bets. Epstein also wanted Hill to transport cash, diamonds, and furs across state lines, which was a federal offense. To accomplish this task, Virginia needed to improve her appearance so that she could wear the stolen property and travel unnoticed. She also had to toughen her demeanor to fool customs inspectors and federal investigators.

Joey Ep bragged about his protégée and made it his personal quest to become her "Henry Higgins." He bought her the most expensive clothes on Chicago's Michigan Avenue, showed her off in the best Loop and North Side–area restaurants, and introduced her to upper-echelon underworld cronies. He even set her up in an expensive North Shore apartment and gave her upwards of $3,000 a week spending money over and above the amounts she was given to launder. He worked with her on what to say, when to say it, and how to keep her mouth shut. In other words, he taught her the racket. The sweet southern girl had become a Chicago "Mob Queen" who threw lavish parties, sought after by Chicago's wealthy on both sides of the law, all bought and paid for by Epstein. Virginia Hill was on her way.

Hill and Epstein insisted there was no sex in their relationship. She told reporters that he was not her "fellah" but "more like a big brother." He described her as "a good kid who's trying to make a living." Both were probably correct. There were rumors around Chicago that Epstein was gay, and in the mid-1930s homosexuality was frowned upon by the general public. Admitting to such a life in the underworld amounted to a death sentence. Virginia helped Epstein put on a more socially acceptable front. It would also explain why Epstein always remained at Hill's side during her numerous love affairs and even promoted her sexual encounters with others connected to the underworld.

Virginia and Joey Ep frequented a northern Indiana club called the Plantation Club, a gambling casino that resembled Tara from *Gone With the Wind*. The Plantation Club was the out-of-state hideaway for the Capone gang. The gang was so entrenched there that Big Al himself had a specially built soundproof room in the back. It was at this club that Capone mercilessly beat to death the three men who had tried to kill him in a foiled assassination scheme. It was here, out from under the scrutiny of Chicago cops and newspaper reporters, that underworld associates unwound. There was one rule in the public room of the club: no business discussions. All business was relegated to the soundproof room. There was one rule in the back room: Anything discussed in that room remained there.

In the summer of 1935 the men who composed the core of the Chicago mob known as the outfit invited a woman into that male-Mobster "back room" domain. Virginia Hill was asked to sit at the table to discuss business. Hill had passed the first round at the tracks. She was about to be promoted.

Virginia was by now well known in underworld circles as Epstein's girl. She also had well-earned notoriety as a top-notch money launderer in racing scams. The glamour girl had gained social grace and confidence and lost most of her "innocent waifishness" by the time she was nineteen. She developed a sharp edge and a quick tongue. She looked and acted like a woman at least ten years older.

At the Plantation Club, Hill now held court with the same men who, only a year or so before, had tried to hustle her as a cheap pickup at the San Carlo Italian Village. Charlie Fischetti, Frank Nitti, and Paul Ricca swapped vulgar stories with her, talked of murder, and laughed at women. Hill's conversation usually kept pace, which impressed the boys. She had now formed and solidified ties with the real power of the Chicago mob that eventually allowed her to become the most dangerous woman in the underworld.

Virginia went out of her way to separate herself from the Mafia wives and girlfriends who socialized in the public room of the club. She saw that they were usually treated as window dressing or used as an excuse to avoid other romantic attachments. She called them "dumb fucking dolls" foolishly waiting to accept whatever love or money their husbands or boyfriends threw their way. She also saw the way the wives were usually abused, verbally and physically, and how mistresses were flaunted. Hill vowed she would have none of that.

She told a friend of Epstein's, "I grew up with that crap from my father and got away from it. Why would I put myself back into it now? Especially when I don't have to?" Any romance, she boasted, would only be for her convenience and for whatever purposes it could serve at the time. Finally, she found both the right time and the right purpose for a romantic entanglement.

She always arrived at the Plantation Club on Epstein's arm, but she played the room, flitted from one table to the next, and wisecracked with, flirted with, and enticed Epstein's cronies. When Ep introduced her to Major Arterburn Riddle—Major was his first name—Hill quickly sized him up as a big spender but something of a chump. Epstein advised Virginia to act especially nice to Riddle. He had millions that the mob wanted to get its hands on. Once again, Virginia did as she was told.

Riddle was a trucking-company tycoon from Indianapolis whose bank account bounced from millions to bankruptcy and back again. Among his holdings were the Riddle Oil Company, several racehorses, and a stable called the Green Grass Stables. The horses made for a natural common ground with Epstein.

There were rumors Riddle had backed part of the Century of Progress, including the San Carlo Italian Village, and was part owner of the Plantation Club. Riddle allegedly fronted other mob rackets by lending his name as a key investor, though the bulk of the investment money came from mob coffers. He had worked closely with Epstein to keep his mob-related investments as well hidden from public scrutiny as possible. Epstein worked well with Riddle, and together they increased their income. Though many connected with the Chicago gang suspected that Riddle's financial involvement was considerable, no one was able to determine exactly how much money Riddle had invested in and for the underworld. Regardless, Capone's boys wanted to make certain that Riddle's cash supply continued.

Riddle was the Chicago mob's number-one front man, and the boys needed to make him happy. Virginia said she thought Riddle was "nice looking in an older sort of way" and went to work—and worked him over.

Major Riddle showered Virginia with expensive gifts, furs, jewelry, cars, and clothes, which she gladly accepted. She convinced him to hand over large sums of cash, which she, Epstein thought, would invest for him in Chicago-area or mob-controlled businesses. Epstein later claimed that Riddle turned over tens of thousands of dollars to Hill. She handed the money to Ep, who laundered it for the mob; all the while, Riddle believed his money was making money. Whether Riddle ever saw any of it again, let alone a dime of profit, is a matter of speculation. Riddle, though, insisted he never gave Virginia money; he believed that giving cash to any woman was cheap and vulgar.

Within weeks of their meeting, Riddle was Virginia's steady companion, sugar daddy, and sex partner. While Riddle surpassed Hill in terms of education, business achievements, and social acceptance, she made his head spin with a whirlwind of parties and nightlife.

The friendly rivalry between Joey Ep and Maje, as Hill sometimes called Riddle, sparked a running gag that made the rounds in Chicago. Virginia once wore a silver-fox cape and diamond pendant. A friend approached her and inquired about the source of the luxuries. Pointing to the cape, he said, "Epstein?"

"No, Riddle," Hill answered.

Pointing to the diamond pendant, he asked, "Riddle?"

"No, Epstein."

But Hill was not greedy when it came to receiving the gifts. She was a woman of discriminating tastes. Riddle said that once when he offered Virginia a diamond watch, she threw it in the toilet and screamed, "What kind of a girl do you think I am?"

Riddle took it as a pang of conscience on Virginia's part, that she felt a little guilty about the implication that she was trading sex for diamonds. Actually, there were rumors that the diamonds were not the best quality and that Hill was insulted by the junk jewelry. She was acutely aware of the image she may have presented to Epstein's mob friends, men whom she knew she had to impress if she wanted to remain on the underworld fast track and continue to advance.

The relationship with Riddle deteriorated and finally ended after about eighteen months. Virginia said it was simply that she grew tired of a monogamous relationship, which for Virginia was hardly the case, as she had numerous brief affairs on the side. Men connected to the mob claimed Riddle had been pretty well "tapped out" and would have had to cash out holdings unless the mob eased up on its squeeze. Riddle never said much of anything and continued to pal around with the Capone squad for a short time after the breakup. But even this relationship ended once Riddle had served out his usefulness.

Epstein promoted Virginia to higher-stakes money-laundering scams within weeks after the end of the Riddle affair, most likely as a reward for her part in the Riddle squeeze. She went from bets of several thousand to bets of tens of thousands of dollars on baseball games, football games, horse races, and the most lucrative of all, boxing at Chicago Stadium.

Epstein covered most bets of more than $50,000 that were placed both locally and nationally. That amount was often considered too hefty a wager for small-time bookmakers. Epstein and his racketeers always cleared a 20 percent cut off the top before any money was laid down. To ensure that their business remained profitable in high-stakes wagers, they usually only covered so-called sucker bets, which guaranteed that the bettor would lose all or most of his money. It was with these sucker bets that Virginia fit into the scheme.

The plan was simple. Epstein used two types of systems. In one, bouts were fixed (sucker bets) and were, of course, sure wins for the bookies. But the odds were preset to lead the gambler to believe he would almost certainly win. In unfixed bouts, called wild cards, the racketeers took their 20 percent of the wager, then gave a narrow spread, which was usually two rounds on either side of the round and the call, a knockout or a decision. The bettor wagered against the bookie, who always had the spread in his favor.

Hill fit into the plan as a grifter, to coax high rollers into sucker bets and place and collect the wagers. She was also a money carrier who passed the receipts from Epstein to the various bookies and vice versa. The police could never directly figure out when and where the money had changed hands, failing to suspect that a pretty young woman was the carrier pigeon.

Hill moved into another area and violated federal law when she began transporting stolen merchandise across state lines into Indiana, Michigan, and—several times—as far away as Miami. After the mob staged a fur or jewelry heist, usually perpetrated as an insurance-fraud scam, the stolen goods were delivered to Virginia's apartment in Chicago. Plane or train tickets were bought in her name. Virginia wrapped herself in as much jewelry and fur as possible without drawing attention, carried the rest of the merchandise in a suitcase, and boarded a plane. With her elegant looks and obvious wealth she appeared as just another rich Chicago socialite who overpacked for the

purposes of showing off. State police and federal agents had yet
to catch on.

Hill had done so well that Epstein convinced his Mafia pals
that it was time for Virginia to move into even bigger and more
dangerous territory. She would infiltrate the inner circle of, and
act as a liaison with, the New York Luciano family, which was
still in the midst of a cold war against Capone's Chicago clan.

4

Virginia Hill was smart, independent, beautiful, sexy, rich, and aloof. She was one of the few women ever allowed to "sit at the table" with gang leaders when they mapped out plans for takeovers, hits, and business ventures. Virginia learned how to grift for the mob, launder money, and skew the odds at the track and at ringside. She knew how and where the top bookies operated and details of the bank accounts of their most secret "upper world" gambling clients. Virginia also learned how the outfit infiltrated unions, owned politicians, and stole businesses they then used as fronts for illegal purposes. Through her work with Epstein she became aware of how the books were juggled, how much money had been cleaned, and what business ventures had been fronted.

She learned it all from those who mastered the art of racketeering: Joey Ep; Jake Guzik, who had ordered the execution of several racetrack wire-service rivals and claimed at least $150 million in cash tucked in several safe deposit boxes; Charlie Fischetti, who had taken over the North Shore gambling, ran the city's "white slavery" prostitution racket, and had at least fifteen murders under his belt; and Paul Ricca, who would work his way up to boss of the Chicago syndicate. She quietly listened as they schemed and plotted and played dumb so as not to let on that she understood their business. To the inner circle of the outfit, Virginia Hill was no threat. She was a "smart doll" who passed around dirty money as quickly as she passed around men.

By 1936, Virginia had enough facts, figures, and details of the most intimate workings of the Mafia to bring down the Chicago hierarchy. She knew it, and they knew it. If she ever said anything to anyone, even in passing, she understood she would die.

By the time Virginia turned twenty, she had associated so closely with ruthlessly cold murderers and vice mongers that she became a chameleon at will, assuming an air of impenetrability and a tough, hard edge when around the group but all fire and desire, "all woman," when she was alone with one man or two. Many who knew her even thought she was sweet and compassionate, and she made a point of buying gifts for friends or introducing them to people who could help them find work, loans, or whatever they needed.

While Virginia earned a reputation as a smart woman and "tough cookie," she also earned another reputation: as a mob whore. She had no compunction about sleeping with a man to gain information if ordered to do so by Joey Ep or others in the rackets. At times, she did it for nothing more than carnal desire and laughed to the other men in the mob about her latest lothario's sexual performance, often right in front of the man she was insulting.

One story best illustrates how Virginia was transformed from a sweet southern girl into a tough-edged mob Queen.

One day in December 1936, Virginia and several other "mob women" were at a Christmas party thrown by Charlie Fischetti and his wife. Virginia arrived with Epstein, but they quickly separated as she worked her way through the party, flirting with and coming on to just about every man in the room. Several of the men, including Fischetti and Guzik, started daring her to, as they put it, "put her money where her mouth was." Virginia thought it was a challenge she could not resist and answered back, "I'll put my mouth where the money is."

She walked over to Fischetti, who was leaning against a wall in the living room, unzipped his pants, and performed fellatio in front of the entire room. Most of the men laughed, but the women found it disgusting and made their feelings known, calling Hill a "cheap tramp" and "white trash." Fischetti's wife reportedly even tried to toss her out.

Then someone in the room challenged Hill to "work the

room." Within minutes Virginia was crawling on her knees from man to man, except for one, Joe Epstein. He found the incident disgusting and retired to the kitchen. Several others followed his lead, and the orgy quickly ended. One woman called Hill a whore to her face, which triggered Virginia's temper. She slapped the woman, grabbed her by the hair, and proclaimed, "I'm the best damn cocksucker in Chicago, and I got the diamonds to prove it. I ain't doing nothing that you haven't done and I don't see any diamonds on you." Though vulgar, Virginia did have a point.

After the Fischetti party, she kept her distance from other mob women and made it clear she considered herself "Queen of the Mob" in Chicago, a title she was well on her way to earning. Charlie Fischetti called her "a right broad." Epstein said she had become "tougher than any guy I'd ever want to cross." Jake Guzik and his wife, Alma, had dinner with Hill one night and offered to put her in charge of several of their brothels that had been problem spots.

The Guziks ran a white slavery system in which girls were literally abducted off the street or lured to Chicago from farms, imprisoned inside brothels, beaten, and forced into prostitution. Rebellious, they continually tried to run away. Guzik told Hill, "If I put a doll like you in front, every John with a roll would come drooling. A tough dame like you'd also keep the whores in line." As he finished the last part, Guzik laughed and slammed his fist on the table, implying that Hill would think nothing of belting a girl if she had to.

Virginia replied, "I don't shill for nobody no more." And she meant it. She earned a place of her own in the gambling rackets, and working for Guzik would have been a loss in status and profits.

But Virginia was bored—with Epstein, Chicago, the men, the lifestyle. She wanted a change. She wanted to meet new people, see a new city, and try her hand at bigger rackets. The Chicago gang found the perfect way to make Virginia happy. It also found a way to use Hill to get inside the Luciano gang so as to keep the Capone boys informed of any expansion plans or threatening moves by the New York clan.

With Al Capone in prison, the Luciano mob believed it could reason with Frank Nitti and Charlie Fischetti, Sicilians who,

Luciano assumed, shared his views on life, loyalty, and crime. Luciano thought that common Sicilian blood ultimately created a tighter bond than one established only by friendship. Nitti had been Capone's barber and was elevated to his second-in-command on the basis of friendship. Both sides agreed that there had to be communication between New York and Chicago; they had to do business together and intermingle if the Mafia was ever to have total domination over the country. The men chose gambling as the bargaining chip. What Nitti hid from Luciano was his vow to make good on Capone's threat to get even with the New York vice lord.

The plan was to allow the Luciano family to buy limited shares of Chicago's North Shore gambling parlors and brothels; the operations, though, remained under Fischetti's control. New York already had gained some control of the Chicago rackets, but by allowing the New Yorkers to expand their reach, Chicago, in turn, could further muscle into some East Coast rackets, through racetrack wires and limited shares of narcotics trafficking. To do this, Chicago knew it would have to do business with Brooklyn's top racketeer, Joey Adonis, "Joey A" to those who knew him, a vain, pompous, heartless, arrogant man who had no respect for anyone, especially women. Epstein and the others knew Adonis was self-serving and would betray his mother for a dollar. Once he got a toehold in Chicago, he would push for more, then try to remove the midwesterners ensconced in the East. He clearly could not be trusted.

Adonis was the undisputed overlord of the gambling and numbers rackets for the entire East Coast. His interests also spilled over into other states. By 1936, Adonis not only controlled vice for the Luciano mob but personally owned every gambling joint in northern New Jersey and several brothels and nightclubs all along the eastern seaboard. Like an octopus reaching out its tentacles, Adonis wanted to grab some of the more lucrative betting and prostitution operations in Chicago. If he could infiltrate the rackets there, he would boost the worth of his underworld empire past $10 billion, making him one of the wealthiest gangsters in history.

FBI files show several variations on the last name of Joey A: Joe Dodo, Joseph P. Doda, Joseph Doti. But most who knew him claim his real name was Doto and that he changed it in the

late 1920s during his days as a triggerman for and later head of
Murder, Incorporated, New York's bloodiest and most terrify-
ing execution squad. He dropped the name Doto because of
continual teasing from friends and gang rivals who called him
"Joey the Dodo" or "Doo-Doo." The name he adopted reflects
perfectly his self-righteous, superior attitude toward himself
and others. "Simply," he smugly told anyone who asked,
"because I'm good-looking." He had a criminal record that
dated back to 1926, served time in the penitentiary, and would
pistol-whip or kill anyone who disagreed with him on anything.

Almost no one dared call Joey A anything but Mr. Adonis or
Joe to his face. He preferred Joey A from associates. There were
only two people who brazenly stepped across that line with
Adonis: East Coast gambling underling Ben Siegel, who
despised him, and, later, Virginia Hill. Both called him Doto to
his face to needle him and arouse his wrath.

Virginia always thought it funny that these so-called tough
guys would be so sensitive about what she considered minor
things, such as nicknames, and often played to that weakness.
Hill always believed she would never be killed or maimed, and
anything less than that, such as a rape or beating, was part of
doing business with the organization. The angrier these men
became at her teasing, the harder she would laugh.

A deal was struck between Fischetti and Adonis that allowed
Joey A to move in on Chicago's rackets in exchange for shares
in East Coast operations. The outfit rightfully assumed Joey A
would skim and cheat Fischetti out of whatever money he could
by shaking down bookies for extra protection money and jug-
gling profit sheets, which was, and continues to be, common
practice in the underworld. Keeping tabs on operations in Chicago proved no problem. But what the Chicago gang needed
was someone to shadow Joey A on his home turf, someone he
would least suspect but who was cunning enough to keep records and make sure Chicago received its share of the take.

Epstein knew that Joey A was a bastard with women: he
slugged them, slapped them, abused them, cheated on them,
and ultimately dumped them. No one ever jilted Joey A.
Epstein said he had a gut feeling that Adonis would meet his
match in Virginia, that the fire smoldering just below the surface in the "southern belle" would ignite, consume, and finally
burn the New York lothario.

"The whole thing was a setup," Epstein joked to associates, " and both Virginia and I knew it. I wanted to teach that fucking bastard Doto a lesson and make him eat some of the shit he always handed out. I hoped he'd choke on it."

Epstein's hatred for the man he called Doto ran deep. The details of Epstein's scheme were laid out in detail, independently, by three men who had firsthand knowledge of the operation. Their stories differed only slightly, on minor points, but the basic plot was consistent.

Virginia Hill was ordered by the Chicago mob to move to New York as its representative, to stick close to Joey A's side and follow him everywhere he went. Hill was supposed to find out if Joey A cheated on his deal with Chicago and, if so, obtain enough proof to have him killed, which some believed was the real thrust behind Fischetti's agreement with Adonis. With Adonis out of the way, Chicago would be able to tighten its grip on East Coast gambling.

Jack Pignataro was an underworld associate close to Joe Epstein and Jake Guzik and knew of the mob's plans for Virginia. He said she was told of the dangers but didn't seem to care. "Virginia," he remembered, "was a real live wire, a lot of fun."

In fact, she seemed to get a real kick out of the fact that she was doing a little spying. She said that she always wanted to see New York as high society and that fucking over Joey A would be interesting. I think she meant it both ways, too, fucking and fucking over. Joey A was a pompous ass.

Adonis was married but never spent much time with his wife and appeared with her only when it was necessary for show, such as on formal functions or holiday parties. A notorious playboy, he was an easy mark for someone like Virginia Hill, who knew how to handle even the toughest men.

Virginia arrived in New York decked out like royalty. A full wardrobe, complete with cosmetics and intimate apparel, had been shipped ahead. Epstein made sure she was well taken care of and sent her envelopes stuffed with a minimum of $1,000, in cash, which arrived in the mail each week, enough to represent Chicago in proper style and to keep up with Adonis's lifestyle. Hill had to appear to be her own woman and not become one of

Adonis's kept women. She hid the real purpose of her assignment from Joey A, and he was led to believe she was there simply to carry profits and launder money for Chicago, not to spy. If the truth had been known, Hill would have been executed.

Hill quickly went to work laundering money. Epstein kept the money flowing. Sometimes the cash shipments were exorbitant, in excess of $10,000. The money was shipped in plain boxes, marked as prescription lotion or drugs, and Virginia laundered the mob's loot in gambling rackets or invested in nightclubs, restaurants, or other businesses, as she was ordered to do. Laundered money was shipped back in the same box in which the dirty money had arrived, with the box marked Delivery Refused/Return to Sender.

If the authorities in New York or Chicago ever suspected anything about Hill, they said and did nothing. Though she was by now a known associate of mobsters and gamblers, she still had no formal police record, no federal file, nor was she under investigation for anything. She moved and operated as freely as any citizen.

Virginia was ordered to meet Adonis in the dining room of the Algonquin Hotel. Adonis was told to expect her. Hill, he was told, would be carrying $10,000 in stolen jewelry, to be fenced in New York. Adonis agreed to arrange a meeting with a fence. Those who knew Virginia said she described her first meeting with Adonis as "electric." There was an instant sexual attraction, and they quickly played out that electricity. Adonis called Hill "insatiable." Within weeks the two were a well-known couple. Virginia had gotten close to Joey A, as ordered.

They quickly teamed up in the gambling rackets. Hill, a top money launderer, worked for Adonis in much the same way she had served Epstein. She pulled her usual racetrack scams, fixed the odds posted at wire services, and helped him collect mob bribes and payoffs. She also transported stolen property between New York and Chicago for both Adonis and Luciano in New York and Fischetti and Epstein in Chicago. Virginia was usually one place or the other and did a lot of mob-related commuting in the late 1930s as the liaison between the two crime cartels.

Adonis did not immediately figure out, if ever, that Hill had actually been spying for the Chicago mob. Virginia Hill had quietly become the outfit's "money-running Mata Hari."

Then she started keeping records of the transactions in a secret diary. The diary was not filled with flowery prose or notations of where she went or who she slept with. It was a ledger of how much money Adonis had given her to launder from the Chicago interest, how much she received in clean money in return, and who had been receiving bribes. She wrote in code, referring to Joey A as "Doto" or "Dot" and Luciano as "Sal." (His birth name was Salvatore, but he had changed it to Charles when he immigrated to New York.) There is also a reference to "F," which is assumed to be Frank Costello. Lesser-known bookmakers, gamblers, pimps, and drug dealers were also noted. Next to each name was a dollar amount, five figures or greater, with a red arrow pointing left or a green arrow pointing right. The red arrow meant dirty money coming in to be laundered; the green was clean money going out.

But gangsters and their underworld associates were not the only names jotted down in the diary. Hill had also kept track of bribes and payoffs delivered to politicians. The diary listed such people as Illinois attorney generals John Cassidy and George Barrett, New Jersey governor Alfred Driscoll, and several prominent and powerful Washington legislators from the Midwest and East Coast.

Virginia was well aware of the risks in keeping such incriminating records, for Adonis, Luciano, or anyone would certainly have seized her book and most likely eliminated her. More interesting, she made similar notations for Chicago money operations. "Ep," "Trig" (Charlie Fischetti's nickname was Trigger Happy), and "Jake" (most likely for Guzik) were listed prominently. If her diary was strictly intended for recordkeeping and spying for Chicago, she would not have included Chicago gangsters. It seems clear that Virginia Hill had plans of her own and suspected she was on to something that might eventually prove valuable.

Epstein had reportedly asked Virginia to keep track of the money and taught her how to do it, since that was his field of expertise. But whether he had requested her to keep a ledger or it was something Virginia decided to do on her own is not clear. It is a safe assumption that if Epstein knew about the diary, he did not know just how detailed Hill's notes were, because it would have incriminated him as well as others if the records fell into the hands of federal authorities.

Hill was considered "Joey's girl" in New York. They dined together, danced together, slept together. He cheated on her. She cheated on him. They traveled, broke the law, fought, and got rich together. It was a business relationship as well as a friendship, but love never entered into it. Adonis was married, and Hill could never emotionally attach herself to any man. That is, until she met Ben Siegel.

Previously published accounts maintain that Virginia first met Bugsy Siegel in California. Some insist it was on a movie set, others say at a party, still others that it was in a bar on the Sunset Strip. But FBI files on both Siegel and Hill also back claims by several members of the Luciano—now Gambino—Mob that Hill and Siegel first met in New York, sometime around late February 1937. Oddly enough, their first encounter was at a Brooklyn bar when Hill was with Joey A.

Siegel and Adonis had met regularly to discuss gambling and wire interests, with Siegel reporting to Adonis. Because of the close nature of their business it would seem logical that Siegel would be aware that Adonis had become involved with someone like Virginia Hill, who was so well connected to the mob and so strikingly beautiful. Given their positions in the underworld, Siegel most likely knew of Hill, and Hill of Siegel, before they actually met. Hill had known Costello, Lansky, and Luciano well enough to make note of them in her diary. Given her position in the Chicago underworld and her work with Adonis, it would make sense that she would also meet other members of the New York Mafia. FBI files show that she had sufficient information about these men and their activities to take over Luciano's gambling interests for a time after he was deported to Italy after World War II. There is absolutely no way Hill would have such connections without knowing Siegel personally, or at least knowing about him.

Siegel, who openly loathed Adonis, deliberately planned to do the one thing that would not only insult Adonis's masculinity but label him a chump in the eyes of the organization—steal his woman. Siegel was a plotter, a thinker, and a schemer. Most likely he calculated his conquest of Hill long before he actually seduced her.

Whether Siegel arranged to meet Adonis in the bar with the aim of getting close to Hill or it was just a fluke of timing remains unknown. What is known is that when Siegel walked up to Virginia at the bar, he turned on the charm, flashed his blue eyes, kissed her hand, and swept her off her feet. The gruff and swarthy Adonis was no match for the suntanned, smooth-talking Romeo.

Siegel left alone that night, but he made his intentions clear. By the next evening, Ben reportedly accomplished what he set out to do: He spent a night making love with Virginia Hill. Hill had committed the one unpardonable sin: She had slept with the enemy.

Though having dalliances with other men, even sleeping with them, might be overlooked, depending on the man and the status of the girl, bedding down with a mobster's rival was considered an act of betrayal. Siegel won his point.

Joey A told others that he noticed the difference in Virginia after she first met Ben. She seemed aloof, distracted, and uninterested in anything Adonis had to say. Though Adonis maintained he did not care, that his relationship was business and that "one broad was as good as another," it was clear that Siegel had stolen his woman. Joey A was diminished in Siegel's view.

After the incident, Adonis maintained his working relationship with Virginia, but sexually he drifted and escalated his affairs with others. But he apparently kept a soft spot in his heart for his former paramour, because he helped her when she struggled with financial hardship later in life.

In any event, Adonis blamed the affair on Siegel. It is likely that Adonis and Siegel shared a common history with women that preceded the Virginia Hill affair. It is also likely that Adonis ordered Siegel out of New York because of the incident.

Days after the liaison, Bugsy left New York in a hurry and relocated his base of operations to Hollywood, California. His instructions were to supervise and consolidate gambling, racetrack, and bookmaking rackets on the West Coast. Siegel, who never trusted airplanes, took the train.

Had Virginia "blown it" in the eyes of Joe Epstein? Probably. Immediately after the Siegel affair, her money supply dwindled, her racetrack "winnings" were reduced, and she was given less responsibility carrying stolen merchandise across state lines. In fact, Hill had relocated to the Savoy-Plaza Hotel, which cost at that time fifteen dollars a day, whining that she could no longer afford more luxurious Park Avenue digs. Within weeks she asked the front desk to move her into a smaller room at the hotel that cost only thirteen dollars a day. Her six-figure income plummeted to $15,000 gross per year in 1937, with Hill placing the exact same wagers on specific bets and winning the exact same amount each time, never being allowed to increase her winnings to fatten her profits. Hill was on a tight budget and on probation.

By 1938, Hill was again part of the social and financial scene. Her benefactor was Joe Epstein. But her usefulness in New York had pretty well soured, and she needed to distance herself from the Luciano mob. In May 1938, Hill went back to Georgia to regroup and recharge.

Adonis meanwhile continued his relationship with the Capone gang and built his multi-billion-dollar gambling empire along the North Shore. He aligned himself with Charlie Fischetti and split profits equitably. Though never friends, they had reached a peaceful accord, but Epstein still scrutinized every penny that crossed Adonis's greasy fingers. There is no recollection of bad blood between Adonis and Fischetti.

But Adonis was not the only one working the Chicago rackets. Frank Costello had joined with Paul Ricca in 1935 and was already cutting separate deals for himself. Ricca had begun plotting against Frank Nitti to take over control of the Capone mob. He became an ally of Costello, who also sought to overthrow Nitti. In fact, Costello and Ricca were eventually arrested together in a police raid on a Blue Island, Illinois, gambling casino. But Costello's visits to Chicago were not entirely friendly. The two sides were bracing for a bloodbath over gambling interests in Broward County, Florida.

The New York cartel had heavily infiltrated the vice and narcotics rackets there by 1934, and the Chicago mob was encroaching on its territory. The New York cut came to 30 percent of all money collected in Miami-area vice. Chicago, through a plan worked out ahead of time by Nitti and Ricca, sought a split and refused to back down until Luciano's goons let them take a slice of the East Coast unions. Luciano refused to give in, but Costello believed that conceding a small portion of the union profits would force the Chicago mob to give New

York clear control in Miami. Luciano stood firm. He knew, with Capone, that nothing was ever as it appeared.

Neither Costello nor Luciano realized Miami was merely a smokescreen put up by the Chicago gangsters. Though the Capone gang presented the unions as a "concession" for backing down in Miami, the unions were what the Capone gang had wanted all along. There was a much bigger scheme brewing, and it involved a move west.

5

Virginia said she never thought she would be happy to return to the South. But Marietta, Georgia, looked to her like a slice of heaven. No hustlers, no mobsters, no con men. Just honest, hardworking people who valued family, God, and a good job and nice home.

Hill had sent her family money ever since she moved to Chicago and allied herself with Epstein. Thanks to Virginia, her mother moved from the boardinghouse to a small cabin to a large home on Powder Springs Street, now Forest Avenue. Each time the family moved, it was either to a better house or a better location. Her mother never questioned where or how her twenty-two-year-old daughter obtained the money that arrived in the mail on a regular basis.

Virginia later told Los Angeles associates that Marietta was the one place where she felt comfortable; there was no one she had to answer to and no one she needed to be wary of. Upon her arrival, she immediately rented an apartment in a large boardinghouse at 202 Church Street, across the street from the First Presbyterian Church. She would not move in with her mother because she did not want her to know about her friends. If living so close to a house of worship seemed an odd twist in Virginia's life, it was not an indication that she had reformed and repented.

A woman who had lived across the hall said Virginia was on the hall phone all day and all night, that the conversations were loud, demanding, and often peppered with profanity. She seemed obsessed with the arrival of the daily mail. Virginia regularly received boxes and bulky envelopes from Chicago.

Virginia bought her mother expensive jewelry, took her family out to the best restaurants, and purchased the finest china, linens, and clothes for herself and her mother. She bought her siblings whatever they wanted—watches and suits and dresses and shoes. Virginia always paid cash. She seemed to have an inexhaustible money machine. Once again, no one questioned where she obtained her funds.

By July 1938, Virginia felt rested and was anxious to get back to work in the rackets. She made one quick trip back to Chicago, reportedly to meet Ep, then returned to Marietta to pick up her brother Chick, who had also wanted to leave home. Virginia would be twenty-three years old in another month, and she was ready to conquer new territory.

They climbed into a convertible and roared out of town. Virginia was once again about to embark on a dangerous and possibly deadly "mission" for the mob. But before she went back to work, she and Chick headed south to Mexico to work a racket run by vicious men who had no respect or fear of the Mafia.

Mexico had long been a weekend bedroom community for California. Californians thought nothing of rising shortly after dawn and driving across the border to Tijuana, where they could bargain for anything, from two-dollar shirts to tacky souvenirs to discount booze and fifty-cent hookers. The air was clean, the beaches empty, and the cantinas hopping. In Mexico, Americans relaxed, threw their money around, and often landed in jail.

Even though many gringos went south to go wild, the Mexicans usually assumed a demeanor of hospitality and tolerance; however, they often showed little respect to the foreigners behind their back. The country became a playground for Virginia, who chugged tequila and did the rumba barefoot in cantinas from Tijuana to Guadalajara. She found herself uncontrollably attracted to Mexican men, an attraction that remained with her through the rest of her life, although she ended her days with a very different type of man. She later told girlfriends in California that Mexican men knew how to treat a lady, that they were animals in bed and gentlemen in public and a little old-fashioned, which, at first, she found endearing. She also warned that they could never be trusted to keep a secret. She promised herself that she would never get close to any Mexican man. It was one of the few promises she made to herself that she broke. And it nearly cost her everything.

Still filled with the excitement of Mexico, Virginia and Chick arrived in Hollywood in late August 1938, where they rented an apartment on Havenhurst Street, off Crescent Heights Boulevard in a cluster of buildings called the Garden of Allah. The apartments were considered a gathering place for the Hollywood movie crowd, where celebrities like F. Scott Fitzgerald lived, and had earned a reputation as an orgy-crazed, drug-filled hideaway for some of the industry's more flamboyant characters. The apartment the Hills occupied was adequate, clean, and large enough to accommodate Virginia and her brother.

Virginia took time to play and party. She slowly began grifting and money laundering again for the mob, still cautious after her New York experiences. Hill knew few people in Hollywood and had not yet been given a prearranged entrée into the movie crowd. When she went out, she usually did so either with Chick or alone. Though she knew Ben Siegel was in town, she had yet to look him up, probably because of some directive from Epstein or Fischetti. Virginia rarely made a move without orders.

Decked out in diamonds and furs, she dined and danced at popular night spots like the Trocadero, the Mocambo, and the Brown Derby. She quickly became known around the nightclub set as a big tipper, often dropping gratuities equal to the tab. She often caught the eye of wealthy men, who bought her drinks, and asked for a dance, dinner, or more. She seemed indifferent to their attention and had no one special in her life for the first few months.

She was apparently so eager to impress and blend in with high society that she invented a background, afraid that she would be shunned if her true origins were ever known.

"I was born in Holland," she purred. But she also accounted for her drawl, knowing her deep southern accent was a giveaway to her true heritage. She claimed her mother was Ameri-

can and her father a half American, half Indian, who sailed back
to the United States and raised her in Georgia. "Father hit a
gusher . . . oil. That's where we got our money," she said, insisting she was an heiress to an oil fortune worth several million
dollars. She also claimed she was a countess. Then, when she
caught the attention of gossip columnists, she reverted back to
the George Rogers story of being his beneficiary. Only by now
the $50,000 inheritance had swelled to hundreds of thousands
of dollars.

It did not take long for the jet set to realize that Virginia Hill
was a comer, even if she could not keep her stories straight. She
had a steady cash flow that allowed her to maintain appearances
and keep pace with the wealthy, or at least those whose credit
was still good around Los Angeles.

Errol Flynn was one of the men who had tried to squire Virginia around town. For some unknown reason, Flynn crossed
her, and they ended up in a drunken brawl at the Brown Derby.
The battle started over dinner when both drank too much. Virginia started to scream at Flynn, disrupting the other restaurant
patrons. There are variations as to what happened next. One
gossip columnist reported that Hill threw her drink in his face.
Another claimed it was a raw egg. Both said that when Hill got
up and left, some of the diners in the restaurant applauded the
fiery redhead, giving the egocentric movie star his comeuppance. The incident made the local newspapers and movie-
industry trades.

Virginia Hill was now somebody, and Hollywood gossip columnists and radio show hosts reported on this mysterious sexpot with the bankroll. Those who knew the underworld, such as
Walter Winchell and Ed Sullivan, were aware of the truth
behind the facade and that she was on her way to becoming a
celebrity, albeit a notorious one. Winchell and Sullivan were
among the first to nurture a relationship with her and the only
male reporters in Hollywood and New York that ever got close
to Virginia.

In the fall of 1938, Virginia spent an increasing amount of
time in Mexico meeting mysterious Hispanics believed to be
connected to crime and drug dealing, disappearing for days.
When she reemerged, she said little to anyone, not even Chick,
about what she had been doing in Mexico.

In Hollywood she often dined and drank at small Mexican

bars and restaurants and met Mexicans in dark corners and spoke in hushed tones. Clearly there was something going on, but Virginia kept her business to herself. One of her favorite spots was a tiny Beverly Boulevard diner called the Mexican Kitchen. Marguerite Collins, who had worked in the restaurant and knew Virginia on a limited basis, said she always sensed a certain uneasiness about her. She said Virginia would usually meet a man, and they would sit in the back of the restaurant and drink. She never knew what was being discussed, because all conversation stopped when Collins approached.

> "It was always a different man," she remembered. "Once she said she was meeting her brother, but the man who came in was very dark. I knew they weren't related. But Virginia was always very nice, somewhat lonely, I think. She drank tequila and left me a big tip. She loved hot peppers, and I always put a lot out for her."

Another of Hill's haunts was the Serape Club, a small, dusty night spot with a floor show that consisted of rumba dancers, bongo players, and mariachis. During her first night at the club she became captivated by a baby-faced dancer with slicked-back jet black hair, baggy trousers, two-toned shoes, and a small turned-up nose. She asked the waiter to invite Miguelito Carlos Gonzales Valdez* to her table. He joined her the moment he finished his set and returned to Hill's Havenhurst apartment when the restaurant closed.

Valdez moved his clothes into the apartment that following afternoon and lived with Virginia and Chick for the next two weeks, until his engagement at the Serape Club ended. He then packed his bags and moved on. The two kept in loose touch, linked up in Mexico on occasion, and remained friends. But their romance did not cause a stir until December 7, 1938. That is when Virginia's reputation as a whore with the underworld caught the attention of the federal authorities and the national newspapers.

---

*There are conflicting stories about Valdez's real name. Some accounts list him as Carlos Valdez, others as Carlos Gonzales Valdez. Other publications insist that Carlos Valdez and Miguelito Valdez are two separate people. But friends of Hill's, newspaper columnists of the day who knew both Hill and Valdez, and the FBI files indicate that Carlos Valdez and Miguelito Valdez are the same person.

Hill and Miguelito had vacationed together for several weeks in Mexico. Virginia had received a phone call from Epstein, asking her to return to Chicago for a social visit and, supposedly, to transport some jewelry to Los Angeles, where the Chicago mob had already made significant inroads. Among the many stops along the route was a layover in Brownsville, Texas, where Customs and Immigration had the option of inspecting luggage, passports, and passengers.

The passengers deboarded, as was customary, and waited in the terminal until cleared by the authorities to return to the plane.

U.S. agents became suspicious of Valdez, who spoke broken English. They questioned his visa and rifled through some papers. It is not clear why they suspected that Hill and Valdez had been living together in Hollywood, but Virginia was called into one office, Valdez into another, and the subject of their living arrangements was broached in questions that were none too delicately phrased.

Virginia denied they were living together, that she was "harboring an alien," or that she was involved in any sort of espionage. They commented on her appearance and expensive clothes and asked point-blank if she had been sleeping with the Mexican for money, and if so, what had been the extent of their sexual involvement.

Finding the questions not only rude and insulting but clearly understanding the implication that she was a prostitute, Virginia vehemently and angrily denied the charges and exploded into a stream of expletives.

Valdez, who had been receiving the same grilling in another room, took the questions as a testament to his manhood, proud that such a good-looking, wealthy woman would invite him into her bed. He brazenly told the customs agents that they *had* been sleeping together and that there had been a long line of men before him. Was she a prostitute? No.

Valdez was denied entry into the United States on the grounds of moral turpitude. Virginia laughed, joking that she was unaware that one "had to prove virginity to get into America." She promised to take care of Valdez, but whether she actually sent him any money is anyone's guess.

Hill flew on to Chicago alone, wrapped up her business with

Epstein and Fischetti, and headed home for the holidays to Marietta. Chick followed her home a short time later. Once there, her life took yet another turn in a multitude of bizarre twists. She met and married a local boy.

Few would claim that Virginia Hill was impulsive; she rarely did anything without forethought and purpose. She could be irrational, hotheaded, stubborn, and driven by sexual desires. But this time she did something that even her closest friends could not understand. She ran off with a University of Alabama football player named Osgood Griffin, a bright and good-looking nineteen-year-old who came from a wealthy family. Virginia was chronologically only four years older than "Ossie," as she called him, but decades ahead in life experience. It is a safe statement that Griffin had never encountered anyone like Virginia Hill in his life.

Virginia said she met Griffin in a bar and bought him a drink. She said they had sex in his car and became engaged that night. A pathological liar when questioned about her past, Hill may have made up the story. She probably knew Griffin long before she moved to Chicago, for he had played fullback for Bessemer High School, though Virginia did not attend that school, and was popular around town. Virginia Hill and Ossie Griffin were married on January 13, 1939.

The Reverend O. B. Sansbury performed the ceremony in Birmingham, Alabama. Sansbury related the incident to Bill Kinney of the *Marietta Daily Journal*.

> They came driving up in a beautiful big car, and she was wearing the prettiest mink coat I'd ever seen. I almost refused to conduct the wedding when I looked at their marriage license and it stated that both had been married before.

Hill apparently tried to pass off the license she received when she had married George Rogers/Randell as the document issued for this marriage. Sansbury was suspicious, but the fast-talking Hill convinced him to perform the ceremony.

Hill told Sansbury that she and Ossie were being remarried and wanted the ceremony conducted by a minister. Sansbury capitulated. "They paid me five dollars," he said, "and left in that shiny limousine."

Virginia refused to offer any details about her life with Griffin, but it could not have been pleasant. The union was annulled six months later, most likely because the blushing bride could not find enough to do to keep her happy in Alabama. Ossie never joined his wife on her frequent trips to Chicago, California, and Mexico. Her continual absence may also account for the annulment instead of a divorce.

Those who knew Virginia later said she constantly changed her story about the Griffin annulment. Depending on her mood and the amount of alcohol consumed, Hill said that he abandoned her and left her with no alimony, no financial settlement, and no further contact. At other times, she said he made irregular cash payments or gave her a lump-sum payoff. Griffin's father, Osgood A. Griffin, who owned a large lumber company in Bessemer, claimed that Ossie was nothing more than a student at the time of the marriage, had no personal income, and could not make any cash settlements. The senior Griffin even said he picked up the $100 attorney's fees to pay for the dissolution.

During the latter part of 1939, Virginia and her brother Chick frequently commuted between Chicago, Los Angeles, and Mexico. Virginia adapted to the Hispanic culture, learned to speak enough Spanish to get around, and worked her way into the inner circle of the rich and influential. She became intimate, both socially and physically, with at least two powerful men: Chato Juarez, who was the son of the minister of finance, and Major Luis Amezcua, a rising political figure. Both reportedly knew about the other, and neither reportedly cared. She also ran with high-ranking Mexican authorities, politicians, and thugs. These men of seemingly varied occupations belonged to the same social circle.

Previous accounts maintain that Hill was welcomed into the this group because of an introduction by a girlfriend. Others insist it was simply because she threw a lot of money around and caught the eye of these men. But personal sources close to both Hill and the Chicago mob tell a far different and more believable account, one that explains exactly what she was doing south of the border so often, why Epstein had continued to send cash, not bank drafts, and why Hill had money to spread in nightclubs but not enough to put herself up in a lavish apartment or purchase a mansion in California.

With a clear understanding of Virginia's Mafia background, factoring in the vast sums of money that Joe Epstein continued to send, and considering the fact that Virginia rarely did anything that was not calculated to the last detail, though her reasons for doing certain things were known only to herself, it is certain that Virginia was not in Mexico strictly to swill tequila and to rumba. Virginia Hill was there on business for the Chicago mob.

Since the collapse of the bootlegging industry with the repeal of Prohibition, the American Mafia was desperate to tap new sources of income. Americans, trapped in a depressed economy, turned to drugs for a quick, if not cheap, escape. By 1934 the New York and Chicago mobs had entrenched their narcotics trafficking into territories outside the United States. Emissaries from both gangs headed south to escalate South American and Cuban drug manufacturing and northbound shipments with Hispanic drug lords. This was the beginning of the emergence of the South American drug cartels that have so completely overrun the U.S. narcotics rackets.

The New York mobsters did greater business with the Colombian and Cuban cartels that specialized in cocaine and heroin running through Miami. The Chicagoans pushed more cocaine and marijuana that came up from Mexico. Eventually, both Mafia groups would join forces and meld their narcotics operations. But at this time, the two ran independent narcotics rackets. This is why Miami had been of such interest to Chicago during its dealings with Joe Adonis.

By the mid-1930s the Capone mob was operating regular drug-producing factories and farms in South America, which raised opium poppies, hashish, and cannabis. Though the drug rackets were considered a "man's territory" within the Mafia, women were used on occasion to smuggle the narcotics across the border or divert the attention of Customs away from airline cargo or autoMobiles transporting the drugs into America.

Virginia Hill, who was by now a world-class money launderer and smuggler, once again proved herself a valuable asset to the Capone gang. The vast sums of money Epstein had been sending Hill were cash payments for drugs and bribes to Mexican authorities to "look the other way" during the drug-smuggling operations. Chicago confidants claim that Hill passed out bribes of around $5,000 a week, a sum that seems exorbitant during the depths of the depression but was in reality chump change to the Mafia, which had been collecting millions from the drug trade.

The mob made more than a 1,000 percent profit on drug sales in the United States. American money went far in Mexico; growers and processors made hundreds of thousand of dollars in U.S. dollars and, along with the cash, traded weapons for drugs. Everyone on both ends of the deal grew wealthy.

Virginia's social acceptance by the rich and powerful in Mexico and South America came down to business. She was a money carrier. She was also a lot of fun, good for the restaurant and cantina trade, and with the money she spent on souvenirs and presents for her mother and siblings and friends back in Alabama and Georgia, a boost to tourism.

During one of her trips to Mexico she joined Miguelito Valdez, who, with his brother, was operating a nightclub just over the Texas border. The nightclub was struggling, and the brothers fought between themselves. Valdez wanted to quit but was once again refused entry into the United States because of the "moral turpitude" incident. Valdez had been Hill's ally in Mexico and told her of his plight. There was only one way to get Valdez legally across the border.

On January 20, 1940, Virginia became Mrs. Miguelito Carlos Gonzales Valdez. The friendship rapidly deteriorated as the battles grew as frequent and loud as the lovemaking. It seemed that Miguelito had changed from an understanding boyfriend who accepted his wife's sexual dalliances, wild nightlife, and ties with unsavory characters into a domineering husband. He demanded she stay home and do things wives are supposed to do: cook, clean, and have babies.

When the parameters of the relationship changed, so did the emotions. Love, at least Virginia's version of it, degenerated into apathy, then finally into loathing. She refused to tell Valdez about her real business and often told him she married him only to help him get into the country. As far as Virginia was concerned, Valdez should have acted as an indentured servant and errand boy. Valdez mistakenly tried to act as a husband.

Hill called a few of her mob buddies and asked them to book

her hot-tempered husband into their supper clubs. There was no need for her to explain her true purpose, to keep her husband busy, miles away and out of her hair. The boys put Gonzales on tour through the Midwest and East Coast doing his rumba show. Virginia made sure he was rarely home in their Havenhurst apartment. She believed that their separation would diminish hostilities. It worked for a time.

As part of their trade accord with New York, the Chicago gang was allowed to invest in a nightclub called the Hurricane Club, at 1619 Broadway in New York. It had all the promise of a money-maker and could prove a great way to launder money as well. The Chicago mob was, of course, a silent partner, and the names of the backers were not to appear in any legal registers. Virginia was ordered to act as the front and travel to New York to work the deal.

Depending on who told the story, Virginia put down anywhere from $6,000 to $60,000 cash, but for some unexplained reason her name never appeared on the license as an owner. There was probably no need, because the books had nothing to do with the license.

Fronting the club turned into a double-edged sword for Hill. It not only solidified her position as a mob insider and socialite; it brought her under the watchful eye of the federal Bureau of Investigation. The FBI had been keeping tabs on Hill as a mob associate. Up until this point she was never considered important enough to merit her own detailed FBI probe, nor was she placed under federal surveillance. But when she fronted for the Hurricane Club, federal agents activated the Virginia Hill file: no. 136246. She was "elevated," if one can call it that, from "known associate of gangsters" to "suspected racketeer." In her own way, she had been "made."

She and Miguelito also appeared in newspaper columns and on magazine covers as they danced together at the club's grand opening. Hill rumbaed barefoot in a two-piece, bare-midriff white cotton dress, her red-painted toenails standing out against the wooden dance floor. Miguelito wore a three-piece suit with two-toned black-and-white shoes, his white pocket handkerchief perfectly folded. If any pictures could express the vast difference between the pair, these photos did.

Two days after the opening, Virginia waited in Valdez's backstage dressing room in a club in which he was appearing. She thrust a paper and pen at him and abruptly ordered him to sign. She supposedly told him that it was yet another booking contract. He knew better than to read the fine print on any bookings that came through his wife's associates. He signed. It was a legal draft agreeing to an uncontested divorce. Hill headed back to Los Angeles and never set eyes on Miguelito again.

There is one footnote to the Valdez affair. The following morning, Ed Sullivan reported that the pair had gone their own ways but her "valedictory gift to him was a $7,500 diamond watch and matching ring." Another columnist named Danton Walker wrote: "Virginia Hill has been discovered by Gene Krupa—or vice versa. Miguelito Valdes [sic] is now out of the picture."

Virginia did not want a husband whom she continually had to support and promote and whose feet were stuck in second-class mud. She was now a celebrity in her own right and needed to move with a faster crowd. She needed a man of power who understood her business and stayed out of her way. She needed someone exactly like herself. She was ready to close in on the Hollywood elite that thrived in one of the most politically corrupt and morally decadent cities in the country.

Hollywood was also the battleground for the New York and Chicago mobs. Hostilities had been steadily escalating and were about to explode. Lucky Luciano vowed to "have blood flowing in every gutter in every street of America," and Virginia Hill knowingly walked smack into the middle of the battle zone, playing each side against the other.

6

The battle over Hollywood between the Chicago and New York crime cartels actually began in the 1920s. Chicago thug Tommy Maloy seized control of Motion Picture Projectionists Local 110 through a common Mafia practice called "inheritance." In Maloy's case, he inherited the local through the sudden demise of its previous president, a street tough named Jack Miller. Maloy's so-called ownership of the union carried the formal title of business agent, though he acted as overlord by approving hirings, ordering firings, and filching a nickel from every dollar of dues. As business agent, Maloy legally collected monthly dues from members and controlled the union pension funds and treasury. In effect, he had an open license to line his pockets at the union member's expense.

Maloy knew his business well, and he ruled through the use of tommy guns, blackjacks, and brass knuckles. His business formula was simple: A projectionist who refused to pay union dues would be out of a job. If a theater owner refused to hire union operators, the film would disappear, the theater would burn down, or the manager would vanish forever.

Maloy operated freely in Chicago during the 1920s. Territorial wars between Capone, Moran, and other factions had yet to be resolved, and the bootlegging wars had gangs hopping. Few had the foresight to think in terms of more legitimate business, such as unions, except for Al Capone, who realized that someday Prohibition would end. He was always searching for new ways to do business. He had already taken over several unions as well as seemingly legitimate enterprises. But Capone wanted more.

During Maloy's reign, from 1920 to his murder at the hands of a Capone henchman in 1935, the motion-picture industry took off. Maloy was shrewd enough to ride the wave of opportunity. Hundreds of new theaters opened every day around the country, but membership in Maloy's union never increased. Instead of padding his union membership list, Maloy issued work permits to nonunion projectionists, with union and nonunion projectionists earning the same weekly wages.

At first, this move would appear foolish for someone with street-smart logic. But Maloy's angle was simple. Union members had to kick back only three dollars each week to the local, while nonunion "permit" workers kicked back 10 percent of their salaries. With some projectionists earning the then astronomical sum of $175 per week, no one complained, and Maloy's personal income grew along with his power.

With the onset of the Depression, theaters could not afford to pay such high salaries for projectionists and would not raise ticket prices on an already strapped public. Owners took a stand against Maloy, and one by one they began dropping union operators and permit workers.

Many Chicago theaters were firebombed, and scores of nitrate-stock films destroyed. But as quickly as one theater went up in smoke, another dropped from union influence. At the insistence of a group of irate theater owners, the Illinois State Attorney General's Office began an investigation of Maloy's union practices. The owners believed they would finally get a fair deal and legal help against the union thugs. What they did not realize was that the office had long ago been corrupted by Al Capone.

With an "irreproachable" attorney general's office closing in and theater control ebbing away, a panicked Maloy turned to the one man who would restore his control and power: Big Al. Capone did not need to be briefed. He had been watching Maloy ever since he inherited the union.

Capone and his men had slowly taken control of Chicago as

their enemies died or found other rackets. The combine was slowly corrupting various unions and had already "owned" the meatpackers, butchers, and dairymen's unions and controlled the garment industry, liquor trade, and restaurant-related operations. There was not one business in the city in which Capone did not have a stake. The projectionists' union was a plum that Capone and Frank Nitti had sought for some time. Maloy delivered it gift wrapped.

In May 1931, Capone had been convicted of income-tax-fraud charges and was residing in the Atlanta Penitentiary. But he still managed to wield his power through Nitti, Guzik, Epstein, Fischetti, and the gang. When Maloy approached the gang for help, the group moved quickly.

Using a legal maneuver through a bought-and-paid-for Illinois legislature, Capone's lackeys rammed through the passage of a bill requiring each movie theater to hire two projectionists "for safety's sake." Operators also had to be certified by the union. That kept renegade theater owners from hiring outside help and guaranteed union work in the city. In return, Maloy was asked to make a $5,000 contribution to Chicago mayor Tony Cermak's Democratic "fund." Maloy remained union business manager. Capone needed him to do the dirty work, and he had not yet outlived his usefulness.

With his newfound power and the backing of the Capone organization, Maloy expanded his union throughout the entire Midwest, South, and East. The holdout was New York. (The West Coast was controlled by numerous craft guilds, and projectionists there were members of IATSE, which recruited members from the stagehands' and craftsmen's guilds.) Nitti, through Capone, decided he would move against New York after he consolidated the various unions under one banner and had the clout of a megaunion backing him.

First Nitti folded the projectionists' union membership into the International Alliance of Theatrical Stage Employees (IATSE). That step automatically gave Chicago leverage in Hollywood, which was Nitti's real goal, as well as control over nearly every aspect of the film industry's workers: from production to distribution to projection. Then he placed his own man in charge of the operation, a slovenly thug named George Browne. Maloy objected strenuously and demanded that he be kept in control of his union. He believed he molded the union into its current structure and should be able to reap the rewards. Nitti said he would think it over.

Maloy received his answer on February 4, 1935, when a speeding car drew alongside his Cadillac on Chicago's Lake Shore Drive. Machine guns opened fire. Maloy's bullet-riddled body was later found slumped behind the wheel of his car.

With Maloy out of the way and George Browne poised to muscle in, Nitti had to force the holdout East Coast projectionists to come under his control. Under the guise of "Sicilian camaraderie," he approached Lucky Luciano and offered to cut him in for a large slice of the Hollywood pie if he threw control of the East Coast unions to the Midwest.

Luciano held out, believing that the other powers in New York, Dutch Schultz, Albert Anastasia, and Leo Lepke among them, would back him. Luciano believed that if the East Coast families joined forces, they could move in on Capone's operation and seize control of the racket for themselves. Luciano did not know that the others had already turned over their shares to Nitti in exchange for a portion of the Chicago and Midwest vice action, along with Chicago's agreement to keep out of Miami. Luciano stood alone.

The unions under Luciano's domain were powerless against the megamonster of the Capone-controlled unions. Capone's men had already worked deals with other East Coast mobsters and struck an accord. By the time Luciano decided to join with Capone, the Chicago mob really did not need his approval. It could take over his unions anytime it wished.

But Luciano was a deadly force and had the muscle of Costello, Adonis, and others behind him. In effect, he had the backing of the Mafia, which Al Capone and Nitti, his right-hand man, could never get. To keep peace and to thwart any Mafia interference, Nitti agreed to give Luciano a cut of the Hollywood bonanza in exchange for merging his unions into the IATSE. Luciano agreed. But Nitti had no intention of keeping his end of the bargain.

In order to gain access to another area of Hollywood, Luciano actually needed to retain some control of the unions. Like Nitti, he realized the money that could be made in the untapped drug, prostitution, gambling, and restaurant trade. If Nitti had kept Luciano frozen out of the studio takeover, his entrance into the other West Coast rackets would prove all the more difficult. Nitti believed he had outsmarted Luciano, while his New York nemesis assumed he had outwitted Nitti. Both now looked toward Hollywood.

Nitti was ready to make his move west to Hollywood to take over the movie studios, which seemed to be a never-ending source of money. His mob would also gain access to movie stars, many of whom were drug addicts, drunks, free spenders, and most of all, gullible. As Nitti told friends, "The goose was ready to be cooked."

George Browne, who was Frank Nitti's underling, teamed up with a Chicago pimp and racketeer named Willie Bioff, who was never quite liked or accepted by the Chicago underworld because he talked too much and thought too little. But Browne and Bioff had done business together for years when they were shaking down merchants and produce peddlers in Chicago's Fulton Street Market. They clicked as a team.

Bioff and Browne went after the biggest exhibitors first, the Balaban and Katz (B & K) theater chain.

As a representative of the Chicago mob, Browne demanded $20,000 from Barney Balaban to "offset treasury cuts from recent theater-employee layoffs." Browne also explained that unless the exhibitor ponied up, every projectionist would be pulled off the job. To underscore his point, he ordered some thugs to burn down several B & K theaters. Others were smoked out by a stooge, who would take a tightly rolled reel of nitrate film and ignite the end. Because the film was tightly wrapped, it would not necessarily burn but send pungent and toxic smoke billowing throughout the theater. Patrons would flee, and the health department would have to inspect the building before the theater would be allowed to reopen. Business would be lost.

Leo Spitz, Balaban's attorney, who would later serve as corporate head of Columbia Pictures, suggested that Balaban hand over the cash as well as an additional $150 weekly kickback to keep peace with the Chicago boys. Willie Bioff laundered the money through Capone's soup kitchens and appointed himself labor-relations counselor to the IATSE.

With the Balaban and Katz chain setting the pace, the pair

pulled the same stunt with every other theater chain, getting equally good results. Once they had the exhibitors under their control, they went after the studios. Their leverage was simple enough. Without a place to show the films, the films would sit in the cans, no one would see them, and the studios would be forced to close. In addition, because the mob controlled the IATSE, no film would go into production, because every studio worker would be taken off the job. They also threatened to pull every projectionist out of the theater and shut down any movie house that hired scabs if the studio heads failed to capitulate. No one found a flaw in their logic.

The major studios paid out as much as $150,000 each. The smaller operations kicked in $25,000. The money was again laundered by Bioff and Browne. Many of the filmmakers accounted for the bribes in their books by listing them as expenses for the purchase of film stock or props.

Bioff and Browne made sure that the studios or exhibitors kept the cash flowing and insisted that they become involved in the studio's business. They merged the IATSE under the American Federation of Labor (AFL), which supervised the other various studio crafts guilds, and put themselves on the board of directors.

When the studios objected, Browne used the clout of the AFL to threaten a massive, industrywide strike that would not only shut down but completely bankrupt every studio in Hollywood. Hours before the strike was called, the studios surrendered. Browne not only smugly accepted their apology but demanded they each kick in another $50,000. Browne convinced his union members that the studio bosses had tried to take away their representation and that the fifty grand was to be put in a special fund that would help strikers if the studio tyrants ever tried to silence them again. He never explained that the special fund was divvied up between himself, Bioff, and the Chicago mob. The scheme is known today as "The Million Dollar Movie Shakedown" because the Capone mob figured it could realize a steady income of $1 million a year from the scam.

The year was 1935. The Capone gang was now well entrenched in Hollywood.

Once the mob had controlled the studios, it was not about to kick back any profits, as promised, to Luciano. Nitti and his boys never intended to make good on their conciliatory promise to cut Luciano in on the action. They made good on Al's vow to "get even" with the New York crime king.

Not only had Luciano been forced to hand over his unions to the Chicago mob; he now had been swindled and risked losing face within the underworld. Once he lost face, he would be personally vulnerable and at the receiving end of the same criminal justice he had ordered against so many of his enemies. Charlie Lucky understood he had to personally stop Capone from taking over the other rackets in Southern California. He had no choice but to fight back, and he took that fight to Los Angeles.

Perhaps no town was a more perfect setting for an organized-crime takeover than Los Angeles. The residents were nonchalant about nearly everything, and just about everyone in town was either trying to get into the movies or worked in some movie-related industry. It was a company town, all fun and glamour on the surface but seething with corruption at its core.

Unlike Chicago and New York, where territories were divided up and disputes settled in bloodshed, Los Angeles was a cowboy town that seemed to spring into a big city over night. Gangsters just moved in, rigged elections, and took over. No argument, no shooting, no killing. And to the underworld, what was taken once could be taken again.

Hollywood in the 1920s and 1930s had become the mecca for movie-star scandals: Starlet Olive Thomas was found dead of a heroin overdose; Mary Pickford's brother Jack became a drug addict; Roscoe "Fatty" Arbuckle was framed by Paramount Studios chief Adolph Zukor in a bizarre rape-murder scandal; director William Desmond Taylor was found murdered, with Paramount's top actresses named as prime suspects; heartthrob Wallace Reid died in a sanitarium when he slid into a coma after the heroin to which he was addicted was abruptly cut off. The list was endless. Each studio had its own "Dr. Feelgood" who set up camp to keep the stars in their drug-induced state. But the decadence did not stop at the studio gates.

Los Angeles district attorney Buron Fitts was already well on his way to becoming one of the most corrupt D.A.s in history. His predecessor, Asa Keyes, who was kicked out of office, ordered Fitts to continue to scuttle evidence on several top

Hollywood murders and suicides. Fitts continued Keyes's modus operandi.

Buron Fitts did not even come close to cornering the market on corruption. The chief of police, Jim "Two Gun" Davis, was a loudmouthed braggart who pretended he was still in the Wild West and carried two pearl-handled pistols at his sides. Davis feigned innocence as he stuffed his pockets with bribe money from brothel owners, rum runners, outlaws, and gamblers. He even promoted men through the ranks of the Los Angeles Police Department on a bribe system: Five dollars secured a detective's license, twenty would buy a lieutenant's position, and fifty would mean an immediate promotion to captain. The bribe scale was even posted in his office. Davis often boasted that "the law is where you buy it in this town."

Davis answered to L.A. mayor Frank Shaw, who perfected the art of dirty politics. He blatantly admitted to newspapers that he rigged elections, then defied them to prove it. He often said he ran his office out of his pockets, meaning that he got more business done by opening his suit coat for bribes than opening his office door for a conference.

Shaw appointed his brother Jim head of a special police enforcement unit that was nicknamed the L.A.P.D. Spy Squad. The group literally spied on citizens who defied the Shaw-Davis-Fitts regime. Those so-called troublemakers would be followed and trumped-up charges placed in their "personnel" file. When and if the undesirables stepped over the line imposed by Shaw, they would be beaten, firebombed, or murdered.

The Spy Squad also became an assassination squad. The group ran Los Angeles with a deadly force equaled in style and terror only by that of Luciano in New York. Los Angelinos were afraid to speak out, store owners were terrified about reneging on a kickback, and honest police officers refused to buck the system, knowing better than anyone the consequences of fighting back.

Even if average citizens were unaware of the extent of the evil that had enveloped their political infrastructure, it was certainly hard to miss on the streets and in the water. Brothels ran freely, some even right down the street from city hall. The majority of people carried unregistered firearms, and business boomed in gun stores. The movies reflected drug addiction, boozed-up orgies, and sex parties that were gossiped about so often on the streets that they seemed commonplace.

The West had become easy pickings, with the city caving in under the weight of graft and run by two-bit hoods who never learned how to claw their way to the top and fight gang wars. Chicago and New York had the same idea: Take over gambling, narcotics, vice, and restaurants. Luciano knew that he had been outflanked by Chicago, but he did not realize how far.

Johnny Roselli had been one of Capone's sluggers and henchmen in the late 1920s in Chicago. He had a lengthy police record by the time he moved west in 1924. He carried an unregistered handgun and worked a variety of rackets, from crooked dice games to rum-running to murder for hire. He was friendly, and through his Chicago connections and the tough-as-nails attitude he projected, he easily worked his way through the ranks of city hall and the L.A.P.D. as both a confidant of the Shaw-Fitts regime and an emissary from the outfit.

One of Roselli's first alliances involved "Tony the Hat"— Tony Strella Cornero—a thug, bootlegger, killer, and pimp who earned the odd nickname because of his tendency to sport a white ten-gallon cowboy hat. Strella operated a small string of tugs that shipped whiskey from Canada and Mexico into the United States during Prohibition. The boats also transported prostitutes and stolen merchandise. Always at odds with the law, Strella teamed with Roselli in the late 1920s to gain the Chicago mob's backing and protection in order to keep his racket operating. In exchange, Strella gave a large part of the profits to Roselli and the mob.

Together Strella and Roselli concocted a plan that would siphon business away from every rogue gambling operation in Los Angeles and lure every man and woman, enticed by a game of chance, to their operation. They turned the bootlegging tugs into gambling casinos, which were actually floating crap games. The scheme became an instant gold mine.

When Fischetti was approached about financing the idea, he wasted no time. He quickly put up a $200,000 stake to pay for renovations of the tugs and bribes to keep Davis and his goons out of the water-taxi operations, which took gamblers from the shore to the ships. Fischetti chose Jack Dragna as overlord and sent him to oversee the gambling operation while organizing Chicago's interests in the West. It had become increasingly evident that the mob's future was out West, beyond the studios.

Dragna had a record that dated back to 1915, a hefty FBI file (no. 307014), and a string of aliases: Jack Rizoto, Jack Dania, Jack Drigna, and Jack Ignatius Dragna. He had been arrested for extortion in Long Beach, had served time in San Quentin, had been arrested in Los Angeles in 1917 for a murder in New York but never served time, and was wanted by the U.S. Immigration and Naturalization Service (INS) for entering this country illegally (he was Italian and never applied for U.S. citizenship, which was common in the underworld), and for robbery and tax evasion. The list went on. He had lived in New York, worked with Lansky, and knew Luciano well. He got along with them and was one of the few men trusted by both sides of the Midwest–East Coast Mafia rivalry.

Fischetti and Luciano realized the enormous profits at stake in Los Angeles and saw that any type of open warfare in the West would halt plans for complete infiltration by tipping off the federal authorities as to their intentions. Any problems, they agreed, would be handled by Dragna. At least that was the deal by which Luciano claimed he would abide. But Luciano went back on his promise when Dragna and Roselli went too far.

Dragna moved quickly and ruthlessly murdered restaurant owners, butchers, greengrocers, distillers, vintners, linen-service managers, pimps, brothel masters, and drug peddlers who defied his authority.

He and Roselli then turned their attention to the sea, to expand their water-bound gambling empire. They raided and seized a weather-beaten wood schooner called the *Monfalcone* and docked it in the three-mile "safe" limit off Long Beach. Gambling still was not allowed, legally, within some city limits, but the three-mile distance was beyond any local jurisdiction. The exterior of the *Monfalcone* gave no indication of the jewel that was hidden inside.

There were leaded glass windows and roofs, a lavish ballroom, and room for an orchestra. The 282-foot ship boasted a number of roulette wheels, fifty slot machines, crap tables, card tables, and bookies to cover racing wires. The ship took in money as fast as people could pull it out of their pockets. It was also symbolic—one of the first major steps toward Chicago dominance in West Coast gambling.

Soon after the takeover of the *Monfalcone* (which caught fire in August 1930), Dragna and Roselli seized and renovated other ships, such as the *Rose Isle*, the *Johanna Smith*, and the *Monte Carlo*, all docked off Long Beach harbor in an area known as Gamblers' Row. The *Monte Carlo* was Tony Strella's plum, and he was put in charge of the other two over strenuous objections and subsequent murders of the owners, who had alliances to the East.

But the duo did not stop at gambling ships. Roselli had always fancied himself as a film producer or studio mogul and openly sought out the friendship of various studio heads. One of Roselli's first and closest allies was Harry Cohn, an ardent gambler who became an easy mark for a sucker bet. Roselli lent Cohn money, staked some of his films, and even acted as his "representative" during the ensuing shakedown by Bioff and Browne, whom Roselli was named to replace as Chicago's inside man in the Hollywood studios.

While Roselli kept busy with the ships and the studios, Dragna emerged as the Al Capone of the West, supervising all the outfit's West Coast rackets. The Chicago mob, which was now known in the underworld as the outfit, tightened its stranglehold on the L.A.-area vice and gambling rackets as well as movie-industry labor unions. It proved unyielding, much to the disdain of Luciano, Costello, and Lansky, who had their sights set on the West in spite of the Nitti swindle.

When Luciano learned he had been ripped off by Nitti in the studio shakedown, he personally came west to settle the score. The first man he saw was Dragna, who agreed to ease off on his grab for the restaurant industry and narcotics trade as a concession for the Nitti scam. Though they shook hands, both men knew that the other could not be trusted, and both immediately set out to undercut the other and shatter the alliance.

Luciano had planted two of his men as moles in the district attorney's office. He put Davis and the Shaw brothers on his payroll and strengthened his South American and Cuban drug connections in order to begin drug shipments through the West. Luciano then made a grab for the Hollywood drug, restaurant, and gambling trade.

His attempt to personally control the Hollywood rackets quickly crashed around him and touched off one of the town's hottest and most grisly scandals, including the mysterious murder of actress Thelma Todd. (The murder is chronicled in detail in the book *Hot Toddy*.)

Thelma Todd was a popular comedienne who seemed to make one mistake after another in her personal life. Most of the time she would choose the wrong man.

By 1935 she had married, then divorced, a man-about-town named Pat DiCicco. A playboy, DiCicco was tied to both the New York and Chicago mobs through his dealings as a gambler and vice peddler. He became close to Todd when, in his early days, he tried to break into the movies as an agent. He promoted Todd's drug habit (which had consisted of speed-laced diet pills) and introduced her to Lucky Luciano, with whom she had an affair. Todd was attracted to Luciano's power and forcefulness and was subsequently his entrée to narcotics and gambling in Hollywood.

Thelma owned a popular beachfront restaurant called Thelma Todd's Sidewalk Cafe. The general public was told that the third floor was a storage room, but insiders knew it was really used as a lucrative gambling parlor. Luciano tried to muscle his way into the operation and take over the restaurant. Thelma refused and went to Buron Fitts, not knowing Luciano had already corrupted the office. Thelma Todd was found dead within the week, beaten, then jammed behind the wheel of her car and left to die alone in the garage of carbon monoxide poisoning.

The death was first ruled a suicide, then, after a grand jury probe, listed as accidental. The evidence was scuttled, the medical records altered.

The debacle created such an uproar of bad publicity for Hollywood that Luciano personally fled the West Coast forever. But he needed someone to represent his concerns, and keep tabs on Dragna and Roselli, in his stead.

Joey Adonis suggested that Luciano send Ben Siegel as the mob's man to supervise the gambling rackets. Adonis believed that by banishing Siegel to Hollywood, he would be through with the man who embarrassed him over Virginia Hill. Adonis also believed that Siegel would blend with the movie crowd and therefore gain inside access to the "dope fiends," as Adonis often called addicts, and their pushers. Siegel might also get close enough to the filmmakers to break up Nitti's shakedown scam or fleece studio heads in a separate deal.

Adonis knew what he was doing. He was rid of the mobster he described as "the most dangerous man I know" and who was, he said, "the only man I'm afraid of." Siegel was sent west for another reason: He was "hot" and needed to get out of town.

The New York authorities were closing in on him with a murder indictment. Siegel stabbed a friend to death in a personal feud and dumped the body in the East River. He was so insane at the time of the killing that he stabbed the corpse an extra twenty times in the stomach so that when the dead body became bloated after death, the gasses could escape, and the body would not float to the surface. He also ran afoul of the law for rigging boxing matches at Madison Square Garden and beating a local bookie who allegedly held back on Siegel's cut. The bookie went to the authorities, and Siegel ordered his execution.

In early 1937, Bugsy opened shop in Beverly Hills. He leased a thirty-five-room mansion on McCarthy Drive that had been owned by opera star Lawrence Tibbett and quickly established his presence in the city. He joined with Roselli and shared ideas with him about running the studios. Together they schemed to consolidate the racing wire services and take over movie producer Joe Schenck's Tijuana racetrack, called Agua Caliente, which was a popular hangout for Hollywood stars and had been ordered closed by the local government. Siegel and Roselli controlled the horse racing at Santa Anita and boxing bouts at the Olympic Auditorium and ignited a wave of terror that had more than four hundred bookies lining up behind him. Chief among them was Mickey Cohen, a fat, pug-ugly swindler who "owned" the bookmaking operations in the Los Angeles city limits. With Siegel and Roselli working together, while keeping an eye on one another, an apprehensive peace was once again struck between the two factions. But, as usual, it would not last.

Siegel was erratic and irrational. He rarely kept his mind on business and took off on tangents that confused Roselli and Dragna. Siegel was moody, and his moods were quick to change. Roselli and Dragna knew they always had to be careful with him.

Bugsy courted such movie stars as Jean Harlow, Al Jolson, George Raft, John Carroll, Sophie Tucker, John Garfield, and Mae West. He became a companion of leather-goods billionairess Dorothy Dendice Taylor DiFrasso, who obtained the title Countess when she married Italian nobleman Count Carlo DiFrasso. Siegel hosted $10,000 parties at Ciro's and the Mocambo and threw week-long orgies at the Garden of Allah. (Virginia Hill had yet to move in there.) He screwed both the women and men; the women sexually, the men financially. But he was "a gangster," and that made him all the more exciting to the naive stars.

There are rumors Siegel even took a screen test as a lark, considering a sidelight as a movie extra. Though he never appeared in a film, Bugsy did consider himself movie-star material. He often said that if the cards were dealt differently, he would have been a leading man instead of a gangster.

He was so enthralled with the business that he seized control of the unions that had not surrendered to the Chicago gang. Siegel lined up the Screen Extras guild, a slew of craft guilds that had remained independent of the IATSE, and supervised the Teamsters trucking and shipping operations at the studios until the outfit took control of the Teamsters after his death. And he did it all behind Roselli's back.

One story describes a clash between Siegel and Warner Brothers over the Extras Guild. Siegel demanded a "payment" of $10,000 to the guild's pension fund. Warners, already browbeaten from the Nitti shakedown, refused. In an unusually controlled manner for Siegel, he calmly laid out the plan.

"I guess you just don't get it. Take your next picture. You've got the script written, the director on salary, stagehands set, all getting paid. So when the cameras roll, the extras walk out. What have you got? Nothing. Just a lot of empty space. No extras, no picture. No money, no extras."

Warners paid.

Bugsy even shook down many of his so-called movie-star buddies for four- and five-figure "loans," which he never repaid. Those who had known of Siegel's loan scams have said that nearly everyone was afraid to say no to him. They knew he had murdered dozens of people and savagely beaten scores more. His favorite pigeon was George Raft, whom Siegel bled. In one year Siegel boasted to Lansky that he fleeced the Hollywood suckers for more than $400,000.

Within six months of his arrival, Bugsy Siegel had became a one-man Mafia terrorist and had crowned himself "King of Corruption" in Hollywood. He had scores of women, a wild nightlife, and constant attention from the wealthy, famous, and infamous. His picture was continually in the newspapers glad-handing and back patting with Hollywood moguls and stars, and his name was on the lips of Hollywood gossips, who adored the bon vivant gangster.

He took over city hall, and local politicians came to him before making a move. Siegel said that "out here the politicians don't run for office, we run the politicians."

But he wanted more. He wanted Jack Dragna, John Roselli, and the Chicago clan out of Los Angeles and made threats against them. Siegel felt he had his own power base and they were no longer assets and allies but hindrances.

Dragna saw Siegel as nothing more than a flamboyant two-bit hood whose control began and ended with the racing wires and gambling rackets. He believed Siegel was too loud and obvious for his own good, focused too much media attention on the underworld, and was too pushy and greedy. He knew Siegel hoped to trigger a gang war. As a final thorn, Ben Siegel prevented Chicago from taking complete control of the local gambling, for the bookies, through Mickey Cohen, had aligned with the Bug. Dragna also knew that only one person could get close enough to Siegel to throw him off guard, trip him up, and get him out of the way—Virginia Hill.

Virginia Hill had been busy running money and fencing property between Mexico, Hollywood, and Chicago and between Chicago and New York. During her stay in Los Angeles, she kept in close contact with Dragna and Roselli. There are stories that she and Roselli had a lengthy affair. She was ordered by Charlie Fischetti to "play socialite" and get the lay of the land.

Siegel had arrived in Los Angeles about one year before Virginia. Bugsy was well entrenched in the Hollywood set, the nightclub crowd, and the underworld when Virginia began to make her own mark. She quickly spotted the movers and shakers and sized up Siegel as the one to watch. Hill studied him but held back on joining him until she had the nod to do so from Dragna. She knew exactly what Siegel was doing, how he was operating, and with whom. She also remembered the affair in New York as the best sex she had ever had and pressed Dragna to move against Siegel. The thought of working for the outfit in some capacity other than laundering and fencing excited Virginia. So did the prospect of sex with the Bug.

Dragna needed someone to get close enough to Siegel to learn his wire-service and bookmaking operations, his political contacts, and the names of his business partners. He also needed to find evidence to use against Siegel once he learned all he needed to know to take over Bugsy's operations.

When Dragna told Virginia to go after Siegel and spy on him, she had no objection. Dragna gave her only one piece of advice. It was meant as a warning. "Don't get too close."

7

If Lucky Luciano thought Chicago was a "goddamn crazy place" where "no one's safe on the streets," it would be interesting to know how he viewed Los Angeles. Jack Dragna, who insisted to federal authorities that he was a banana importer, was gunning after Bugsy Siegel, who wanted to be a movie star. Johnny Roselli, who wanted to be a movie producer, was going after Mickey Cohen, who fronted his bookmaking empire through a Sunset Boulevard haberdashery store. Reformist groups were attacking one another to win the honor of nailing the Shaw brothers, Police Chief Davis, and Buron Fitts. Meyer Lansky and Luciano were plotting to kick Frank Nitti and Paul Ricca out of Hollywood.

Virginia Hill arose out of the chaos. By now she was the most trusted and highly placed woman in the underworld, compared to other mob women, who ran brothels or were hooked up with small-time bookmaking joints. Her elevation in the mob also put her on equal footing with many of the men, something that no other woman had been able to do before or has done since.

Hill was one of the few people who moved freely between the New York and Chicago gangs. When she needed something done, she phoned Adonis or Luciano in New York, Charlie Fischetti or Joe Epstein in Chicago, or Jack Dragna or Johnny Roselli in Los Angeles. Calls were first met with the usual mob question: "What's the matter?" Then whatever Hill needed was done, whether it was money, access to a politician, travel arrangements, or palms crossed with a few bribe dollars.

By this time the FBI was well acquainted with her underworld business. She was also the envy of many street punks who were trying to move up in the criminal ranks. Virginia complained to Joey Ep that she had been followed in Los Angeles and Chicago and that she believed she was being shadowed as the first step in a holdup. Ep told her she had become paranoid. He added that no one would dare rob someone so highly placed in the Capone mob. He was wrong.

Hill was so busy as a money carrier and money launderer by 1939 that she spent little time in one place and had keys to several gangsters' apartments. While in Chicago to either pick up or deliver money or stolen merchandise, she usually stayed in Epstein's suite in the Sherman House Hotel or in his North Side penthouse. One evening in March 1939, Hill had a late dinner at a Clark Street restaurant near Epstein's office. She finished her meal and headed straight to Joe Ep's hotel suite. Shortly after she unlocked the door, two gunmen shoved her inside and stuck a pistol in her face.

One of the men slapped her and shouted, "Where's the money?" Virginia pointed to a dresser. While one held the gun, the other rifled through the drawers, where he found nearly $2,000 in cash. Then they stripped Virginia of her fur stole and jewelry, its value estimated somewhere between $8,000 and $10,000. It was stolen merchandise, of course, which was to be carried to Los Angeles the following week. Two days later, eighteen-year-old James Drobvonick and twenty-year-old Tony Porcher were found dead—one hog-tied and stabbed and left in a trunk of a stolen car, the other dumped in a corn field near Schaumburg, just outside the city.

How these two gunmen were identified as the criminals and who killed them remains a mystery. Undaunted, Virginia Hill had the nerve to report the robbery to the Chicago Police Department, which duly recorded and filed the complaint. She later explained that she made the report in order to be able to declare the theft as a loss for income-tax purposes. Epstein was apparently behind the idea to report the crime, and there are suspicions that the robbery itself was staged, the thieves killed as a cover-up.

Epstein and Luciano kept Virginia busy with the South American drug rackets and money laundering and used her to front nightclubs and other business ventures in New York, Chicago, and Los Angeles. But when Dragna sent word that he was having problems with Ben Siegel, Hill was ordered to stay in Los Angeles. Virginia obliged. Dragna gave Hill the highest commendation possible in the underworld: "She was the only woman who could be trusted to keep her mouth shut."

There are different versions of how Virginia Hill and Bugsy Siegel reunited. Several mob historians insist they met for the first time ever at Warner Brothers on the set of George Raft's movie *Manpower*. They claim Hill had been a bit-part actress and caught Siegel's eye and that from the instant they met, Hill and Siegel were lovers.

This scenario seems unlikely for a number of reasons. Chief among them, as previously explained, was that Hill must have known Siegel in New York if she had consorted with every one of his criminal friends. It is impossible to believe she would have known everyone but Siegel.

It also seems unlikely because there are doubts as to whether Hill had even been an actress at all. Several accounts claim that Hill and her brother Chick, who had lived with Virginia in Hollywood, enrolled in the Columbia Pictures Acting School together sometime around 1941 and that Hill appeared in *Ball of Fire*, a Barbara Stanwyck–Gary Cooper movie (for which she did do a screen test); signed, then bought out, a seven-year contract at Universal; unsuccessfully tried to find a talent agent; and had dreams of being a big star.

If Virginia had real movie-star aspirations, she certainly would have been one. The Chicago mob still owned the movie studios and unions. All Hill had to do was say the word and she would have been featured in any movie she desired. Ben Siegel owned the Screen Extras Guild. He would have done the same for Virginia upon orders from Adonis or Luciano, or even Jack Dragna, whether Siegel knew Hill or not.

In Hollywood, nepotism continually takes precedent over talent. Hill had the looks; talent was inconsequential. Virginia was too well connected in the mob to be frustrated at any ambition. Setting her up in a movie, especially in the 1940s, would have been one of the easiest favors granted.

A thorough search of the records in the Academy of Motion

Picture Arts and Sciences Library in Los Angeles produced absolutely no mention of Virginia Hill in any Columbia Pictures Acting School, Universal Studios Acting School, or the credits of any motion pictures in the late 1930s and early 1940s at Universal, Columbia, or Warner Brothers. At best, she worked as an uncredited extra, more as a lark than any desire to be an aspiring actress.

This version gives more credence to the story of what Hill was actually doing in Hollywood and how she reunited with Siegel, as related independently by Harry Brescelli and "KJ" Stimpson, who knew Hill in Los Angeles.

By 1939 and 1940, Virginia was well known around Hollywood as a free-spending socialite who threw $10,000 parties at Ciro's and the Mocambo, had her own box at Santa Anita, and was on the "A" list at Hollywood parties. She was the idol of the gossip columnists, who hinted at her mob connections, which many found glamorous and intriguing, and who liked to gossip and make up stories about her background, which Virginia hid from guessing reporters. Virginia hobnobbed with celebrities and the wealthy businessmen of California, including newspaper tycoons Chandler and Hearst, but considered George Raft among her closest friends in Hollywood.

Raft had become notorious throughout the movie industry as a crony of Lucky Luciano, Meyer Lansky, Charlie Fischetti, and Ben Siegel. It gave him an air of authority both on-screen and off and set him apart from the countless other stars who were magnetically drawn to the underworld but could not break into the inner circle. Hill was introduced to Raft by a mutual friend, Pat DiCicco.

If life imitates art, then the maxim is certainly true for George Raft. He made his career as a screen gangster and built his reputation on the fact that he played the parts so convincingly. In Raft's mind, he was never acting. He was such a gangster wannabe that he actually became Lucky Luciano, Meyer Lansky, or any of the other criminals he idolized when he stepped before the cameras. But Georgie, as his friends called him, was so eager to please the mob that he was considered a pushover and an easy mark for a loan. And the underworld never ceased leaning upon him for loans and favors, which ranged from money laundering to fronting businesses to helping secure the mob's grip on the studios. Though Raft perceived himself as a Mafia insider, he was ridiculed as a "groupie" and a "pigeon" by those really on the inside who bled him dry.

Ben Siegel and George Raft were mirror images of one another. Raft imitated Siegel on-screen; Siegel imitated Raft off camera. Siegel dreamed of being a movie star as much as Raft dreamed of being a gangster. Raft taught Siegel how to dress. Siegel taught Raft the machinations of the rackets. The two quickly became inseparable from the moment they met in late 1938.

In the spring of 1939, George Raft threw a party at his home in Coldwater Canyon and invited the Hollywood crowd, which included George Jessel, John Garfield, Wendy Barrie, Milton Berle, Eddie Cantor, Ray Danton, writer Gene Fowler, Errol Flynn, Betty Grable and Harry James, and a few sports figures, bankers, and mobsters, among them Ben Siegel and Virginia Hill. Hill reportedly knew Siegel would be at the party and used the evening as the catalyst to continue the affair that first ignited in New York.

They stayed behind after the rest of the guests left and spent a long and amorous weekend in Raft's guest bedroom.

Raft welcomed the liaison and considered it an honor that the two underworld figures chose his home to resume their romance. Hill liked Raft's house because of the privacy, away from her brother Chick, and Siegel claimed to his wife that he was there only to play cards and gamble with Raft and his buddies. It was the perfect setup for both, and Raft was trusted to keep silent about their affair.

Hill was such a frequent guest at Raft's home that she checked in for the weekend with her own satin sheets, pillowcases, and personalized towels. She even brought her own maid on occasion. Hill had a key to the house and came and went as she pleased.

Raft said that Hill and Siegel spent at least two weekends per month at his house; they would show up separately and disappear for several days. He would see full meal trays brought up and empty ones carried back down. Other than that, he never knew he had houseguests.

By May, Siegel and Hill were nearly inseparable. They maintained separate quarters at first, for appearance sake, because

Siegel was still married to Esta, though he left her and the children in New York. Esta knew about her husband's affair. It certainly was not his first. But she also knew that as the wife of a mobster, infidelity was the price for a home, car, clothes, and food on the table. Esta remained in the background and never pressured Ben in his outside affairs.

In front of the children, they insisted that their father was in California on business, and his affairs were never discussed on his infrequent trips back East. The Siegel children were not allowed to read newspapers unless Esta prescreened them for articles about their father.

Hill and Siegel joined forces at the racetracks, working the betting scams, setting up sucker bets, and fixing boxing matches. The two played the horses with Gary Cooper, Clark Gable, and Cary Grant, who had nearby boxes at Santa Anita and ringside seats at the Olympic Auditorium. There was no better match sexually, personally, and professionally. They were experts in the drug, money-laundering, and gambling rackets, shared common friends, and were both hungry to move up in the underworld. Siegel thought he had found the perfect woman.

The two seemed to represent exactly the common ground that Luciano and Fischetti (and Jack Dragna) had hoped to find—strong, trusted emissaries who worked well together, enjoyed one another's company, thought alike, and yet would remain firm in representing each side's gambling concerns. Luciano felt he could let his guard down, if ever so slightly, with Siegel running the family's wire, racetrack, and casino operations. Fischetti felt confident that Hill would get close enough to Siegel to ensure that he would not try to swindle the outfit from its share of profits and to find an opening for the Chicago clan to muscle in on his operation.

Virginia took Ben Siegel with her on one of her excursions to Mexico and introduced him to many of her Mexican contacts, both personal and "professional," those with whom she did drug-related business. They roamed Baja, Tijuana, and Rosarita Beach and, with East Coast and Chicago money, financed several Mexican casinos, including a large operation at Rosarita. They worked the drug rackets and meshed the Chicago and Luciano operations into one major Mafia narcotics operation, though the two factions still held opposing views on drug users. Chicago had a policy of never doing business with drug users; Luciano's gang had no such qualms.

In exchange for Hill's bringing Siegel into the center of the Chicago mob's drug racket, Siegel cut Chicago in on a piece of the action at Agua Caliente in Tijuana. It seemed, for a time, that the hostile undercurrent between Chicago and New York had begun to fade, that the two sides could work together for the common corruption of the town and the "greater glory" of the Mafia. Virginia Hill was doing her job. Ben Siegel believed he was in love and had the hottest romance of his life.

While in Los Angeles, Ben and Virginia moved frequently from hotel to hotel, friend's house to friend's house, rented home to rented home, almost as if they were running from something. They shared a room at the Sunset Plaza Apartments on Sunset Boulevard, then moved across the street to apartment 6-D at the tony Chateau Marmont Hotel, where they registered under the name Mr. and Mrs. James Hill. They stayed at the Towne House Motel on Wilshire Boulevard and the Ambassador Hotel, where a top-floor suite plus room service cost Virginia more than $1,200 per week. She rented Rudolph Valentino's old hilltop home, Falcon's Lair, then a penthouse on Wilshire Boulevard. Hill and Siegel leased a ranch home in Coldwater Canyon, just down the street from Raft's house. Hill used a variety of aliases, more than twenty five by the time the FBI gave up counting. And she usually picked up the tab and paid cash, mostly hundred-dollar bills, all coming from her never-ending money machine, Joe Epstein and commissions for her work.

Siegel was usually broke and often let women pay for his company. Where his money went remains a mystery. But Siegel finally decided his affair with Virginia was serious and that it was time for him to pay the bills. He bought a home at 250 Delfern Avenue and immediately ordered in carpenters and designers to decorate it. He thought the address and home were both swanky enough for the girlfriend of Hollywood's most flamboyant man-about-town. Siegel had two special sets of keys made, one for him and one for Virginia. Both were cut from solid gold.

Chick Hill moved into the Delfern house and did odd jobs and errands for Ben. Chick later said that he thought of Siegel as a combination big brother and father figure. Siegel made sure the young man had plenty of walking-around money, girls, clothes, and cars and introduced him into the underworld rackets. (Chick was arrested several times during his adult life on various charges and ended up with a lengthy police record, which he blamed on Siegel's corrupting influence.)

Virginia and Ben represented the glamorous side of the underworld, characters that Hollywood so ineptly portrayed in early movies: free-spending, well-dressed, sharp-talking wise guys with the world at their feet. When they entered a nightclub together, they were instantly recognized from the countless newspaper and magazine stories; every head turned; waiters fawned over them, knowing that a hefty tip awaited them; movie stars, politicians, and the wealthy and powerful of the country paid their "respects." Within one year, Virginia and the Bug ruled Tinseltown.

Hill always tipped everyone, from store clerks to delivery boys to waiters, with brand-new, crisp hundred-dollar bills. She rented out Sunset Strip nightclubs and showered her friends with expensive gifts of diamonds, clothes, and cuff links or perfume.

Siegel was not as generous with servants but more of a showman than Hill. He usually flipped a gold coin or silver dollar in one hand, then sent it spinning for someone to catch as a tip, a trick that Raft imitated and later claimed he copied from a number of gangsters. Gifts for friends were usually small tokens, wallets, stickpins, or brand-name watches. No one complained.

They had accounts at nearly every store in Beverly Hills. Ben Siegel, Esq., had tailor-made suits, gold cuff links, and fancy, two-toned Italian leather shoes. He had his initials embroidered on his shirt cuffs and used silk handkerchiefs and designer stockings.

Hill had a closet stocked with Persian lamb coats, mink stoles, and a cache of imported suits, dresses, and shoes. She decorated the Delfern home with the best that money could buy: fine bone china, Tiffany vases and lamps, cut crystal, sterling service dinnerware. She always drove a Cadillac convertible, never more than a year old. And she always made sure she sent several hundred dollars back home to her mother in Marietta each month. Virginia apparently managed her money well, because all this was done during the period that she insisted to the Internal Revenue Service that her annual income was less than $16,000.

While Hill and Siegel found an uncertain harmony working for the Chicago and New York cartels in Mexico and Hollywood, they ran into some trouble when they expanded their reach into Miami, Florida.

The New Yorkers had already infiltrated nearly every racket in Miami, from greyhound racing to nightclubs. Joe Adonis had a stake in at least four popular nightclubs and even used his own name as one of the owners of the Colonial Inn, which personally netted him $685,000 yearly. Siegel was ordered to shape up the racing and wire services and consolidate the bookies into one operation, much as he had done in Los Angeles, where he put Mickey Cohen in charge of the mob's interests.

Virginia traveled with him and bought a furnished house on Sunset Island No. 1 in Miami Beach. The home had been owned by Randolph Hearst, heir to the Hearst publishing fortune. Hearst later insisted that he thought Virginia Hill was just some "nice old lady from Pasadena" and claimed he had no clue that the renter was the notorious mob Queen.

Siegel fronted the down payment of $30,000, and Hill picked up the monthly mortgage of $180. The house was bought more on a whim than for anything else. Hill and Siegel used it only as a vacation getaway to relax and enjoy the sun, until Hill got wind that a contract had been put out on her life.

Once she was tipped off to the plot, Virginia wired the house like a fortress with electronic surveillance equipment, alarms, and floodlights and kept a private detective on retainer. She never traveled without a bodyguard.

The newspapers had a field day with the Hill house and splashed pictures of it across its front pages. "Bugsy's Girl Trapped in Miami Beach Fortress" . . . "Bugsy's Baby Buys Bunker." Gawkers lined the front wall, and tourists slowed down their cars to stare at the house, hoping to see *the* Virginia Hill.

The chief of police was angered by the bad publicity and ordered Hill to get out of Miami Beach, saying that if she was going to get killed, she had "better do it in California and not here."

The publicity forced the hand of the FBI, which was already

investigating mob connections in Miami. With the flashy Hill buying property, there was no question that Ben Siegel was somewhere nearby. The FBI put a twenty-four-hour tail on Hill and bugged the house, hoping to get evidence against Siegel to crack the New York's gambling operations.

If Chicago had hoped to become involved in the Miami rackets by riding on Hill's and Siegel's coattails, the scheme failed. Hill was ordered out of Miami, and the Luciano family blamed her for bringing out the FBI. The family froze Fischetti and his goons out of a possible stake in the Miami businesses.

But the story also has an odd twist. The contract that had supposedly been put out on Hill never materialized. The twenty-four-hour tail by the FBI scared off any gunmen who would have tried to kill her, so the FBI had inadvertently saved the glamorous gangster's life.

Virginia rarely returned to the Miami Beach home after the debacle, and the incident seemed forgiven and forgotten by Fischetti, who used it as leverage with Adonis, Costello, and the New Yorkers. Fischetti said that in exchange for the ill-fated shares in Miami he wanted to put all Los Angeles gambling and wires under Dragna. The New Yorkers held firm against giving up any shares of the empire. Fischetti ordered Hill to move in against Siegel and collect enough evidence to wrestle Siegel's gambling power base away.

Hill called Siegel "Baby Blue Eyes," a nickname she had heard George Raft call Ben in jest. Hill later told a reporter from the *Chicago American* newspaper, "I called him that because I liked the name. It fit. And Benny hated it. So I called him Baby Blue Eyes to get him mad, too."

She called him Baby Blue Eyes for another reason. It made for convenient shorthand in her secret diary.

The diary shows a gap between 1937 and 1939. The last entry prior to the gap indicated a payment of $27,000 from Epstein to Adonis for something listed as "g.r.t." The cryptic notation remains a mystery to those who have seen the diary or are familiar with Epstein's and Adonis's business transactions. But the diary resumes on December 9, 1940, with the name "Baby Blue" and an arrow after the amount $40,000. The arrow points to the initials "BF." If speculative accounts offered by several people connected to the Los Angeles and

Chicago underworld are true, the notation gives a clear example of the far reaches of the mob into Los Angeles city politics.

Siegel had been indicted for the November 22, 1939, murder of Harry "Big Greenie" Greenberg, a muscleman for Louis Lepke and Murder, Incorporated, until he threatened to squeal to the FBI to try and stave off his deportation. His execution was ordered by the cartel of Lepke, Lansky, and Luciano, and Siegel was directed to carry out the hit.

Siegel was suspected from the moment Greenberg's body was found, but the authorities had to build their case before making a murder indictment stick. They had also been looking for any excuse to put Siegel behind bars and shut down his gambling operations in Los Angeles.

In addition to seizing the racing wire services and bookmaking rackets, Siegel had lured Tony Strella Cornero away from the Chicago duo of Dragna and Roselli and muscled in on the two most profitable of the Southern California gambling ships: the *Rex*, which was an opulent ship docked three miles off Santa Monica pier, and the *Lux*, docked three miles off Long Beach. The two literally put Roselli's and Dragna's ships out of business. Strella, under orders and with the protection of Siegel, refused to cut the Chicago team in on any ship action. The freeze-out infuriated Dragna and Roselli, who now threatened an all-out war, a threat that had first been made by Luciano against Frank Nitti in the 1930s.

FBI files indicate that Roselli had come within days of carrying out his plans to blow up the *Rex* and the *Lux* and ignite that war against Siegel and the East Coasters when L.A. city politics took a drastic turn.

Reformist groups, led by cafeteria owner Clifford Clinton, successfully won a campaign to boot Shaw and Davis out of office. They installed their own man, Fletcher Bowron, as mayor in 1938. Bowron threw the Shaw gang out of office, physically kicking Frank Shaw down the steps of city hall. Bowron's second show of power was the destruction of the gambling ships; the *Rex* was dynamited before a crowd of newspaper and newsreel reporters. Bowron beat Roselli to the punch and put a serious but temporary crimp in Siegel's gambling operations.

Though Bowron was "untouchable," corrupt Los Angeles district attorney Buron Fitts was still in office. But his days were numbered. Riding the crest of success in their Bowron campaign, the Clinton-backed reformists went after Fitts, promoting their own man for district attorney, John Dockweiler, who beat Fitts in the November 1940 election. Though his administration proved to be rocky and short-lived, Dockweiler was considered by many a cleaner district attorney than Fitts or his predecessor, Asa Keyes.

But before Fitts stepped down, he allegedly made good on a secret deal with the mob. Siegel was jailed for Big Greenie's murder on October 7, 1940, and served approximately two months. The short term was supposedly agreed to by Siegel and the mob as well as Fitts and Bowron. Bowron had made verbose statements about "ridding the city of gangster vermin" and vowed to keep Siegel in jail for life. But Fitts allegedly had his office infiltrated by, and had been on the take from, Luciano's men, who made it clear that Fitts was not to present a strong enough case to put Siegel behind bars for any length of time. He was caught in the middle, and the compromise deal was struck.

Siegel was in jail, Borwon made his point, and Fitts wiggled off the hook. Siegel was released on December 11, 1940, for lack of evidence.

There are several men who insist the "BF" in the diary is Buron Fitts and the $40,000 was a bribe. Though there is no evidence of this beyond the diary, they claim Siegel's jail term is proof enough. They also claim that the money was put up by the New York gang, which would make sense. Hill must have known about the bribe from Siegel and duly noted it. She never knew what information would come in handy and took copious notes on everything, just in case.

When John Dockweiler took office, the gravy train ended. Siegel was reindicted in September 1941, but the case dragged on and was eventually scuttled in February 1942 for lack of evidence.

While Ben Siegel was dodging the law over the Big Greenie murder, Virginia Hill was making detailed entries in her diary, listing the names of Siegel's business partners, following the money, and unlocking the secrets to his empire. She was now free of other obligations to the Chicago mob, such as money laundering and fencing, and was ready to devote herself full-time as the lover of Ben "Bugsy" Siegel, Baby Blue Eyes, Hollywood's sexiest man. Or so Siegel believed.

8

The rough edges of Virginia Hill's personality had been fine-tuned into a tough outer shell that very few people were now able to penetrate. She used sex to toy with men's emotions, keep them at bay, but entice them into hovering around her, ready to jump at her slightest whim. She enjoyed her life as a social butterfly and nightclub queen in Los Angeles. She also seemed to enjoy her life with Ben Siegel, though she had remained anything but loyal to him.

Virginia was still involved with Johnny Roselli, who had affairs with numerous other women, to keep him occupied. She spent weekends with her Mexican lovers, sneaked off for a quick tumble with drummer Gene Krupa, and even had several steamy affairs with Bugsy's best pal George Raft, right under Siegel's nose.

Raft claimed that many times when Ben was downstairs in Raft's Coldwater Canyon home, Raft would go upstairs while Virginia was still in bed, "draped in lace and buried in those satin sheets," as he described it, and made love. Raft said he would do his imitations of Siegel for Virginia, which always made her laugh.

Siegel did suspect that Virginia was passing her favors to other men and one evening told Raft that he would kill any man caught with Hill. Raft said it was one of the few times he was actually frightened for his life, because Siegel never made a threat he did not plan to carry out. But it did not stop Raft from sneaking into Hill's bedroom. In fact, Raft later said, it made their "screwing all the more fun, knowing that at any second Benny could burst through the door and kill us both."

If Siegel ever suspected that his biggest threat was his friend, he never let on. He was so trusting of Raft that he even asked him to follow Virginia around for a few months to see if he could find out who Hill was seeing. Raft thought that was quite funny, too.

The part of the life Hill did not enjoy was the endless army of newspaper and magazine reporters that always seemed to know where she would be ten minutes before she ever arrived anywhere. Virginia was big news, and the reporters never held back.

A March 1942 article in the *Los Angeles Times* portrayed Hill as a calculating woman with a backbone of steel who "tossed around 100 dollar bills as if she had a money machine stashed in her bedroom," adding that Hill "was a gangster's moll in the truest sense of the word, running around, painting the town with Ben 'Buggsy' (sic) Siegel, the two-fisted gunman from the East Coast."

Virginia said she found reporters disgusting men who were "always digging for the worst filth to fill up the pages, no matter who they hurt doing it." The only reporter she ever trusted and spoke with was Los Angeles newspaperwoman Florabel Muir, who had close ties with Mickey Cohen and Ben Siegel and usually played straight with the underworld.

Muir was one of the few reporters to whom Virginia Hill actually granted interviews. Hill said she had a lot in common with Muir. They were both women trying to claw their way to the top in a man's world; Hill in the underworld, Muir in the newspaper business. Both were highly successful, and both shared a mutual respect.

But the newspapers of the period preferred to dwell on the sensational, if not glamorized, side of Hill's life and published numerous photos of Hill covering her face, fleeing reporters, turning her back, or shaking a fist. The stories that followed were usually peppered with such lines as "gangster's girl Virginia Hill" or "Bugsy's baby, Virginia Hill, on another shopping spree" or "Hill has a field day slugging it out with the press."

The reporters often tried to goad her into a fight by verbally accusing her of sleeping around and prostituting herself or speculating on where and how she got her money. The reporters' accusations usually worked. Virginia took more than one swing at a reporter and smashed scores of cameras and tape recorders.

Siegel recognized the pressure Hill was under and took her away to Mexico in July 1941. They spent one month in a villa somewhere near Rosarita and partied, drank, and made love to their heart's desire, away from the media microscope.

One evening, while swilling tequila with some of the locals on the beach, someone called Virginia "a flamingo," and the nickname stuck. There are as many stories about why she was given the nickname as people willing to offer an explanation. Among the many: When Hill drank, her face turned a reddish color, like a flamingo, and she did a lot of drinking in Mexico. She had long, slender legs like a flamingo and paraded them around much as the bird does; her reddish hair was so striking that in the sun it gave off a glow much as the feathers of a flamingo in the sun; or she strutted around and was a showoff like a flamingo. One of the versions may be true, all may be true, or none may be true. Nonetheless, before long she was called the Flamingo by nearly everyone in Mexico, and soon the name followed her among the underworld in the United States.

Siegel liked it, and called his sweetheart the Flamingo. Whenever he asked Chick where she was, he would speak of Virginia as a bird rather than a woman, such as "Have you seen the Flamingo" or "Is the Flamingo here?" Virginia thought the name was funny, and she believed it set her apart from other, more common "Virginias."

By that June, Virginia even had vague entries in her dairy about "Flamgo," which could easily be assumed to be the Flamingo. The entries showed five-figure amounts going to "Flamgo" from "Ep" and others and back out from Adonis and the East Coast boys. Virginia's diary was growing thicker, and the notations more incriminating to the New York and Chicago mobs. If Siegel ever suspected he was being carefully documented, he kept it to himself. If Epstein had realized the extent of Hill's notations, he surely would have confiscated the diary. But Virginia's scribbles were allowed to continue, with erratic entries every several weeks or so.

Many suspected that Hill was falling in love with Siegel, violating Los Angeles kingpin Jack Dragna's order "Don't get too close." From all outward appearances, they certainly had a strong mutual attraction, which was evident to everyone who saw them together.

Ben and Virginia often visited movie sets while Gary Cooper and George Raft were filming. The two sat near one another but rarely engaged in any public displays of affection. However, they would always keep an eye on what the other was doing. If a crew member got too friendly with Virginia, Siegel would stare at the man with a look that literally could kill. They were welcomed on any set, and the crews fussed over them as if they owned the studio, which in a sense, with Hill's Chicago connections and Siegel's control of the extras union, they did.

Raft and Cooper both later said that sometimes, for a lark, Virginia would walk across the set during the filming and try to blend in with the extras. Most often these scenes were edited out, which may account for her alleged appearances in some films, without credit.

They also had fun off the sets as well. When they sensed reporters stalking the Delfern home, they camped out at Raft's house, leaving Chick and Virginia's new secretary, Jerri Mason, to fend off the press. They donned cheap disguises, sat in a parked car across the street, and watched the reporters trying to watch the "phantom" Ben and Virginia, actually Chick and Jerri, in the house. Virginia said it was her favorite trick.

She still traveled frequently between Chicago and Los Angeles and visited Marietta several times each year, though she never brought Siegel along on any of those trips. He had his hands full trying to keep Dragna at bay and build his gambling and racetrack wire services in Hollywood.

Dragna and Roselli began to grow impatient as they tried to muscle in on a piece of Siegel's gambling action through the proper Mafia channels. There was no question that Chicago had a rightful stake in the racket. It had pushed deeper into Los Angeles, as far as seizing businesses, unions, studios, and even other sporting events, than the New Yorkers. But Siegel moved faster on the track-related rackets, which infuriated the Chicago outfit.

Roselli and Dragna had lost the gambling-ship income when

the new Los Angeles city hall regime of Bowron and incoming district attorney John Dockweiler blew up the ships and vowed to slam the hammer down on the underworld. Bowron and Dockweiler opened their files to the FBI, which had been building a case against the Mafia for its infiltration of the studio unions.

A punch came from nationally syndicated columnist Westbrook Pegler, a muckraker and so-called yellow journalist who often zeroed in on the underworld. Pegler received a tip on Nitti's shakedown scam and exposed the truth about Bioff and Browne's mob ties. With the columns and subsequent publicity, the pair's usefulness to the mob ceased. Bioff and Browne were booted out of the IATSE and the AFL and replaced by other underworld-backed stooges; Bioff was later executed by the mob, as was Frank Nitti, who took the rap for the Hollywood debacle. Roselli, a latecomer in the shakedown, was later indicted and sent to federal prison for his role as a collector of the money in the scam.

Though the studio shakedown had ended, the Chicago mob still maintained its stranglehold on the unions. However, a steady source of income had dried up. The mob found new income when Dragna and Roselli seized several racing wires in Illinois, killed their owners, and started the *Illinois Sports News*, which provided racing results from tracks across the country and worked with bookies to fleece gamblers.

They started a similar race wire in California; then Dragna and Roselli eventually consolidated all the wires into one megaracket. They called it the *Universal Sports News* and based their operation in Los Angeles. When they tried to strong-arm Siegel's L.A. bookies into joining their service, Siegel knew he was being squeezed out. He schemed with Mickey Cohen to stop them.

According to documents found in the files of the Los Angeles district attorney during the years 1943 and 1944, Siegel plotted to assassinate Jack Dragna and take control of Los Angeles and the West for himself. Purportedly, he hired Mickey Cohen to carry out the hit. It was supposed to go down sometime in July 1944, while Dragna dined at Sherry's, a popular hangout on the Sunset Strip. At the time, Siegel would stay in New York so he could have an alibi. Cohen was supposed to have hired two gunmen, one of whom was believed to be Harry "Hooky" Rothman, who staked themselves outside the café in a parked car and waited. They were supposedly ordered to "shoot to kill" Dragna and anyone who was with him, man or woman.

The D.A.'s reports show that the hit was foiled, and it is believed that Dragna was tipped off to the plot. Not only did Dragna not show up that night; he sent two of his gunmen, one believed to be Eddie Cannazero, who later figures prominently in the story, to kill the goons who tried to kill him. It is unclear if Dragna only suspected Mickey Cohen's role in the scheme or if he had traced its origins back to Ben Siegel.

Insiders say most likely it was Virginia Hill who tipped Dragna off to the plot. She would have been one of the few people who knew of it in advance and was trusted enough by Siegel to be in on the planning. Insiders also believe that she let Ben Siegel believe she was loyal to him and probably even told him of Dragna's dinner plans as a guise to lull him into a sense of security with her. If true, she had indeed become the Mafia Mata Hari.

After the bungled assassination attempts, it was clear that Los Angeles was once again on the verge of a war. Dragna put a price of $100,000 on Siegel's head, and Siegel is believed to have returned the favor by putting a price of one nickel on Dragna's life. Siegel apparently thought the cheap price would be a greater insult to the Mafia don and joked to an associate that Dragna's life was not even worth a "plug nickel" to him.

Dockweiler knew something was brewing and agreed to work closely with federal agents in Los Angeles to either get Siegel and Dragna off the streets and out of Los Angeles or find a way of settling the feud. The FBI pulled in treasury agents and went to work closely scrutinizing Dragna's income, which he reported as $25,000 per year as an "importer." Since Siegel still declared himself a resident of New York, he was now under the jurisdiction of New York-based federal authorities. The agents soon found enough holes in Dragna's declarations that they believed they had enough to build a case against him.

The tide was again turning against the Luciano and Capone mobs. Luciano had already been indicted and jailed for racketeering and extortion. Treasury agents were closing in on Joey Adonis and Jack Dragna. While the treasury men sifted through their legal documents, the government found one common thread with which to tie the knot and, it is believed, get rid of the hoodlums for good: Most were in this country illegally and could be deported as illegal aliens. The government worked deliberately.

The Mafia knew that the last thing it needed at this time was a war in the West. Bloodshed would bring the ever-snooping press to its door, do-gooders would demand swift action against its most notorious leaders, and the few uncorrupted politicians left would use the anti-Mafia clamor to advance their own political careers. New York mobster Frank Costello and Chicago's Charlie Fischetti, who were considered by insiders and outsiders to be "in charge" of the Mafia, came to Los Angeles for a conference.

Federal records show that both men arrived in Los Angeles on July 10, 1944, on separate TWA flights that came in to Long Beach airport. Fischetti arrived in the morning; Costello, three hours later, at twelve noon. But the records stop there.

A source close to Jack Dragna claims that what happened next defused the potentially explosive situation but was the catalyst for Ben Siegel's eventual murder.

Costello, who was always the peacemaker, called Dragna, Dragna's Los Angeles underling Johnny Roselli, and several of their cohorts to a meeting to try and find a workable peace. Fischetti arrived late. Joey Adonis was at the meeting, but it is not clear exactly when or how he arrived in Los Angeles. Siegel was ordered to the meeting but refused to attend. It is believed that he was either in Las Vegas collecting shakedown money from the local gambling clubs or in Mexico with Virginia Hill. Hill was not at the meeting but was a topic of discussion after the New Yorkers left.

Dragna explained the problem he was having with Siegel, who continually blocked Dragna's plans for a unified wire service that would fall under Chicago control but profit the entire mob through its citywide branches. Roselli also complained about Siegel's meddling in the movie studios, which had been Chicago's domain since 1935. Both men made it clear that Siegel was a hot-tempered, conceited, self-righteous bastard who would not listen to reason and thwarted mob infiltration of unions and rackets to bolster his own position.

Dragna laid his cards on the table. The East could continue to run the gambling and track/sporting events in the West as well as its drug and prostitution operations, but Chicago would seize control of the wire services and all studio-related unions. The local bookmaking ventures would answer to Dragna's Universal Sports News but the profits would be divided between the different Mafia factions according to the cities in which the book was made and collected, whether Siegel liked it or not.

Adonis objected but was overruled by Costello, who saw the profit in the bigger picture of a unified wire service. The agreement was allegedly "run past" Luciano, who had been orchestrating out of Italy. Costello and Fischetti shook hands, and Adonis was ordered to get Siegel in tow and consolidate the wires under Dragna.

Adonis spat on the ground. "I'll deal with that Jew bastard in hell, not on this earth." He stormed out. Costello said it would be squared away in a matter of time and that Dragna and his boys should be patient.

When Costello left, five people remained in the room: Jack Dragna, Johnny Roselli, Allen Smiley, and two others. Smiley, whose real name was Smehoff, dabbled in both worlds: crime and cinema.

He began his criminal life as a thug in the teenage Bug-Meyer mob and was considered a longtime pal of Ben Siegel's. He also had ties to Johnny Roselli through the film industry, where Smiley worked odd jobs in the studios and peddled scripts. He combined the two through his operations as a nightclub owner on the Sunset Strip. Though Smiley knew Siegel probably better than anyone and had childhood ties with him, he had his closest adult-life relationships with the Chicago outfit. Smiley often acted as a go-between when tempers flared between Siegel and the outfit. He was asked to serve in that capacity once again.

But Allen Smiley was also asked to do another errand for Dragna: to keep an eye on Virginia Hill. Though Hill had always done as she was told and had tipped Dragna off to the hit, Dragna had reason to believe that her alliances were moving toward Ben Siegel. Dragna suspected that Hill had tipped off Siegel and Mickey Cohen about Dragna's retaliatory hit. Dragna had another reason to be concerned.

Virginia was still laundering money at the Santa Anita race-track and making money runs to Mexico. She had also traveled extensively between Los Angeles and Chicago and New York delivering stolen merchandise. But she had swindled Epstein and the Chicago mob out of tens of thousands of dollars, claiming she lost shipments or had been cheated by bookies when in fact she had collected the money. Virginia took a little here and a little there. She said later in a *Herald Examiner* newspaper interview that she did it to "show Joey E he was a chump. The dumb guy just kept sending more."

When word got back to Epstein in Chicago that Virginia was in possible danger from Dragna and that she may have been getting romantically involved with Ben Siegel, Epstein intervened. He asked her to move back to Chicago.

Virginia swiftly gave Joey E her answer. "I work where I want and when I want. I don't dance for nobody." Epstein backed down but agreed with Dragna to put Smiley to work on Virginia. There is no indication that Hill ever suspected that she had come close to being killed or that she was being watched by Smiley.

The money kept coming from Epstein, and Hill kept spending it. Hill later said that she hated Epstein for making her work for the money and also for trying to orchestrate her life. He had been controlling her life since she was seventeen years old, ordering her around, dictating where she went and with whom she could associate. Though Virginia complained loudly and angrily about Epstein, she never once sent his money back, nor did she ever confront him about her feelings.

Virginia Hill was a user who had no loyalty to anyone and who now seemed to understand her power within the mob. When Epstein backed down on his request that she move back to Chicago, Virginia realized that she had the upper hand. From that day forward, she lost all respect for and fear of anyone in the mob except for one man, Ben Siegel, the man Dragna called the Bug.

Virginia said she was uncontrollably attracted to him but "scared stiff." She had been at the receiving end of Bugsy's fists more than once in their relationship. They had screaming matches, and she had been pummeled by Siegel when he caught her with other men. She also beat Ben in violent and bloody attacks over other women, his wife and his refusal to divorce her, and his jealousy. In fact, the two frequently wore heavy facial makeup to cover the bruises and wounds from their fistfights and clawing bouts. But only once did Siegel threaten to kill her. And Virginia knew he meant it.

9

Not satisfied with cheating bookies on the wires, gambling fixes, and racetrack swindles and rigging sporting events, Ben Siegel decided the time was ripe to expand his reaches, regardless of what edict came down from New Yorkers Costello or Adonis. Siegel was a wild card and a wild man who refused to work with Chicago-backed mobsters Roselli or Dragna or siphon off any segments of his West Coast empire.

In 1944 the Bug opened a large warehouse in the Los Angeles suburb of Cerritos and stored more than $6 million worth of scrap metal and machine parts. The owner of record was a company called California Metals Company, which was much like the hundreds of other surplus and scrap-metal operations that emerged across the country during the war. The company bought most of its materials from airplane manufacturers and the government at five to ten cents on the dollar. But the FBI files show that the name was nothing more than a front for Siegel and his partner in this venture, Allen Smiley.

Siegel and Smiley saw the profit in doing what many companies do to the government today: They bought the surplus at wholesale prices and then resold it retail to the government or to other firms needing parts. The scheme was perfectly legal and promised to make millions for Smiley and Siegel. Smiley also secretly kept Dragna apprised of the operation.

Smiley also kept the outfit's Dragna and Roselli informed about another scheme of Siegel's, one in which Hill was involved as a money collector. This was the formation of the *Trans-America Race Wire Service*, which was in direct competition with Dragna's venture. Hill believed Ben and another partner, Moe Sedway, started the service not only to make money and capitalize on the fact that they controlled the bookies in Los Angeles but to show their disrespect to Dragna. She also gave the outfit detailed reports of Ben's activities and to-the-penny accounts of how much Siegel had earned and skimmed from the service.

Many previously published accounts claim Dragna, Chicago's West Coast overlord, was in on the Trans-America wire from the beginning and that he had used it as muscle to get bookies to join his service. But insiders close to the Chicago mob staunchly deny those claims. They said that Dragna was not part of the initial setup, that it was Siegel's and Sedway's, and that Mickey Cohen and his goons had been the sluggers that terrorized bookies into joining.

Their method was simple. Though most of the bookies had subscribed to Dragna and Roselli's operation, Cohen ordered them to hand over an additional $150 per week to operate the phones or they would be shut down. Few stood up to Cohen.

Siegel expanded his service to Arizona and Nevada, where bookies had been aligning with another hood named Gus Greenbaum, who had learned his craft from Siegel. Once Trans-America was up and running, Greenbaum threw his bookies in with Siegel.

Ben Siegel now had only one area left in which to expand his gambling empire, Las Vegas, Nevada.

One of the Bug's first investments in that desert town involved a small club called the Northern Club, which offered a little gambling with dinner and drinks. Siegel reportedly invested $50,000 in the club and put Sedway in charge of running the operation. Sedway was to report to Siegel if anything went wrong and make sure the books balanced at the end of each pay period. Other than that, Sedway was on his own.

Siegel later added two more people to his payroll for his Las Vegas enterprises: Sollie Soloway, who was his brother-in-law, and Dave Berman, an ex-con who had worked for Siegel in the

East. Gus Greenbaum was also sent to Las Vegas to supervise gambling and other mob-backed investments, such as the Frontier Turf Club, the El Cortez Hotel, the Golden Nugget, and the Las Vegas Club. Siegel was either the outright owner or had a stake in the business.

His power grew in increasing proportion to his profits. With a monthly income estimated at more than $100,000, Siegel bought a share of several Mexican racetracks and a major piece of the Clover Club bar, which was a popular and illegal gambling den in Hollywood notorious for its mob ties and rigged tables. Virginia Hill also had a stake in the Clover Club and fronted a share for the Chicago boys as well.

But Siegel habitually broke the one rule that any gangster always lived by: Never become your best customer. Ben Siegel was one of the shrewdest entrepreneurs ever born. He could turn a dime into a dollar in a second. But he was also a compulsive gambler who lost far more than he ever earned. He hit his friends up for loans. At the top of his list, as always, was George Raft. Second was Virginia Hill.

Raft said Ben Siegel would have taken every dime he had if he did not squirrel some away and not tell Siegel about the hidden cash. Raft sold off watches, jewelry, and stock and reportedly even traded down cars several times to come up with the cash Siegel demanded to cover bets. Raft later claimed that Ben had even pressured him to remortgage his Coldwater Canyon home so that Siegel could put $30,000 cash on a horse at Santa Anita. Raft refused, and, he claimed to friends, Siegel slugged him and refused to speak to him for nearly one month because the horse won.

Hill kept Ben at bay by giving him lump sums of $10,000–$20,000 upon demand. She always seemed to have the cash on hand, ready to turn over at Siegel's slightest whim. Virginia later said the money she gave Ben was what she had been skimming from Epstein, so the loss did not matter to her.

When questioned by federal authorities in 1951, she initially claimed she skimmed the money to make a chump of Epstein. However, shortly before her death, Virginia said she took the money out of fear of Siegel and that Epstein knew about the payments to the gangster.

On February 6, 1944, Virginia recorded in her diary that she made a personal payment to "Baby Blue" of $26,000, a sizable amount of money but not more than Hill or Epstein could cover. She showed a similar payment to "Baby Blue" two weeks later. If Siegel had been fleecing Hill, he was doing a good job. If she had continued to pay him the amounts out of fear, she was clearly being terrorized by the gangster.

There is speculation among some members of the underworld that Ben Siegel had suspected that Virginia was spying on his bookmaking operations and wire service and reporting his activities back to Fischetti or Dragna. Siegel must have suspected that someone had been leaking personal information to the Chicago mob, because every time Ben made a move, placed a bet, opened a nightclub, even with a "front," or collected profits, Dragna, Roselli, or someone connected to the Chicago outfit knew about it, down to the penny. The only two people who would have had such intimate knowledge were Allen Smiley or Virginia Hill. One he trusted; the other he loved.

Ben and Virginia had been together for five years, but Virginia's love for Siegel was waning by the spring of 1944. If the mob Queen had "gotten too close," as Dragna had warned, she now sharply veered away from the man they called the Bug. She told associates that she had enough of Ben's hair-trigger temper, his continually soaking her for loans that he would never repay, his paranoia about other men, and his distrust of her. Virginia knew Siegel had her followed not because he suspected she was not dealing squarely with him on a business level but because he was convinced she was seeing other men behind his back. And she was.

Virginia repeatedly said that the best sex she ever had was with Ben Siegel. She said she also had the most fun with him and got a certain sexual-sensual thrill out of living on the edge with Ben. But the downside of the relationship, other than the underlying purpose of her liaison with him, was that he was married and had repeatedly and steadfastly refused to divorce Esta. In fact, Siegel lied to both women about the relationship.

When he went back home to New York, Siegel told Esta that he and Hill were "business associates," that she was a "good friend," or that he was keeping an eye on her for Joey A. Esta read scores of articles about the Hollywood gangster's moll and knew more than she cared to about Hill's relationship with her husband. Whether Esta bought any of Ben's malarkey is unclear, because she remained loyal to him, though she did finally agree to a divorce.

Siegel told Hill that he begged Esta for a divorce but that she refused. If he pursued the matter, he told Virginia, he would never see his children again. He convinced Virginia that Esta was a shrew and a tough lady who kept the marriage together only because she needed someone to pay the bills.

Unlike Esta, Virginia did not believe his story, and the two ended up in a violent argument. Virginia stormed out of Siegel's home and threw his gold key in the dirt.

According to close associates of Siegel's, Ben literally chased after Virginia and pulled her out of her convertible just as she was about to start the car. He dragged her into the house while she screamed out every four-letter and foul expletive imaginable. Once inside, he slammed the door shut, threw her to the floor, and kicked and slapped her until she was nearly unconscious.

Virginia kept shouting that he was only using her for her money and that he had turned her into a high-priced mobster's whore. Then she insulted his masculinity, claiming she saw other men only because Siegel was a lousy lover and the joke of Los Angeles, that every woman in town knew he was awful in bed and could never satisfy any woman.

With that, Ben Siegel went nearly insane. Siegel's friends claim that if there was any one time Siegel came within inches of murdering Virginia Hill, it was over this incident.

After he beat her nearly senseless, he carried her up into their bedroom. Siegel raped Virginia Hill, then walked out. He went to George Raft's house and acted as if nothing had happened. The incident was never reported to the police.

Several weeks later, Siegel did run up against the law, and there are many who believe that Virginia Hill, or possibly Jack Dragna, was behind it. Siegel had been spending a quiet afternoon at Allen Smiley's apartment on Sunset Boulevard. Along with Siegel and Smiley, George Raft and another friend were there. Raft had just returned from performing in an overseas USO tour and was eager for a little rest and relaxation. Siegel, of course, decided that the best way to kill time was to do a little friendly gambling.

They placed penny-ante bets on horses running at Churchill Downs in Kentucky. Most of the bets were in the $1,000 range and placed through one of Cohen's bookies. Siegel was still on the phone, making the bets, when there was a knock at the door.

Smiley opened it, and one man entered the room, gun drawn. The man was Capt. William Deal of the Los Angeles County Sheriff's Department's vice unit, which had jurisdiction over Sunset Boulevard as an unincorporated area of Los Angeles.

Deal placed Smiley and Siegel under arrest but left Raft alone. The charge was bookmaking.

Siegel protested, claiming that he was placing bets, not making them. But it made no difference.

As they left the apartment, Raft insisted he be arrested, too, out of fear it would appear as if he played a part in a setup. Deal refused.

Court records show that Siegel and Smiley were subsequently charged with bookmaking and conspiracy, which was a felony. The two were in danger of serving time.

The case went to Superior Court Justice Cecil Holland, with former Superior Court Judge and state parole board member Isaac Pacht hired to represent the pair. Raft was called in as a witness, an order with which the star gladly complied over objections from his bosses at Warner Brothers, who thought his public support of known criminals would hurt his popularity.

When Raft, Siegel, and Smiley arrived at the downtown Los Angeles courthouse, they were mobbed by a crush of reporters trying to get pictures and stories. Mixed with the reporters were fans of Raft's, who pushed to obtain autographs and to get a closer look at Raft's friend, the notorious gangster. It was a field day for Siegel, who knew the publicity would make him an even bigger celebrity and swell his already-inflated ego.

Raft smiled, waved and posed for photos, signed autographs, and fired off a few quotes about the hearing.

"Ben Siegel is a good man. He's not a gangster. At least I've never known him to do anything illegal."

On the stand Raft accused Captain Deal of entering the apartment illegally. Apparently he never bothered to obtain a search warrant in his eagerness to collar Hollywood's number-one archcriminal. He also never read the pair their rights. Raft then gave Siegel a glowing testimony.

"I have known Siegel for many years. We have been friends for a long time. We went up to the apartment [Smiley's] and were sitting there discussing things about going to New York, that was all."

The case deteriorated into a nightmare for the law. Felony conspiracy charges were dropped, and Siegel and Smiley agreed to plead guilty to bookmaking charges and pay a fine of $250.

The hearing made Raft an even bigger star. The on-screen tough guy really was a tough guy offscreen as well. His popularity rating in movie magazines reached an all-time high.

But for Ben Siegel, May 25, 1944, was a day he would have preferred to forget. Since the arrest, he was viewed by other racketeers as a two-bit punk who got caught on a cheap charge and did not have enough foresight to bribe his way out of the case. On top of that, the dismissal of the felony charge and the small fine ignited the wrath of local law enforcement officials, especially Deal and Los Angeles Police Chief Clinton Anderson, who now made a point of having Bugsy followed everywhere he went.

Siegel felt trapped. His romance with Hill was on the skids, and his prestige as a Hollywood tough guy was on the wane. He talked about leaving Los Angeles and moving to Las Vegas, where he had the cops on the payroll, his gambling businesses were making money, and he would be out of the newspaper reporter's fishbowl. He asked Virginia to move with him. She laughed in his face and went back to New York.

10

Virginia certainly felt no loyalty to Ben Siegel, especially after the violent rape incident in the Delfern Avenue home. But she was uncontrollably attracted to him. She suffered from the same character trait that afflicted almost all gangster's women, wives and girlfriends—a tendency to equate violence with passion. Siegel was violent, perhaps the most brutal man Virginia had ever met. To her, that made Ben Siegel the most passionate man she had ever known.

But Virginia was also the kind of woman who could dish out abuse as liberally as she took it. She was determined to cut Siegel down to size. Virginia vowed that by the time she was finished with him, the humiliation she suffered after the incident in Smiley's apartment would look like an honorarium. The way to do that was by broadcasting the one thing that triggered his uncontrollable rage, that Ben "Bugsy" Siegel could not satisfy a woman.

When Siegel left for Nevada, Virginia headed to New York and straight into the arms of Joe Adonis. The two quickly picked up where they left off in February 1937, when Siegel spirited Virginia out of Adonis's arms. They went dancing and drinking and carousing at the various mob-backed nightclubs in New York and New Jersey, played the roulette and dice games in Atlantic City, and teamed to work the sucker-bet rackets at

Madison Square Garden. They went to Broadway shows and made a dazzling show at "A" list society parties. They also garnered several newspaper items in the *New York Times*, the *New York Daily News*, the *Herald American*, and several local and national tabloids.

Syndicated columnist Westbrook Pegler, who years earlier had triggered the downfall of the so-called Million Dollar Movie Shakedown with his series of antigangland articles, deliberately baited Siegel with his *Herald American* column. Pegler wrote:

> The hottest criminal couple in New York is Joe Adonis and Bugsy Siegel's former paramour Virginia Hill. The deadly duo have been seen swilling it up with some of the most infamous of the Great White Way who seem to have a knack for picking out and partying with the gutter crowd from the slums and backwoods. Or has the slum gang climbed out of the gutter and into the place of royalty among the theater set?

Pegler certainly knew that Siegel would read the column or at least be told of it. Pegler told friends later that he knew the article would "get Bugsy's goat." He believed a showdown between Siegel and Adonis would fuel the fire of gossip columns and books for years. Pegler must have been disappointed, because nothing ever came of the article that anyone could recall.

Virginia, true to her character, did not limit herself to one man during her frolic in the Big Apple. She flitted and flirted with one man after the next. Adonis did not seem to care.

During one of her excursions to New York in August 1944, Virginia met Carl Laemmle, Jr., son of Universal Studios movie pioneer Carl Laemmle. Laemmle, Jr., was a millionaire. His wealth came from his father's work in Hollywood as well his own as a movie producer. He was also considered "the" catch among the nouveau riche women, married and single, in New York and Los Angeles. But no one woman seemed to capture his attention and his heart until he met Virginia.

Columnist Lee Mortimer always claimed that he introduced the pair at Aqueduct and even took credit for building Virginia into the "darling of the press" with his repeated items about her. But Mortimer actually did more to upset and provoke Hill than any other columnist because of his continued attacks on her character, implying that she came from a "white trash, dirt poor" background and that she was a high-class hooker. It is curious that he would want to introduce such a woman to someone as respected as Laemmle, Jr.

Carl Laemmle, Jr., fell head over heels in love with Virginia. He followed her from New York to Beverly Hills, where she rented a home. He bought her diamonds, jewelry, rugs, dishes, clothes, knickknacks. He spent thousands of dollars chasing after Hill and hoping that he could buy her affection, if not her loyalty.

Laemmle was the first man who probably loved Virginia without any hidden agenda. He wanted nothing from her in the way of favors, as did Epstein, or sex, as did Adonis, or money, as did Siegel. He did not need her money, and there was nothing in the way of criminal activity that Laemmle needed or wanted any part of. Laemmle was a lovesick puppy around Virginia. And she treated him like dirt.

According to Dean Jennings in his book *We Only Kill Each Other*, Virginia often conspired with her brother Chick to make a chump of Laemmle. Once, Jennings writes, when Laemmle showed up at the Hills' front door, Chick raced around from room to room, turning the lights on and off and knocking things over. Virginia screamed and pretended to be in fear of her life, making Laemmle believe she was being stalked by Mafia hit men. Laemmle was duly frightened.

Jennings also claims that when Laemmle gave her an expensive bracelet with "I Love You" engraved on it, she called him a "corny jerk" and flushed the bracelet down the toilet while he watched.

He also related a story that highlighted the extreme humiliation Laemmle suffered at the merciless hands of Virginia Hill. Jennings wrote that Virginia and Laemmle got into a loud argument over something while parked in front of the Hill home. Virginia literally ripped from her earlobes a pair of earrings that Laemmle had given her, hurting herself in the process. She threw them out the window and stormed into the house.

About one hour later, George Raft drove by and spotted

Laemmle on his hands and knees, combing through dirt and trash in the gutter. Laemmle told Raft about the fight and that he was looking for the earrings. Hill saw him in the gutter, too, and her dislike turned into loathing and hatred. She never saw, or wanted to see, Carl Laemmle, Jr., again. The feeling was mutual.

After the Laemmle affair, Virginia decided she needed time to herself, away from friends, the press, and Adonis. She hid out at George Raft's home for several weeks toward the end of September. Though their affair had waned since the rape incident, Siegel still believed he had a claim on Hill. When he heard where Virginia was hiding, he told Raft he would kill him if he made a pass at her and ordered him to follow her to make sure she was not seeing anyone behind Siegel's back. Siegel still had not discovered that Raft and Hill were more than mere roommates.

They almost got caught when Siegel showed up one night unannounced. Fortunately it was one of the few nights that Virginia decided to sleep alone. Ben climbed into bed, and the two made love on Virginia's satin sheets, which she usually carried with her. Siegel returned to Nevada the following morning, none the wiser. He left Raft and Hill with the same threat about fidelity and pulled Raft aside to remind him to keep close tabs on her. The actor delivered one of his best performances and promised to do as Ben requested. As Raft later told friends, "We laughed like hell over that one."

Siegel finally decided to cut his ties with Los Angeles once and for all and put his Delfern Avenue home up for sale. Wanting to avoid the throngs of "lookey-loos" who would come to gawk at the gangster's home, with absolutely no intention of buying, Siegel told only one person about his intent to bail out of Beverly Hills, his attorney Jerry Geisler, who had gotten the Bug off the hook for the Big Greenie murder a few years back.

Geisler was notorious for his dealings with movie stars and the underworld and getting them out of trouble. One of his first cases was the Alexander Pantages rape trial in 1929–30, and he later represented nearly every movie actor charged with everything from drunk and disorderly conduct to paternity suits to murder (e.g., the case of actress Lana Turner, who was accused of murdering gangster/lover Johnny Stompanato). To Geisler, Siegel was just a face in the crowd.

Geisler arranged for actress Loretta Young to purchase the Delfern home for nearly half of its real value, somewhere around $85,000. Siegel was anxious to bail out, and as he later said, "It didn't matter what I sold it for. I woulda spent the money at the track, anyway."

It has been the law in California for years that a home could not clear title without a termite inspection; the owner was usually expected to pay for it and make repairs. A report found $475 worth of termite damage to the subflooring around the kitchen and near the garage. Siegel refused to pay, claiming that Young and her husband were getting the home for a song and enough was enough. Young backed out of the deal, which triggered Siegel's notorious temper.

First he threatened to kill the actress, but Geisler talked him out of it. Ben ordered Geisler to handle the case through legal channels, though Young was within her legal right to back out of the sale.

An $85,000 damage suit was filed in Los Angeles Superior Court. The judgment was in Young's favor. Siegel appealed, lost the second round, and finally gave up and sold the house to someone else.

Before he cleared out, he hit up Raft once again for money. He telephoned the star and ordered him to drive to the house and take a look at some old, weather-beaten gardening tools and lawn furniture. Raft said he did not want the junk, but Ben made it clear he was not asking the actor, but ordering him, to buy it. Raft reluctantly agreed. Siegel swindled his "best friend" out of another $500. Raft knew Siegel would bet and lose the money as quickly as he had conned him.

Once he felt clear of Los Angeles, Siegel devoted his energies to building his Las Vegas businesses. Though Las Vegas was nothing more than a cowboy town, he saw his income from his gambling clubs skyrocket as the war neared an end. People needed recreation, a place to cut loose and celebrate the wave of postdepression and postwar giddiness that was sweeping across the country. He also saw the crush of people pouring into California, the scores of G.I.s who had been stationed in the state, and decided to settle down there. He suspected that he had in his hands the future of the underworld in a town in which what little law existed looked the other way.

Feeling secure with his dream of the future and at peace with his "escape" from Los Angeles, Siegel moved to patch things up with Virginia. He promised to divorce Esta, and he laid out the details of his dream to Hill. He assumed Virginia would be forgiving and want to move out of Los Angeles and join him.

Siegel never suspected that Hill had a hidden agenda, that everything he said or did was being reported to the Chicago boys, especially after the attack in the Delfern home. He naively assumed he had been forgiven when Virginia took him to her bed in Raft's home. Ben Siegel also assumed that when he promised to divorce Esta, Virginia would be all his.

Siegel set up camp in the dusty Vegas desert with plans of building an empire and notions of being the gambling mogul of the West, with his queen at his side.

One part of his plan proved to be costly. The other deadly.

11

Virginia was loath to become involved with Las Vegas. To her it was a dirty town crawling with vulgar, sweaty men who never shaved or bathed and treated their horses better than their women. It was hot, dusty, and more rural and remote than anything she had ever seen in the South. Worse for her, she was allergic to the cactus and broke out in hives.

Ben pleaded with her to accompany him on one of his numerous excursions to Nevada. Virginia flatly refused. Instead, she remained in Los Angeles and enjoyed the Sunset Strip nightlife, dancing, and gambling. She continued placing bets on horses at Santa Anita while pocketing hundreds of thousands of dollars in cash, collected from the track and from Epstein, who still sent her "dirty" money to clean for a profit. And she still covered bets for Siegel when he, as usual, lost at the track.

The racetrack scam was a curious enigma for both legitimate gamblers and those hooked up with the underworld. It has long been believed that the Mafia was able to somehow "fix" the horse races, for quite often, when someone needed quick cash, they told that person what horse to bet in which race and the horse usually came in as predicted. But to guarantee a horse would finish first across the line, every other horse in the race would either have to be drugged, or every other jockey would have to be in on the fix.

Usually the mob only skewed the odds and used people who studied the ponies. If the races were fixed, Siegel, who lost a small fortune at the track, was never let in on the scam.

In the summer of 1945, Siegel was gearing up to play the biggest score of his life.

Las Vegas was known not only for its frontier lifestyle but its legal prostitution and, of course, gambling, which attracted professional gamblers, but not necessarily the so-called high rollers, who lost most of their money in Atlantic City or Reno, which was at the other end of Nevada.

Siegel had the Last Frontier, the Monte Carlo Club, the El Rancho, the Las Vegas Club, and the Golden Nugget under his control. He now raked in more than $1 million each year from the casinos. To Siegel, however, that was chump change, slightly more than $200,000 per club. He knew that higher stakes awaited him.

He and Moe Sedway drove to the outskirts of town, down Highway 91, about seven miles past Freemont Street, which was the center of the casino strip. Ben stopped the car in front of a shanty motel reminiscent of the thousands of ramshackle one-room cabins that dotted the interstates in the 1940s. It was owned by a widow named Margaret Folsom.

Siegel had become paranoid that he would be recognized from the hundreds of newspaper articles and photos that had appeared over the past decade. He ordered Sedway to front for him and con the woman out of her property. Sedway carried out Siegel's instructions, and Folsom quitclaimed thirty acres of "useless" desert land to Sedway, who turned around and quitclaimed the property to Siegel. Ben "Bugsy" Siegel took the first giant step toward opening the hotel that would stand as a monument to corruption, the Mafia, murder, and unrequited love.

Siegel rushed back to Los Angeles and laid out his plans to Virginia. He gave her details of how he and Sedway swindled the little old lady out of her Las Vegas land, how he planned on selling shares of his dream to help finance its construction, and how he would make millions from this one operation. He gave her details of what money changed hands and who he hired, who he fired, and who else he swindled to get his dream off the ground.

A better actress off-screen than on—Virginia Hill in a posed glamour shot.

One Virginia Hauser)   Anne Virginia Hauser)

(Fingerprint Classification—Not Known)

WANTED

For: FEDERAL INCOME TAX EVASION

VIRGINIA HILL HAUSER——Alias Virginia D'Algy,
atson, Juan, Dietah, Dagby, Reid, Onie Brown, Betty Hood, Ona V. Hill, , Mrs. W. Hall, Mrs. Norma Hall, Mrs. Onie V. Reid, Mrs. H. Harper, , Mrs. Jamison, Mrs. J. H. Herman, Mrs. Ona Virginia Herman, Mrs. , Mrs. J. H. Hoff.

: White; female; age 39; height : complexion fair; hair auburn;

ty American; born in Lipscomb, August 26, 1916. Last known United States was Spokane,

Hill Hauser was indicted on June a Federal Grand Jury at Los An-

geles, California, for income tax evasion. At the time of her indictment, she was reportedly residing in Klosters, Switzerland. She is presently married to an Austrian-born ski instructor. Hans Hauser, and has a 5-year-old son, Peter Jackson Hauser. Virginia Hill Hauser was formerly a paramour and associate of gangsters and racketeers.

URNISH any information which may assist in locating this individual to the telligence Division, Internal Revenue Service, Washington 25, D.C., or the Assistant ransissioner, Intelligence, listed on the back hereof, who is nearest your city.

mber 1, 1955, by: gust. Director, Division

INTERNAL REVENUE SERVICE
U. S. TREASURY DEPARTMENT
WASHINGTON, D. C.

1955 "Wanted" poster.

Charlie Fischetti, Al Capone's cousin, who pulled the strings in both Chicago and L.A. (C&C photo)

L.A. crime boss Jack Dragna. (Chicago Crime Commission photo)

98015
LA 12 6 46

The Bug in Hollywood, August 17, 1940. (Bettmann Archives/UPI photo)

Hollywood wannabe and gangster wannabe—Ben Siegel and George Raft outside the courthouse at Siegel's bookmaking trial. (AP/Wide World photo)

The Flamingo, in the upper left, open for business. The Dunes, lower right, nearly completed, circa 1954. The rivalry between New York and Chicago came to a head in the desert. (Photo coutresy The Flamingo Hotel/Las Vegas)

The Flamingo, shortly after its opening. (Photo courtesy The Flamingo Hotel/Las Vegas)

A side view of the front entrance. Bugsy's private suite that he and Virginia Hill shared looms above the front door. (Photo courtesy The Flamingo Hotel/Las Vegas)

Premiere

GRAND O~~P~~
of Las Vega
$5,000.0

Tonight and Tomo

THE ~~Flamin~~

Owned and
THE NEVADA PRO.

With the Greatest Array of Cafe Ent
Anywhere for Your Ent

JIMMIE DURANTE
XAVIER CUGAT &
ROSEMARIE   TO
THE TUNETO

SATURDAY NIGHT THE
OPENING
Stars and Personalities from Hollywoo
Up in a TWA Constellation

THE BIG NEW YEAR'S
More Fun Than You Ha

THE FLAMINGO OPENS
Music and Dancing in Cafe-Loun
Main Dinning Room Open

Phone 4000 or Apply in Perso
for Tickets of Rese
NO RESERVATION REQUIRE
COCKTAIL LOU

No. 810 N. Linden Drive, Virginia and Bugsy's Beverly Hills love nest. Brother Chick and Jerrie Mason are seated on the outside railing.

aby Blue" gunned down the Beverly Hills home rented with Virginia ll, June 20, 1947. (LAPD oto)

Beverly Hills P.D. Officer W. L. Ritchey points to the spot where Bugsy's killer probably stood. (LAPD photo)

Virginia Hill arrives in New York, August 8, 1947. (Bettmann Archives/UPI photo)

Adonis testifies before the Kefauver Committee. He would not
[test]ify against [himself] in any respect." (AP/Wide World photo)

Hill smiles for the camera as she leaves the Federal Courthouse in
New York, May 15, 1951. She defeated Kefauver and his committee,
but it was the beginning of the end for her. (AP/Wide World photo)

Auctioneer G. T. Gre[...] puts Hill's coat on the auction block in Spo[...] Washington, August [...] 1951.

Hans Hauser, Virginia Hill Hauser, and Peter Hauser relax ove[...] dinner, circa 1960.

Virginia Hill took copious notes, made notations in her diary, and reported everything to Dragna and Fischetti.

The Chicago mob had been slowly working its way toward the Nevada desert for the last two years and knew exactly what Siegel was up to. Dragna decided he would let Siegel clear the way, take the initial lumps while getting a new venture off the ground, and pick up the financial slack before curious gamblers became regular customers. Then Dragna and his men would close in. They sat back and waited for Siegel to move forward.

To help finance construction, Siegel sold shares of the hotel to associates and friends, including Meyer Lansky and his New York thug-associates, who invested on behalf of the Luciano mob; Sollie Soloway, Siegel's brother-in-law; Billy Wilkerson, who owned the movie-industry tabloid the *Hollywood Reporter;* and Allen Smiley, who kicked in for a token fifteen shares. The shares were sold for $250 each, and Siegel raised about $1 million right off the top. He incorporated the venture and called the investment group the Nevada Projects Corporation.

He hired Del Webb to help design and build the casino, which Siegel now envisioned as a "jewel in the desert . . . one of the classiest gambling casinos in the world . . . to rival Monte Carlo . . . to keep gamblers inside and betting once they walked in the door." He told reporters that the hotel would offer everything, "from the world's best food to the world's most comfortable beds." What he did not mention was that there would be enough diversion from high-class hookers to ensure that gamblers got their money's worth.

He then unveiled his grandest plan. He said the name of his paradise would be Ben Siegel's Flamingo Hotel. Once again the love-struck gigolo had gone too far.

Joey Adonis and Meyer Lansky flew to Las Vegas for an emergency meeting with Siegel. At all costs he had to keep his name off the marquee. There were very few people, especially gamblers, who did not know who Siegel was and what he was. They believed it was bad business to advertise that a hotel and casino were openly run by a gangster. They argued it implied an immediate swindle and probably bloodshed. Siegel refused to give in. Lansky threatened to pull out of the deal and shut Siegel down. After a heated debate Ben Siegel agreed to take his name off the title. But he insisted that "Flamingo" be retained. It was.

But Esta had enough. She knew full well who the Flamingo represented and felt it was a deliberate slap in the face. She flew out to Nevada to inform her husband that she was filing for divorce. Esta filed suit in Reno. The demands were uncontested by Siegel, who agreed to pay her $600 per week for life. Though Esta herself put several thousand dollars into the casino, she naively expected her husband to make good on his promise to pay. She never saw a dime and was even forced to pony up $45,000 of her own money to help finance the casino or Siegel said he would refuse to agree to the divorce.

Esta already believed she was the laughingstock of New York, with her husband building a monument to his mistress and flaunting the affair in the papers. She reportedly went straight to Adonis, whom she had known through her husband but with whom she had few personal dealings, and made a scene over the $45,000, threatening to talk to the press about her husband's business dealings, that is, the little she knew about them, and the casino. If nothing else, she allegedly decided, she would embarrass Siegel and his friends the way Ben had embarrassed her.

Associates say Adonis reimbursed Esta the $45,000 in cash. She in turn would agree to remain silent about Ben, her life, and anything she might know, or think she knew, about the Flamingo Hotel. Esta agreed.

Though Adonis's maneuver put out one fire, it reignited Joey A's wrath for the Bug. Adonis believed that he had been called upon too many times to clean up messes that Siegel had made. And Siegel never seemed to care about anyone else.

He was also indifferent about the continual threat from Jack Dragna and Johnny Roselli to Siegel's racetrack wire service. Dragna's men had ceremoniously beaten or intimidated book-ies into either dropping their alliance with Siegel, who focused all his energies on the Flamingo and seemed to let his Trans-America service slip away, or subscribing to both services, which was costly.

In Chicago, Fischetti and his goons had bought out the *Continental Wire Service,* which was one of the last "rogue" book-making phone operations remaining. Shortly after its purchase, the outfit murdered its former owner, James Ragan. The only other major wire service not under the outfit's banner was Siegel's, and Dragna was determined to correct that omission.

Siegel was too busy supervising construction at his dream casino. He flew in carpenters, plasterers, electricians, and decorators from all over the country, paid them exorbitant amounts for their suggestions, then nonchalantly fired them and hired others. Many who knew Siegel at this time believed that he had truly lost his mind, that he had taken on a dictator-type mentality in which he barked bizarre orders and expected everyone to jump without question.

He demanded that walls be double and triple thickness to hold up against wind, sandstorms, and earthquakes. That part of the bill came to $138,000. He designed the dining room with one plan, then abruptly changed his mind and told contractor Del Webb to redo the blueprints for an extra $75,000. He wanted a header beam raised because it was too low. That cost an additional $23,000. An expanded kitchen passageway put an extra $35,000 on the tab. Then he enlarged the boiler room for $115,000. The curtains were wrong, the silverware was wrong, the glassware was wrong. All were changed on a whim.

Anyone who could swindle a buck or pad his expenses did so freely. Siegel was too busy building his empire to notice that it was crumbling beneath his feet. The bills skyrocketed. What was originally set to cost $1 million doubled, then tripled, then quadrupled. The investors saw their shares in the debacle dwindle into oblivion.

There is a common misconception that Virginia Hill was not only a constant companion of Siegel's at the construction site but that she had a say in the building as well. Both are false. Hill rarely, if ever, visited the site and positively had no hand in its development. She had nothing to do with the bookkeeping or with its expenses. The logic is simple: Few businessmen take their mistresses along on business ventures, especially of this magnitude, and in the Mafia, women, no matter how respected or powerful, would never be included or involved in business. Virginia had no place in Siegel's affairs.

Virginia also detested Las Vegas and now saw Siegel only when he came back to Los Angeles. They stayed at Hill's rented Coldwater Canyon home. Virginia later said that when Ben would visit, they would spend the entire weekend in bed together, read poetry to one another, and dream about the hotel. He would tell her details of the construction, where and how the money was being spent, or at least the money he had kept track of, who was paying off what inspectors, and who was putting money into the project. Virginia played dumb and acted interested.

She grilled Ben about details, especially those concerning money and the investors. She had also learned that Siegel himself was dipping into the financial well and skimming $10,000 here and $10,000 there. She took mental notes, then transcribed them in her diary.

The bulk of Virginia Hill's diary focuses on the dates between December 1945 and December 1946, when the casino finally opened. It is filled with cryptic notations about money transfers from Adonis and Lansky, Smiley and Wilkerson. It also indicates when and how Ben Siegel ripped off the Nevada Projects Corporation.

Though Siegel's continual building of the casino, then tearing it down, seemed an odd and obsessive quirk to nearly everyone, Bugsy knew exactly what he was doing. Virginia's diary shows that Ben Siegel was not a man with a will-o'-the-wisp personality. He used the constant alterations in construction as a method of skimming.

When he needed something redone—a beam moved or a wall replastered—he charged the Nevada Projects Corporation $30,000. But the actual cost was only around $20,000. Siegel pocketed the extra $10,000 for himself. His mistake was confiding his scheme to Virginia.

There is also another misconception: that when Siegel built the casino and the cost overruns started mounting, the Mafia threatened to shut him down, that the underworld still suspected his "dream" was a lot of malarkey. Nothing could be further from the truth.

Las Vegas was on the verge of a major tourist explosion and well on its way to becoming a resort town when Siegel first laid out his plans for the Flamingo. He picked a site more than one mile out of town, but the town was already encroaching upon Siegel's land by the time the workers broke ground.

A local newspaper, the *Las Vegas Review Journal*, paints a clear picture of the desert at the time Siegel moved in.

For the past year rumors have been flying thick and fast that the "greats" of movieland and speculators from all parts of the nation are contemplating investments in Las Vegas.

A round-up of the resort hotel picture today shows two enterprises actually under construction and one starting.

The article mentions the El Rancho, on a thirty-eight-acre tract owned by a Marion Hicks and Clifford Jones. Another unnamed forty-eight-room hotel was planned slightly to the north of the Last Frontier. The million-dollar New Horizon was just to the west. Frank Sinatra reportedly had a stake in that hotel and allegedly planned to install a radio station inside so that he could perform live broadcasts as a tourist attraction. The article also mentioned another unnamed hotel that was estimated to cost nearly $2 million. Construction of a massive underground water well was already under way. Cowboy actor Roy Rogers had begun to build a dude ranch several blocks from Siegel's Flamingo Hotel. And another ranch called Wolfe-Best intended to hire top singers and movie stars; their names would appear on the marquee.

The hotels open for business by the time Bugsy finished building the Flamingo included the Frontier, Club Savoy, Last Frontier, Monte Carlo, Pioneer Club, Nevada Biltmore, El Rancho, Las Vegas Club, Kit Carson Club, and the Golden Nugget. Absolutely no one thought Siegel's idea was out of line or crazy. The newer operations mentioned in the newspaper had cost well over $2 million each.

Though hardly an innovation for the mob, graft and skimming always seemed to go hand in hand on any construction project. But what made Lansky and the Luciano clan angry was that Siegel did it to them. He was cheating his own kind. Adonis knew Siegel was going too far, and he continually needled Lansky, Luciano, and Costello to do something about it.

But there was another more pressing problem to contend with. Chicago's West Coast boss Jack Dragna made a stand and called for a meeting on November 5, 1945, in New York with Costello, Charlie Fischetti, Joe Adonis, Meyer Lansky, and Ben Siegel. Siegel refused to show. Dragna said that the racing wires had to be incorporated under one banner and he would seize control of the Trans-America Race Wire Service. Rather than just muscle his way in, Dragna convinced the New Yorkers that he wanted to do it peacefully and avoid bloodshed.

He also made it clear that there could be an even bigger battle over control of Las Vegas if a concession was not made. Costello and Fischetti reportedly agreed to consolidate the wires under Chicago's control, with a 25 percent cut going to the East. Siegel had no say in the matter. When told of the deal, he barked to Costello that "things stay as is. No deal with any of the Chicago dagos. If they want the wires, let them try and get them. They'll have to go through me." Siegel also said he had no time to deal with it now. He had other problems brewing at the Flamingo.

Though the East Coast mob was by now firmly entrenched in Vegas and with the multi-million-dollar Flamingo Hotel promising to be a gold mine, the Chicago mob went forward with its plans to rival the Flamingo. It mapped out designs for several hotel/casinos to be built: the Desert Inn, about a long block down the road from Siegel's Flamingo; the Thunderbird, which was closer to the center of town and the other casinos; and the Dunes, which would be adjacent to Siegel's dream resort.

If the Flamingo proved profitable, Chicago would ride its coattails. Almost everyone assumed that it would probably take a little time before the idea of a high-class gambling joint caught on in the cowboy town, but no one figured that it would collapse. Anyone involved in the rackets saw the potential in Vegas. They also saw Siegel's obsessive-compulsive behavior over his hotel and knew he was speeding toward the edge of destruction.

There are published reports that claim Siegel and Virginia flew to Mexico in September 1946 to get married. The stories even claim that Siegel bought Virginia a ruby and diamond ring and that she even mentioned the ring as her wedding ring to a newspaper reporter who asked about it several years after Siegel's death.

If this is true, absolutely no one connected with either the Chicago or New York mobs can offer any insight. Even those men who were close to Joe Epstein seriously doubt the story's validity. If Virginia had married Siegel, she certainly would have sent word back to Epstein, and he would have cut off his money shipments. It would also have been a flash point for the simmering feud between Dragna and Siegel. Virginia was supposed to keep an eye on Siegel, and a marriage, no matter the reasons behind it, would have immediately put Hill's trust in question because it could have been interpreted as a switch of alliances toward the East Coast.

If she did marry Siegel, as several writers claim, it was definitely not out of love. Over and over people who knew her have stated flatly that she was terrified of him since the rape incident. But she might possibly have gone along with Siegel's marriage proposal as a ruse to get even closer to him in order to gain even greater intimate knowledge of his financial and personal dealings and to report back to the Chicago outfit. Her diary indicates no marriage but shows that she must have had considerable inside information, obtained directly from Siegel, concerning his money skimming from the Flamingo and dealings with the Luciano gang.

By the end of 1946, Virginia Hill had enough evidence in her diary to send the Mafia crashing, including details of bribes of city officials and law enforcement agents in Las Vegas, swindles of contractors, and accounts of rigged sporting events and skimming from the wires. More significantly, the diary notations indicate how much Siegel had ripped off his own people. The various entries, when added together, indicate that Siegel had embezzled somewhere near $2 million from the Nevada Projects Corporation.

Again, rumors persist that Hill herself took the money without Siegel's knowledge. Inasmuch as she had no direct dealing with the finances of the hotel, it would have been impossible for her to get any money from the operation, let alone have enough access to steal $2 million without Ben knowing about it.

Associates of Siegel's say the diary is correct; Siegel stole the money. They also maintain that he gave the $2 million to Hill for one, or all, of several reasons: to buy her affection, to hide the embezzlement from the corporation, or to bribe her into remaining silent about his crooked dealings with the hotel and the wires. If he gave her the money, it would also explain how Hill knew about the swindle. She supposedly kept the money in a Swiss bank account. But details of the account, if true, are sketchy at best and probably more speculative than factual.

By November 1946, with cost overruns, the free-for-all graft from contractors, and the embezzling, Siegel had sunk more than $5 million into the Flamingo. He was deeply in debt; his investors were irate and knew they had been cheated. He had no money to hire opening acts, and his dream had become a nightmare.

Ben Siegel needed another half million dollars, at the very least, to open the casino doors. His anticipated grand opening on Thanksgiving weekend was a lost cause. He wanted to shoot for the Christmas holiday, but even that date was in jeopardy.

Siegel had sold off all of his shares in the Nevada Projects Corporation months before, when the overruns were hovering in the $4 million range. His only interest now was personal; to see his dream reach fruition and his sweetheart's name in lights, as he had promised. Ben Siegel's ego was on the line. If the Flamingo did not open in time for the big holiday season, backers would toss Ben Siegel out of the corporation and put Meyer Lansky in charge to straighten out the mess.

The Chicago mob was also eyeing the situation, eager to see Siegel fail so that they could move in on the operation. Ben Siegel had only one place to turn.

In an act of desperation, he went to his friend Billy Wilkerson and asked him to pay off the rest of the debt in exchange for a greater share in the hotel. He also needed Wilserson's Hollywood clout to ensure that opening night would be packed with celebrities and big names would appear on the marquee for a good draw and good radio and newspaper coverage.

Wilkerson agreed to kick in the extra money and promised Siegel to hide his additional investment from the mob. Siegel knew that if anyone found out that the hotel had now cost more than six times its initial estimate, questions would be asked, and his bilking could be uncovered. He also knew it would give Dragna the ammunition he needed to undercut his power and seize his racetrack wire racket.

12

With millions lost in graft and bilking scams, $2 million given to Hill "in trust" by Siegel, and nearly $1 million buried through the last-minute bailout by Billy Wilkerson, the Bug was ready to put the finishing touches on his casino. The last detail was his personal suite, situated above the entrance so that he could see who came in and out without being observed.

The suite was perched four stories up and dead center over the front cement entrance. It was built to withstand any earthquake or attack by any underworld enemies. Siegel demanded that the outside walls be four feet thick; the glass overlooking the exterior was to be double paned and bulletproof. Siegel later removed some of the double glass because he said it obstructed his vision.

Inside the suite he had a specially built clothes closet that had a thick bolt on the interior of the door. Inside that closet he had an escape hatch constructed under the right corner of the floor. The hatch itself also had a lock that could be secured from the underside, slowing down anyone who tried to pry it up from the outside. All Siegel had to do in case of attack was lock himself inside the closet, lift up the carpet, open the trap door, and scurry down a wooden ladder. The ladder went five floors down to the basement, which was a maze of dank tunnels and pipes.

The maze split in two directions, again giving Ben Siegel a

chance to escape his pursuers. At either end a bodyguard and a driver were ordered to stand ready to whisk Siegel to safety in case of attack. Bugsy Siegel believed he was well prepared for any emergency, though he always maintained to associates that he was not in the least bit paranoid.

He often bragged about his alleged invincibility. "Anyone who tries to kill Ben Siegel will find himself eating dirt before he gets off the first round," Siegel boasted to a *Herald* reporter in Los Angeles shortly before the Flamingo was about to open. "But no one will ever kill Ben Siegel because I've got no enemies on this earth."

Virginia and Chick visited Las Vegas shortly before the casino was supposed to open. Chick moved into the El Rancho, which was one of Siegel's operations, and took a job collecting money from the slot machines.

Virginia moved a handful of dresses, slacks, undergarments, and personal items into Ben's Flamingo suite. She helped Ben furnish the apartment and ordered and paid for expensive bric-a-brac, paintings, and linens to make the suite more of a home than a hotel room.

Siegel spent the last three months of 1946 negotiating for talent to headline his grand opening. Through his clout with the unions in Hollywood, his personal association with entertainers, and his alliance with the powerful Billy Wilkerson, Siegel booked Xavier Cugat and his orchestra and Tommy Wonder, who appeared by "special permission" of M-G-M; the Tune-Toppers, a musical quartet; and, at the last minute, Jimmy Durante.

Siegel needed someone else to round out the bill.

Rose Marie was a child singing star who was, by the 1940s, a popular singer and comedienne who also did impressions of Jimmy Durante for a lark. She had been playing at the Copacabana in New York and had made a big splash. Wilkerson approached Rose Marie with the idea of appearing at the Flamingo. At first, she was reluctant, but quickly changed her mind when she found out Durante was on the bill.

Rose Marie said she had always wanted to perform with Durante, doing her impression with him, and thought it would be fun. She was signed on for four weeks at $3,500 per week.

Ben went out of his way to make sure that opening night

would make a big splash in the press. He sent cases of whiskey to Los Angeles and Las Vegas newspaper offices, flowers to columnists, and even expensive gifts of perfume and jewelry to many of his Hollywood pals, who he hoped would show up for window dressing and to guarantee press coverage.

But two weeks before opening night, December 26, Siegel saw another major setback to his dream. One by one the stars backed out of the invitations. George Jessel, Clark Gable, Spencer Tracy, and Gary Cooper all said they were previously engaged for that evening. The Christmas holiday, it seemed, was the last holiday anyone would want to be away from home, especially when it meant traveling to a desert town to help a notorious gangster save face.

The *Las Vegas Review-Journal* offered one of the first write-ups:

> One of the greatest floor shows to be presented in recent months in Las Vegas will be provided by the new Flamingo Hotel when it opens its doors for business on December 26.
>
> Officers of the new resort hotel has [sic] set their sights high, as far as entertainment is concerned, and had designed its program to suit the "big city" tastes of the Las Vegas and the city's visitors.

The newspaper also indicated that a problem existed over when the hotel would open, which would later cause a great deal of anguish and disappointment for all concerned.

> According to management there has been some confusion regarding the Thursday and Friday night openings. In order to clarify the situation, the Flamingo announces that, due to many requests, it has decided that in order to accommodate all Las Vegas residents who may wish to be included in the opening of the new $5,000,000 pleasure resort, a double opening night will be presented . . . dress will be optional.
>
> There will be another big gala New Year's Eve party and the management is hoping to present one of the greatest evenings of entertainment that ever has been seen in Las Vegas or anywhere else.

It is the plan of the management to open each afternoon at 4 o'clock with the cafe–cocktail lounge and casino running full blast. The big restaurant will open each evening at 6:30, with the entire assembly running all night.

Siegel also spent another $22,000 on newspaper ads, the bulk of which appeared only in Las Vegas. In fact, the opening was virtually ignored in the Los Angeles papers.

One of the first big ads boasted of the $5 million cost of the hotel/casino, which indicates that the mob—the Nevada Projects Corporation—knew full well of the cost overruns (except for the last Wilkerson bailout) and even used it to its advantage as a way to let gamblers know that this would be the finest, flashiest, and most expensive resort in which they had ever set foot.

The ad claimed that the hotel was still undergoing its finishing touches and that completion was expected by March 1, 1947. The ad bragged that "nine big stores, operated by America's leading merchants [would] bring to Las Vegas the greatest fineries of the world," that "there will be a swimming pool area, a health club, tennis courts and thirty six-room luxurious bungalows." It promised

the greatest array of chefs housed under one roof, its casino staffed by experts drawn from all over the U.S. . . . entertainment assembled from the world's stage, from radio and Hollywood's studios . . . top bands of the nation will play music for your dancing.

The Flamingo anticipates attracting many people who have never been to Las Vegas, conducting booking offices in the four largest Eastern cities. Phone 1138 or apply in person for tickets. Reserve now for the big New Year's Eve Jamboree! The Flamingo is for Las Vegas!

No one was sure whether or not Siegel was going to pull it off. His investors, which now included the Chicago, Cleveland, and Miami mobs as well as the New York clan, believed that if the Flamingo could draw, it would lure gamblers and vacationers to the other hotels already operating or in the planning and construction stages. If the Flamingo flopped, they believed it could mean the death knell for the Vegas empire, or at least a serious setback.

As the third week in December approached, the hotel was far from ready. Virginia took a serious interest in the operation because by now nearly everyone knew of her association with Siegel as well as who "the Flamingo" really was. She believed the hotel was her showcase and its appearance a personal reflection. She left Los Angeles and moved into Siegel's hotel suite.

Bugsy took out his stress and frustration on Virginia, and the two ended up in screaming and slugging matches nearly every night. Most evenings before the opening, while crews pounded the last nails and unpacked the last of the liquor, Virginia sat alone in a corner chair and drank herself into a hazy stupor. Then she ambled into the suite and cursed at Siegel and accused him of trying to embarrass her by putting her name on the disaster. Ben reacted with violence.

Their nerves were frayed and their tempers short by the last week. The two were barely speaking; Virginia, who more than likely never really loved Siegel, had had enough of his temper tantrums and threatened to walk out on what she called "his stupid gambling joint that wasn't gonna draw anything more than flies and losers." Ben ordered her to stay with him and see the hotel through the opening month. Or else.

Virginia could not have been too concerned about any threat Siegel might have made. She had details of his swindling and embezzling in her diary—facts, figures, and dates—more than enough to nail the gangster if he dared try to harm her. The diary would be just another excuse Dragna would have for disposing of Siegel and getting the New York gang to back him. Concerned or not, Virginia stayed at Siegel's side.

Days before the opening Siegel made yet another appeal to Hollywood tabloid mogul and financial backer Billy Wilkerson and laid his cards on the table. "If we don't get any stars, we're not going to draw any crowds. If we don't get the crowds, you lose your shirt. We all lose."

Wilkerson used his clout once again and convinced what celebrities he could get to turn out, provided they could spend Christmas at home. Any "movie star" party had to be over the weekend, after Christmas, and the stars had to be separated from the noncelebrity gamblers. Siegel agreed to host a special Hollywood-type weekend beginning on Saturday, December 28.

Siegel and Wilkerson chartered the TWA Constellation plane, which was supposed to be crammed with stars, newspaper reporters from across the country, and fan-magazine photographers. It was scheduled to arrive Saturday and leave on Sunday, the twenty-ninth. Wilkerson kept his part of the bargain and guaranteed George Jessel, who was promised he would serve as master of ceremonies, Veronica Lake, Lucille Ball, Brian Ahern, June Haver, Ava Gardner, Eleanor Parker, Brian Donlevy, Sunny Tufts, Peter Lawford, William Holden, Nancy Guild, and of course, George Raft.

Siegel ordered his publicists to slap together a full-page newspaper advertisement listing the stars who promised to turn out for the "big gala weekend," without the star's knowledge of the ad or their approval. When several stars saw the ad, they backed out in revolt, angered about being used, and spread the word.

Ben thought he had Hollywood sewn up, the underworld bamboozled, Virginia intimidated, and the city gawking at his garish monstrosity. The only one he was not able to win over was Mother Nature, who opened the flood gates on Christmas Day, pounding the desert town with several feet of rain, flash floods, washed-out roads, and a near lake where sand used to blow just days before. To make matters worse, Siegel's specially built airport, planned to welcome the TWA star caravan, had also become a massive mound of mud and was unusable. The TWA flight had to be canceled. A fourteen-car Union Pacific train was leased instead. And more stars backed out.

Siegel redid the newspaper ads once again. The last advertised the "Jamboree Special" train but offered no specific movie-star names other than that the train was from Hollywood. Reservations were sluggish, so Siegel wanted to encourage last-minute tourists. He ended the ad in boldface print, letting people know that they did not need a reservation for the cocktail lounge at any time. Realizing that the Vegas cowboy crowd was shying away from the casino, he also advertised "come as you are," which infuriated Virginia, who feared that the casino would turn into a "low-class cowboy joint with bums and drunks." She envisioned the riffraff scaring away the high-class gamblers the casino initially set out to draw.

Ben stuck to his guns. He even told Virginia that he would

wear a sports shirt and slacks so everyone would feel welcome. Hill insisted he dress properly for the occasion.

When the rain finally ended on opening day, Thursday, Siegel discovered one disaster after another. The roof leaked, the wiring was defective, and the rooms were not ready for either guests or performers. But that was only the beginning of the disaster.

There is a strong belief among the underworld that the opening of the Flamingo was sabotaged by Mafia rivals and professional gamblers, some of whom saw the profit potential in the Bug's operation and wanted to drive him out of business and seize the venture for themselves and others who hoped Siegel would go out of business and eliminate competition with their smaller gambling dens. Still others knew Siegel was so busy with the appearance of the place that he entrusted the hiring to unscrupulous thieves. They rigged the tables, double-dealt the cards and ripped off Siegel for their own profit. Professional gamblers swarmed on the casino and plucked Siegel clean, to the tune of $250,000. The only way he actually made money was by putting his guests and tourists up at the El Rancho and Last Frontier hotels at eleven to twenty dollars a night.

Siegel's only hope was for the Hollywood weekend and the crowds it promised to attract.

On Saturday, December 28, the Flamingo went all out to put on a big show. It worked.

Wilkerson was named general in charge of the hotel and made sure the press had enough "facts" to paint a pretty picture of the casino. He pointed out that the landscaping alone cost $1 million. He shipped in live flamingos from Florida and promised that Frank Sinatra, Lena Horne, and the Andrews Sisters would appear on the bill in the months to come.

Wilkerson made sure the weekend was a success by arranging plenty of press coverage. The Las Vegas air strip had dried suitably to accommodate several planeloads of guests and performers, the train arrived on time, and it looked as if, finally, Siegel knew what he was doing.

On hand for the big weekend were Jessel, Raft, Vivian Blaine, Lon McAllister, Jesse Lasky, Charles Coburn, George Sanders, Sunny Tufts, and the stars of the show: Cugat, Durante, Rose Marie, and the singers and dancers. The house was packed on both Saturday and Sunday night. The Flamingo was a huge success, though there were no rooms to accommodate guests and the casino and dining room were combined for the show.

Rose Marie remembered the weekend as a lot of fun and that everyone both onstage and off seemed to enjoy themselves. She clicked with Durante; she did her impersonation and even sang a duet with "the Great Schnozzola," who even taught her to play the piano in his style. Rose Marie also remembered when she first met Virginia Hill.

"There was no mistaking that she was Bugsy Siegel's girlfriend. They weren't lovey-dovey or touchy or anything. You could just feel it. You just knew it."

She said that when Hill first saw her, she noticed that Rose Marie was "a little fat" around the middle.

I was three or four months pregnant at the time, with my daughter. Virginia mentioned that I looked a little fat. When I told her that I was pregnant, she said she was leaving for Paris to buy wine, I think, and asked me if I wanted her to bring anything back for me. She brought back a beautiful French organdy-and-lace christening gown. There was also some embroidery on it. It was very pretty. I still have it.

She said that Hill basically hovered around the room during the weekend but did not really mix or socialize with the guests. That was left to Ben Siegel, who made it his personal mission to ensure that each celebrity guest and performer felt welcome, or at least enough to return and spend money.

Rose Marie said that when she received her first paycheck, she noticed that eleven dollars had been deducted. When she saw it, she was angry and quickly went to the owner (Siegel) to inquire about the missing funds. Rose Marie said she had no idea at that time that Ben Siegel was the notorious Bugsy Siegel.

I asked him where my money was. I said that if he needed it that bad, I'd give it to him. He didn't have to steal it. He looked at me and said, "You stayed in the El Rancho, didn't you?" I said yes. He said, "Well, that cost eleven dollars a night . . . if it's a problem I'll reimburse you." I told him that it wasn't a problem. I just wanted to know why it was taken out and that was all. I got the eleven dollars.

Rose Marie said that she played baccarat and was given $10,000 to start. She expected to lose the money but build it up to $30,000, then had to go onstage. With nowhere to put the money, she tucked it inside her blouse and performed. She said she was scared stiff and nervous the entire performance. Later, she went up to Siegel and told him, "Don't ever do that to me again." Winning was not worth the agony.

With the stellar celebrity weekend, Siegel and Hill believed their Flamingo would be a winner. The house was sold out for two nights, the casino had gotten back on its financial feet after Hill and Siegel fired or threatened the initial group of dealers who had swindled the casino, and reservations for the New Year's Eve bash picked up. But then the celebrities went back home to Los Angeles. The weekend was over, and so was the party. Reality set in.

"After that first weekend, we played to an empty house," Rose Marie recalled.

Maybe ten to twenty people showed up after that. When the stars left, the only ones there were cowboys, and they didn't know what to make of the place. It was too much for them. They stayed away. Siegel even advertised that they could come as they were, in their cowboy clothes, to try and bring them in. That's probably where the "come as you are" idea started. But it didn't work.

Rose Marie offered to renegotiate her contract for a lesser amount or a shorter run, but Siegel held firm on his initial offer. He refused to believe that business would not pick up, especially with a world-class menu at modest prices.

The Flamingo's restaurant offered hors d'oeuvres ranging from sixty cents for chopped chicken livers to two dollars for cherrystone clams on the half shell and cracked crab to a one-dollar drink called "Flamingo Egg Nog," which is said to be a mixture of conventional egg nog with a drop of cherry flavoring to give it a pink color. The most expensive item on the menu was New York cut sirloin steak for $4.50, and that was served with potatoes and vegetables, soup or salad. Still reasonable for 1946.

The Flamingo lost more than half a million dollars that first holiday week. Word spread around town that the hotel was run by gangsters, that honest citizens would end up in a shoot-out if they went there. Word of Bugsy Siegel's temper and Virginia Hill's questionable morals became common knowledge in town. Virginia told Siegel she had enough of Vegas and went home to Los Angeles.

Virginia rented a home at 810 North Linden Drive in Beverly Hills from a Mexican associate, Juan Romero, who had previously leased several homes to Hill. Hill was quickly back to her old style of high living and free spending, made especially easy because Romero charged her nothing for rent. Virginia insisted Romero never charged her rent out of friendship, but mob associates claim the rent deal was in exchange for sexual favors from Virginia. Hill retained an interior decorator, brought only the best of furniture and decorations, and went on a wild jewelry-buying spree. She installed a wall safe in the home to protect her jewels, which now were worth more than $250,000. The safe also could be used as a cash box. It held the money deliveries from Epstein, which were sporadic but still continued, and her racetrack winnings, which were more regular and profitable.

But disappointment over the Flamingo and the certain pressure she was receiving from Siegel, whom she did not love, and from Dragna and the Chicago mob, which was questioning her loyalty and squeezing her for more information on Siegel's finances and details of his wire services, took their toll on Hill. She flew into violent temper tantrums at the slightest suggestion of anything she did not like. She was insistent that she was being followed, that someone was trying to kill her, and that everyone was using her and no one cared about her.

At dinner one night in her North Linden Drive home, she pulled a gun and threatened to kill Allen Smiley and several others who were there as invited guests. A private detective was called and stopped Virginia before she pulled the trigger.

While Virginia became unglued in Beverly Hills, Bugsy Siegel's emotions snapped in Las Vegas. In a seemingly irrational move, he issued a death threat against his backer, Billy Wilkerson, and his friend Moe Sedway and vowed to put them in their graves before he died.

13

Though business slowly began to pick up, it was still a long way from the Hollywood weekend and the promises of a self-sustaining money machine that Ben Siegel had convinced his investors in the underworld the Flamingo would become. The suites were not yet completed, the lounge still needed finishing touches, and the electricians found flaws in the wiring that called for an immediate shutdown of various parts of the hotel. In short, the Flamingo had laid an egg.

Virginia wanted no part of the operation, and after the holidays were over, she refused to set foot in the hotel again. By the end of January she had completely dissociated herself from the Las Vegas desert and exploded into a rage if anyone dared mention the hotel's name or called her by her nickname. Chick, though, stuck by Siegel's side and remained in Vegas for most of the winter.

To make matters worse, one of Siegel's big investors, Billy Wilkerson, saw the writing on the wall and demanded that Ben buy out his shares. Ben refused and threatened Wilkerson with everything he could, from shutting down his paper to outright murder. Wilkerson knew Ben would do neither because of the monumental backlash any action against him would trigger. Wilkerson realized that if he leaked the fact that he fronted the last leg of the financing, such information would raise further speculation about the cost overruns and certainly cast grave suspicion that Siegel had swindled his friends. He had the Bug over a barrel.

Hill's diary indicates that Siegel either paid off or bought out Billy Wilkerson's share of the hotel for $375,000. Whether he received the other money he laid out remains a mystery.

Then Siegel's original partner in the hotel, Moe Sedway, grew too big for his own good. He raked in a fortune running Ben's other Vegas operations and was the local party boy and the Nevada politician's best friend. He became a desert "mover and shaker" and was considered by many a man of respect. Sedway's newfound status infuriated Siegel, who desperately tried to scrape cash together to make needed repairs and complete the finishing touches on his venture.

When Siegel heard that Sedway wanted to run for state assembly, he went berserk. "Sedway's going legit? Who the hell does he think he is? We don't run for office. We own the office. He'll bring the heat down here faster than anything."

The two came to blows, and Sedway was barred from any of Siegel's Vegas establishments, which did not sit well with the boys from New York, who backed the smooth-talking Sedway because of his ability to get things done.

Siegel also made another mistake. It concerned the long-simmering feud over the race wires.

Lucky Luciano had been deported to Italy from the United States in February 1946, after he served time in prison for racketeering charges. But Luciano did not stay in Italy long. Though he considered his home country just another branch office of operations, Luciano believed he was still too far away from the United States to properly run his Mafia family and its illegal gambling, narcotics, and prostitution rackets. He set up shop in Havana, Cuba, just a short hop from Miami, which had been the base of the Luciano mob's narcotics operation.

Luciano was kept abreast of the Flamingo's progress, or lack thereof, and Siegel's unwillingness to work out a concession with Dragna's boys over a consolidated wire service. The hotel debacle was a sore point with Luciano and his boys. Vegas was a boom town, and they knew it was only a matter of time before the other hotels picked up the slack from the Flamingo and made a profit. However, the wire situation was a powderkeg, and the fuse was lit.

There are stories that Dragna himself went to Cuba to try and strike an accord with Luciano but was told that his hands were tied as long as Ben Siegel refused to compromise. Luciano and Dragna both understood that the wires in Los Angeles and Las Vegas were Ben Siegel's personal rackets. The bookies were in his pocket not through any loyalty on their part but out of fear, and as long as Bugsy held control, Dragna and Siegel would be business competitors, not partners, draining the profits instead of building an empire for bigger rewards. Siegel and Dragna had held one another in check, but Dragna was tired of being thwarted.

Siegel was too busy with his hotel for anyone to reason with him. He rambled on about idiotic improvements, talked nonsense, and became even more paranoid, insisting that he had been sabotaged and that someone was trying to murder him. He finally realized that keeping the hotel open while there were drills, hammers, and buzz saws running was a foolish notion. The noise and dust drove away the few customers who tried to enjoy the facility. Siegel shut everything down except for the coffee shop and part of the casino on February 6, 1947.

When Siegel came to visit Virginia in Los Angeles, she called him a "two-bit loser, a fucking chump who made his friends rich but couldn't keep cab fare in his own pocket." When she tried to throw him out, he dragged her up the stairs, threw her into the bedroom, and raped and beat her on the floor. Like so many others who had crossed the Bug, she had had enough. She vowed to destroy him and told him he was a dead man.

Though the hotel was shut for a month, Siegel worked like a demon trying to drum up publicity and come up with a scheme for a "grand reopening." He worked with the hotel's publicists and cooked up a gala celebration that garnered considerable press and radio coverage. It was Siegel's last shot, and he knew it.

With money borrowed, and never repaid, from George Raft and purchases on credit for fliers, banners, and decorations, Ben Siegel staged one of the biggest blowouts ever seen in Las Vegas. The local newspaper described the ceremony.

The Flamingo, Las Vegas' newest luxury hotel, was formally opened Saturday afternoon with a ceremony in which city, county and hotel officials took part and climaxed by the Andrews Sisters.

Patricia, Laverne, Maxine—cutting a red silk ribbon to open the double doors leading from the patio to the lobby.

The city of Las Vegas was represented by Mayor F. W. Cragin and Frank Gusewelle, chairman of the county commissioners, represented his board. They offered good wishes of the local government for the success of the institution.

The ceremonies, which were broadcast over KENO with Buck Newcome as master of ceremonies, were attended by many Las Vegans and visitors who came here for the opening of the hotel.

The Andrews Sisters were a major draw and helped put the Flamingo back on its feet. They headlined a "star-studded show," as the hotel's press described it, which included musician Henry King; the Ruddells, a tumbling and trampoline act composed of two men and a girl; and Cabot and Dresden, a dance team. The first week was sold out, and the Andrews Sisters continued to pack the house for the remainder of their engagement.

Buoyed by the success of the reopening, Siegel signed on the Ritz Brothers for $20,000 per week, which was a considerable amount of money for 1947. Siegel maintained to backers that the fee was not a problem. He told associates that the hotel was clearing ten times the Ritz Brothers' fee each week from the room rentals, casino, and restaurant. Flamingo investors believed Bugsy. The Ritz Brothers, who had packed the El Rancho to standing room at the same time the Flamingo first opened, were signed to go on in September. Siegel believed he had pulled the hotel, and himself, out of trouble. But the truth was a different matter.

Though the casino was packed every night, the roulette wheels spinning, cards and dice moving quickly across green felt tables, and tens of thousands of dollars pouring in, the hotel was operating in the red. There are some who claim Siegel could not keep his hands clean, that he still ripped off his own business and blew the stolen money on bad gambling bets. Others believe that Dragna and his men had secretly controlled the dealers, who were skimming and turning the profits over to the Chicago outfit. Several others say no one will ever know the real story.

Meyer Lansky made a trip west in late May 1947 to find out

exactly why the Flamingo was losing money when it appeared to be such a success. Most other hotels were raking in profits in the hundreds of thousands to millions. The new resorts were opening to packed houses and swelling cash reserves. But the Flamingo was a losing proposition, the only one in the red in the entire area, if not the country. Lansky, who was by now the only one who could get close enough to Siegel to talk to him, was ordered to Las Vegas by Frank Costello to try and reason with the Bug and get to the bottom of the problem.

Lansky learned nothing as fact but suspected many things; mainly, that Dragna had a meddling hand or Siegel had sticky fingers. Either way, the problem had to be eradicated.

Federal files show that Jack Dragna, Johnny Roselli, and several other Chicago representatives were called to a meeting with Lansky, Siegel, and Joe Adonis, who flew in the day after Lansky's arrival. The meeting took place in the home of a Beverly Hills attorney tied to the Chicago outfit. In that meeting, Dragna and Lansky spelled out their concerns and, for what would be the last time, mapped out plans for expansion of Las Vegas and details of a consolidated racetrack wire service.

The Chicago clan was already involved in several resorts, including the Dunes, planned adjacent to the Flamingo, the Frontier, and the Desert Inn. It also had shares in the Flamingo, the Golden Nugget, and the Las Vegas Club. Siegel refused to cut the midwesterners in on a share of the El Rancho and held firm on his control of the wires. Both Lansky and Dragna saw that Siegel was unmovable and had become an obstacle to greater profits. He had to be removed.

The meeting broke up with hollow promises by Dragna and Adonis to ace Siegel out of Vegas and divide the desert town. They told Ben he would be relegated to operating the L.A wires only. All, including Siegel, knew that the Mafia doesn't vote someone out of power and into early retirement; they are eliminated when they cease to further the cause. Most assume that at this time Siegel knew his days were numbered, but his ego prevented him from accepting the truth and acting, conceding to Dragna and Adonis.

The murder of Bugsy Siegel has remained one of the most puzzling and intriguing assassinations in the history of the underworld, one that has drawn considerable speculation as to who orchestrated the hit and actually pulled the trigger.

In a series of personal interviews, members of the Chicago underworld revealed precise details of the murder of Bugsy Siegel, from setup to execution. The story is published here for the very first time.

Meyer Lansky had too many childhood ties with Siegel to take any direct action against him. Adonis was more than eager to make the necessary arrangements to get his archnemesis out of the way. Because both men were considered of equal ranking in the New York Luciano mob, such a conflict would have fractured the group in two; those backing Lansky in support of Siegel and those backing Adonis against Siegel. Both factions agreed that the hit would have to be done outside the family. It would be Dragna's responsibility, and the Luciano clan would disavow any prior knowledge of the setup.

Siegel's fate was sealed at a meeting held on the last week of May 1947; it was simply a matter of a convenient time and place. The only problem seemed to be Virginia Hill. Her loyalties were in serious question, and there was even a suggestion by Lansky that she be eliminated along with the Bug. Dragna was indifferent. Hill could live or die. The outcome was of little consequence to him. She had done her job, but she had also become too intimate with Siegel and was far too irrational and emotional since the Flamingo disaster to be trusted. They all agreed that Virginia Hill had changed from her old Chicago days. She was no longer the tough-as-nails sexpot who played the rackets for the money and nothing more. Since teaming up with Siegel, she had taken on much of Siegel's personality. She had become a hysterical paranoid mistress who knew too much and called far too much attention to herself.

The only one in the room who defended her was Adonis, her former lover. He still seemed blinded by his sexual appetite for Virginia and could not see that she had changed. He tried to convince the group to delay a final decision on Hill's fate. From that moment on, Virginia Hill became Joey A's responsibility and his liability. In backing her, he made a major tactical error and broke a Mafia law: "*Non sedere mai con la schiena verso la porta*" (Never sit with your back to the door.) In other words, Joey A turned his back by trusting Virginia because of their past. He assumed she would remain loyal to him and eventually win back favor with the underworld. He would later learn the folly of his actions.

Two men who were close to Jack Dragna independently related the next sequence of events.

Virginia received a mysterious telephone call on June 8; the caller ordered her to pack a bag and fly to Chicago in two days. She was only to tell Siegel, if asked, that she was going to Paris to buy wine for the Flamingo, as she had done on previous trips to France. The trip would not be questioned by Siegel or any of his associates, and no suspicion would be aroused. Hill was also reportedly instructed not to ask any questions but to go straight to Epstein's North Shore apartment upon her arrival.

Virginia did as she was told. Epstein met her at Midway Airport in Chicago, and she stayed there for six days. Epstein allegedly gave Virginia $5,000 in "clean" cash, which added to the $10,000 she already had. If Virginia suspected anything was going down, she kept her mouth shut and laid low in Chicago.

While she was in Chicago, the plan against Ben Siegel went into action.

Siegel called an emergency meeting of the local bookies and told them that the price of the wire service was being doubled. Anyone who refused to pay the additional money would be killed. To Siegel's surprise, not one bookie kicked in. All ignored the Bug's demands. Dragna had apparently already spread the word that Siegel was out and Chicago was taking control.

Outraged, Siegel commandeered Flamingo builder Del Webb's private plane and headed back to Los Angeles for a meeting with Dragna. Dragna could not be located, and Siegel and a friend flew back to Vegas. The date was June 13. Siegel had to suspect something, because he surrounded himself with bodyguards, but he carried on his business as usual.

On the morning of June 16, Virginia Hill boarded a plane from Chicago to Paris. She never made contact with Ben Siegel, nor did she send back any word to him. Virginia Hill flew out of town and out of Siegel's life.

On June 19, Siegel and a friend, Swifty Morgan, returned to Los Angeles. Their plane touched down at approximately two-thirty A.M. They took a cab to the Linden Drive home. If Siegel expected Virginia to be there, he was disappointed. Only Chick Hill and Jerri Mason, Virginia's secretary and Chick's girlfriend, were there to meet him. Morgan and Siegel checked into different bedrooms and slept the night. Siegel conducted some business over the phone, then left when Allen Smiley showed up just before ten in the morning.

Siegel and Smiley went to Mickey Cohen's home to discuss the problem with the racetrack wires. Siegel reportedly suggested that Cohen and his men rip out all the phone lines from the bookies who were holding out. Cohen laughed and said he would take care of it, but they had to move slowly so as not to tip off Dragna or bring the New Yorkers down around them. Siegel was angered at Cohen's lethargic attitude and left with Smiley, who stayed in the car during the exchange.

Siegel then went to see his accountant, Joe Ross. In a June 23, 1947, *Variety* article Florabel Muir says that Siegel saw Ross to "map out an advertising campaign for the hotel." She wrote the promotion campaign extending far into the future, but gave no specific dates. Muir also wrote that Siegel met with his publicist, Paul Price, and wound up in an argument over Price's expense account set aside for visiting newspapermen. Price explained to Ben that the hefty tab was necessary to guarantee continued publicity and favorable reviews of the floor shows. Siegel appeared frustrated but made no move against Price and left. Smiley dropped Siegel at the Linden Drive home and took off.

Later that evening, Smiley returned to Beverly Hills, and Ben and Smiley left for a restaurant called Jack's, with Chick and Jerri sitting in the backseat of the car. After dinner they made a few stops, then finally returned to the Linden Drive home.

There are stories circulating that Chick claimed he smelled carnations when he opened the front door of the house, that the odor of flowers was a southern symbol of death or doom. If true, Chick was the only one who smelled anything. The four went inside. Chick and Jerri retired for the night. Siegel and Smiley stayed up and chatted.

While the four were out dining, Jack Dragna put the final phase of his assassination plot into motion. The following has never been offered to the Beverly Hills police or other investigators and had previously only been discussed among those connected with the underworld. But with the permission of those with personal knowledge of the murder, the last pieces of the "Bugsy Siegel Murder Mystery" can finally be put in place.

Dragna phoned Eddie Cannazero, whom he had used as a triggerman on a number of occasions, including the failed attempt on the life of Mickey Cohen, previously described. Cannazero apparently already knew exactly where Siegel would be at any given time. He only needed the final go-ahead from the boss, Dragna. At approximately 9 P.M. Cannazero and four other men boarded two black sedans and slowly made their way from Hollywood to Beverly Hills.

Cannazero rode in the first car with two men. The second car, which carried two men, was used as a so-called crash car, a vehicle that would divert police or any suspicious cars if the caravan was being followed. Unobserved, the caravan arrived at approximately ten P.M. One car parked around the corner from the Linden Drive home; the other, across the street. Both turned off the headlights.

Cannazero loaded a .30-30 carbine and positioned himself behind a lattice divider on the neighbor's property. He was concealed, but he had a clear view of the large plate-glass front window of the Hill home.

When Siegel, Chick Hill, Jerri Mason, and Allen Smiley arrived, they apparently did not see the car across the street or ignored it. Cannazero already had the carbine poised in the lattice when the four entered the home.

At approximately ten-thirty, Smiley opened the front drapes, which allowed Cannazero a clear view of the living room where Siegel and Smiley were talking. Siegel sat down on the sofa, picked up a copy of the *Los Angeles Times*, and flipped through the first section. He was still edgy and became bored with the paper. Siegel told Smiley that he felt he could not trust Mickey Cohen to take care of the bookies and said he intended to discuss the problem with Cohen later in the week. Smiley offered to fix Ben a drink to calm him down. Siegel accepted the offer.

Allen Smiley walked out of the living room and toward the kitchen, turning his back on Siegel. The time was approximately ten forty-five P.M.

At precisely the moment Smiley had distanced himself from Siegel, nine shots rang out in rapid fire, shattering the front window, smashing a white marble statue that many assumed was a figurine of Virginia Hill, ripping apart several paintings, and drilling holes in the wall. Moments later, Smiley heard the screeching of tires.

When the gunfire quieted, Smiley, Chick Hill, and Mason ran into the living room. In the center of the dust and debris was forty-two-year-old Ben Bugsy Siegel, slouched back on the sofa where he had been sitting and talking less than two minutes before. Blood streamed from his head and poured from the sockets of what were once his baby blue eyes. Siegel took four of the nine shots. He died instantly.

At approximately eleven P.M. Jack Dragna received a phone call. A voice at the other end, believed to be that of the trigger-man, Cannazero, informed Dragna of what had gone down. Joey Adonis received a call three minutes later in New York. As he hung up the phone, Adonis said only one sentence to associates in the room.

"The insect was killed."

Adonis smiled and walked outside.

There was no immediate need to inform Virginia Hill of what had occurred that night. She already knew something was going to happen to Siegel when she left for Paris. What she did not suspect was how close she had come to sitting on that sofa next to Baby Blue Eyes.

14

June 21, 1947. Beverly Hills police chief Clinton H. Anderson: Some of the people in this case are too big to be pushed around. There was money—a lot of money—behind this killing. It wasn't just a cheap gambling murder, you know. I do not believe that Siegel was wiped out because of anything which occurred in Las Vegas.

Six days later. Anderson: "Bugsy Siegel was killed over the love of Virginia Hill, and a Chicago racketeer probably engineered the killing."

June 28, 1947. Anderson: "Benjamin Siegel was killed because he demanded hush money from the Chicago mob . . . probably the Fischetti brothers, Charles, Rocco, and Joe."

Two days after that. Anderson: "Bugsy Siegel was murdered over a dope ring. He was apparently trying to muscle in on Mexican dope smuggling when he was gunned down."

August 1, 1947. Anderson:

The killing of Bugsy Siegel has been linked to a jewelry racket. The plan involved the transfer of stolen jewelry from Beverly Hills and Los Angeles to New York and could have netted Siegel and his gang more than half a million dollars.

Others were not as concerned about Siegel after the fact. June 22, 1947. Louis Wiener, Flamingo attorney:

> The Flamingo will conduct business as usual, despite the death of Benjamin Siegel. The Flamingo is owned by the Nevada Projects Corporation, and Siegel was only a stockholder in that corporation, and his death will have no effect whatever on the future operations of this hotel.

While Beverly Hills police chief Anderson and his men ran ragged as they tried to follow up every lead and nail shut the murder investigation of Ben Siegel, Meyer Lansky, Wiener, and two others seized control of the hotel. There was never any hesitation or show of remorse over the death of its founder. The mob knew the resort would be a gold mine if run properly.

In the meantime, the bullet-riddled body of the former Las Vegas playboy lay in the Los Angeles County morgue, unclaimed, on a marble slab, with an identification tag strapped to his left big toe, marked only as "B. Seigel, Crypt 6," his last name misspelled. No one ever showed up to view the body or claim it. The official cause of death given was "cerebral hemorrhage . . . gunshot wound of the head inflicted by person or persons unknown . . . we recommend further investigation."

The only personal effects recovered from the body were a gold key, which Siegel made for himself, similar to the one he had cut for his earlier home with Virginia, and $108 cash in his wallet. Upstairs in Bugsy's bedroom police found a .38-caliber handgun and a little black book, the discovery of which was hidden from the press for several weeks.

While Virginia remained in Paris, giving yet another brilliant acting performance of the hysterical and grieving companion, Esta Siegel flew to Los Angeles for questioning. She told Anderson that she had divorced Siegel in Reno, Nevada, on August 3 on the grounds of mental cruelty, that they had been married on January 28, 1928, and had two girls, Millicent, who was sixteen at the time of the killing, and Barbara, who was fourteen. She also stated that she had never heard of Virginia Hill until her name was brought up in connection with the murder.

While the newspapers painted a sympathetic portrait of the grieving widow and gave her name as "Esther" instead of Esta, the real meat of the murder, they believed, was the mysterious Virginia Hill, who captured more newspaper space than the murder investigation itself. All this while Hill remained in Paris.

The papers gave every juicy detail of Hill's life with Siegel that they were able to find out or print.

A *Los Angeles Times* article obtained a story on Hill from her suite in Paris. It told of how Hill wept as she sat in her hotel room looking out on the Rue de la Paix. She said that she had a quarrel over whether Siegel should wear a sports shirt to a dinner he was attending at the opening of the resort.

Between tears she said:

The last time I saw Ben was three weeks ago at his brand-new gambling casino in Las Vegas, Nevada. He was working hard and I told him he could not come to dinner with all those nice people we were going to eat with in a dirty white sports shirt. I told him it wouldn't look nice.

He barked back I should mind my own business. I am not taking that from anyone, so I packed my bags and left. I phoned good-bye from Chicago last week and said I was going to Europe. He said good-bye, and I never heard from him afterward.

Then she let the tear ducts work overtime.

I can't believe he's dead.

Ben, that's what I always called him, was so nice, and he had lots of friends. I can't imagine who shot him or why.

Hill told reporters she was touring France for three months and wanted to give Europe the once-over. Though she started out alone, Virginia Hill never went solo for long.

While Baby Blue Eyes was getting his in Beverly Hills, Virginia had gone on a wild spree in France with twenty-one-year-old Nicholas Fouillette, son of a wealthy French business family. She spent the weekend on their houseboat in the Seine near Fontainebleau. But she made sure people knew that she slept in the same room with Nick's mother.

When Hill crossed her legs to appear more casual with reporters, some very distinct bruises became evident. They were high up inside her thighs. She yanked her skirt down a notch and explained that she received the bruises "horseback riding in the forest."

When grilled about her alleged affair with the dead gangster, Virginia backpedaled.

> I never was very friendly with Ben, either. I never went with his friends, and he did not know who my friends are. There was no mistress business involved. If anyone or anything was his mistress, it was that Las Vegas hotel. He was killing himself putting it in shape. I never knew Ben was involved in all that gang stuff. He never mentioned anything about it, and I never asked any questions. I never saw him before he got started on the Flamingo.

Hill was a fair liar and getting in some practice for when she later testified at a senate hearing that she was nothing more than an innocent little waif who happened to meet some smart businessmen.

Beverly Hills police were scrambling to bring something to the Los Angeles District Attorney's Office. They had investigated tips that someone had dropped a fortune at the Flamingo the night before the shooting and went gunning after Siegel for revenge. They also checked tips that he had forced local bookmakers to step up their investment in his wire service and that some irate bookie may have been gunning for him. They also checked rumors that the Flamingo was doing such a smash business that it was taking customers away from other Vegas casinos whose owners wanted Siegel out of the way.

Then they called in suspects. Juan Romero was questioned. He owned the Linden Drive home and rented it to Hill and Siegel. He also had managed Valentino's estate and leased Falcon's Lair to Hill before she met Siegel. Nothing was learned, and he was released.

Publicist Paul Price was interrogated, then let go. Chick Hill, who had last been employed at the Flamingo handing out change for the slot machines, said he knew nothing about Siegel or why anyone would want to kill him. They questioned Allen Smiley and suspected he was holding out. The reporters, especially Westbrook Pegler, finally had found something worth pursuing.

In a syndicated column, Pegler laid out Smiley's background.

He mentioned every arrest on record for Smiley, including the May 25, 1944, arrest with Raft and Siegel. Pegler reviewed records of the Immigration and Naturalization Service (INS) and listed Smiley's aliases: Aaron Smehoff and Abraham Smickoff, here illegally from Russia. By age fifteen Smiley had been convicted of robbery and was sentenced to reform school. He also had a string of arrests: for gambling, peddling without a license, bootlegging, and his involvement in other rackets. Pegler also made it clear that the immigration authorities should take a closer look at Ben Siegel's "buddy" and not be swayed by Smiley's "powerful" friends.

Smiley was detained, on and off, for nearly two weeks before the authorities finally decided there was no evidence to book him in connection with the murder, even as an accessory.

They turned their attention to Virginia Hill, who refused to return to Los Angeles for questioning. "If I'm a suspect, tell me how I did it from over here? If ya want to talk to me, arrest me. You pay for my trip home. If not, leave me alone and let me enjoy my vacation."

The papers reported that Hill had left Los Angeles on June 18, one day before Siegel's murder, with Dr. (Mom) Chung, who was considered the "mother" of the Chinese air force. Chung had helped get the famous Flying Tigers off the ground during World War II. The papers gave a fairly accurate account of Hill's background, then went off into wild tangents. Some claimed that Virginia stopped her lavish party-giving lifestyle in 1941 and tried to enlist in the American Red Cross. Others said she designed the penthouse for the Flamingo but agreed that she was nothing more than a casual acquaintance of Siegel's, which also poses the question of what Siegel was doing in her home the night he was killed. Others wrote that Hill was a "thirtyish" Hollywood movie dancer with a considerable number of film credits.

One of the first apparent breaks in the case came through an anonymous tip four days after the killing. The caller claimed that Siegel ran into a mob feud when he considered cutting his ties with the *Trans-America Racing Wire Service* and aligning instead with the *Consolidated Racing Wire*. Consolidated had been charging bookies $1,100 per day to operate their phone lines, and, the tipster claimed, some feared Siegel was well on

his way to becoming the czar of the wires, which already controlled eight states.

Though the caller had slightly jumbled some details, the gist
of the call proved accurate.

Then another tip came from a source through the Los Angeles Police Department, passed along to the Beverly Hills P.D.
The word on the street was that Bugsy died because he was trying to infiltrate the Mexican dope-smuggling racket from Chicago. Police said the same gang behind the Siegel shooting may
have fought a gun battle two days later with customs agents in
Calexico. A few hours after that shoot-out Mexican police chief
Juan Meneses, allegedly an enemy of the smugglers, was shot to
death. The leader of the ring, a man named Martinez, was captured several hours after the Meneses murder and after more
than two-hundred shots were fired and a treasury agent's car
was drilled beyond repair. The agents seized nearly $35,000
worth of opium. Martinez "strongly hinted," as police phrased
it, that he was connected to Siegel's murder.

Finally, police said they were closing in on the killer. They
said that they knew for a fact that Siegel's murder was orchestrated from Chicago by a top Mafia "racketeer" connected with
bookmaking. They said his racketeer was in love with Virginia
Hill and distraught when word leaked out that she had tried to
commit suicide with an overdose of sleeping pills after a fight
with Siegel. This was just one of many so-called suicide
attempts staged by Hill throughout her life. Those who knew
her usually ignored them because she never took the pills when
she was alone or when she would not be "discovered" in time,
and she never took enough pills to do anything more than knock
herself unconscious.

The police went on. They insisted this racketeer called in two
hit men from another state to do the killing. Though word was
sent back to Chicago that Los Angeles and Beverly Hills police
wanted to question this racketeer, Chicago police refused to
cooperate and hand over Joe Epstein. They knew better than to
believe Epstein ordered the murder in a fit of jealous rage over
Hill.

George Raft was cast under a cloud of suspicion, not for any
connection with the killing but for knowledge he may have had
about Siegel's underworld connections, which, police hoped,

could shed light on at least the cause of the murder. Raft bought a ticket for the next TWA Constellation plane headed for Paris. He desperately wanted to talk to Virginia but never made his reasons clear.

Word had gotten around that Hill herself had been marked for death, and possibly Raft wanted to warn her. Or perhaps he just wanted to get out of the fishbowl and understood that Virginia was a friend and lover who knew the score and would ask few questions. Raft was ordered not to leave the state. His attorney, Herbert Silverberg, went to Paris instead and said nothing to anyone when he boarded the plane or when he returned. He would not even say if he saw Hill.

As an odd contrast to all the hype and frenzy Siegel's murder and the investigation had sparked, Siegel's funeral was eerily stark and quiet. There were no sightseers and only seven mourners. Virginia Hill stayed in Paris and did not even send flowers. She later said she could not have cared less "what route the bastard took to get to hell."

The first to arrive for the 9:00 A.M. service was Allen Smiley, who showed up in a black limousine. Then Esta and her two daughters, Millicent and Barbara, whose ages the newspapers kept fluctuating between eleven and fourteen; Siegel's brother, Dr. Maurice Siegel; and Dr. Max Kert, who was a rabbi at the Olympic Jewish Center on Olympic Boulevard. Siegel's sister Mrs. Bessie Soloway arrived last.

Siegel was laid out in a blue suit, white shirt, blue tie, and white handkerchief tucked into his coat pocket. He wore no jewelry. The coffin was sealed, and lit by two amber lights. Dr. Kert read the Twenty-Third Psalm and a Hebrew prayer. There was no eulogy, no comments, and the entire service lasted only five minutes.

Siegel's body was later taken to Beth Olam Cemetery and buried in a plot purchased by Siegel's brother. Rabbi Kert conducted a graveside service. The only one who attended was Siegel's brother.

Raft later claimed he wanted to attend but was ordered by his bosses at Warner Brothers to stay away because it "would have looked bad" for his screen career. The others—Mickey Cohen, Chick Hill, and the rest—offered no excuse. The underworld, which usually turned out in droves and plays a psychotic game of floral one-upmanship at funerals, turned its back on the gangster later dubbed "The Man Who Invented Las Vegas."

Shortly after the funeral Virginia phoned her brother and Jerri Mason at the Linden Drive home. She reportedly told them to pack up all her possessions and ship them to her home in Florida that she had previously wired and rigged with tighter security than a prison. She also gave them instructions to pick up cash and jewelry from various people around Los Angeles. They did as she instructed and asked no questions. Hill made the call brief and cryptic. She was convinced her phones in Paris and in her Beverly Hills home were tapped by the authorities, and she did not want to give them any more information than necessary.

Virginia then frantically phoned Epstein in Chicago. She was told that he was either "out of town," "unavailable," or that "a message would be taken." She reportedly dialed the phone at least fifteen times and each time was put off. She tried calling Adonis and received the same brush-off. Virginia was convinced she had been marked for death.

She took another overdose of sleeping pills in her suite at the Westminster Hotel in Paris. As she was about to drift off, the phone rang. Virginia groggily picked up the receiver. It was Epstein.

Details of the call are not clear. It is assumed he phoned the front desk, because Virginia Hill quickly recovered from her suicidal call for help. But rather than easing her fears, her paranoia intensified, especially when word reached Paris that the police in California were about to release the details of the mysterious Bugsy Siegel diary, confiscated shortly after his murder.

If the diary contained even half of the specifics about underworld operations that Virginia's diary had recorded, the New York, Chicago, Los Angeles, and Las Vegas mobsters were in serious trouble. It would be every man for himself, with murders, betrayals, suicides, and indictments that would not stop with the underworld. If the diary was anything like Hill's, it could topple some of the biggest politicians in the country.

Worse for Virginia, she believed she was a prominent player in Bugsy's diary and would be incriminated in illegal money laundering, racetrack swindling, and bookmaking along with the others. And she feared far more dire consequences. She was terrified that Siegel had suspected the real purpose of her relationship with him was that she was spying for the Chicago mob.

Virginia was both Siegel's confidant and lover—and his Judas. She feared Bugsy's diary could force the New York Luciano family to order her execution, with the Chicago outfit reluctant, or even powerless, to stop it.

15

If Beverly Hills police chief Clinton Anderson was bluffing when he said that he had in his possession one of the most powerful tools to bring down the Mafia, he scored a direct hit in the underworld. No one knew exactly what Siegel had put in his diary, nor did they even know for certain that the Bug had kept such a secret ledger. But the underworld believed it could not take the risk that Anderson was right.

Jack Dragna laid low for more than six months after the murder, leaving the racing wire services as they were before the Siegel hit. He allowed Siegel's bookies to continue to operate under Trans-America and let Mickey Cohen retain his position as the "bag man" who collected the shakedowns and profits from the bookies. Though Cohen was allowed to carry on business as usual, Dragna kept a close watch on him.

Dragna felt the same way about Cohen as he did about Siegel, and for much the same reason: Italians and Jews often did not mix well in the Mafia. Cohen was followed constantly, his haberdashery store under constant surveillance, his telephone line tapped.

But Dragna was not the only one watching the man many called "the Mick." federal agents believed he was a direct link to organized crime, and local authorities maintained he knew who carried out the hit on Ben Siegel. It is believed that all, at one time or another, or even at the same time, had planted taps in his home and business. Cohen became aware of the surveillance. After Siegel's murder, Mickey always answered his telephone with a greeting that soon became a running joke in the underworld and law enforcement. He would pick up the receiver and say, "Hello, everybody!" Cohen said he did not want anyone listening to feel left out of his conversations. Cohen also sensed that Dragna was lying in wait for him and had retained two thug-enforcers, the Seca brothers, who followed him everywhere.

Knowing that he had put the underworld on edge, Anderson started to leak fragments of the Siegel diary to the press. The Beverly Hills police chief made it clear that Siegel had kept detailed records of the personal and business dealings of what Anderson called the Guzik-Ricca-Capone mob. He referred to bribes and shakedowns in "certain Rush Street [Chicago] gin mills" and even sent some of his own men to that city to do some investigating. His men were ordered to make themselves obvious so that members of the outfit knew they were being watched. Anderson said he was now convinced, six months after the hit, that the order came from Chicago. He also said the diary indicated that Joe, Rocco, and Charlie Fischetti, who were still key members of the outfit, played a major role in the killing.

He added that the diary outlined many shakedown scams orchestrated out of Chicago and carried out by Siegel in the West, including one involving bookmaking in Los Angeles that ended up with a $300,000 "kick" from the Fischettis to Siegel, but details never were more specific than that. Anderson also claimed that the diary indicated that Siegel was trying to get even more money from the Fischetti trio when he was killed.

Anderson said the diary also listed the names of Ben's enemies, his business partners, and his contacts. The chief released what he said was only a partial list in the hope that someone would fill in the blanks. That list included Luciano, Adonis, Lansky, Costello, the Fischettis, the Capone boys, and Willie Morietti, who was a cousin of Joey A's.

Anderson told reporters that he had already been contacted by several "top ranking Mafia chieftains" who were ready to talk and plea-bargain with him.

Then the whole scheme blew apart. Columnist Lee Mortimer, who had long been a nemesis of Virginia Hill's, claimed he was offered $50,000 dollars by a "Mafia figure" during a secret meeting at the Ritz Bar in New York. The money would be donated to Mortimer's favorite charity if he could prove Lucky Luciano had threatened to kill Siegel in a phone conversation reportedly made to either Meyer Lansky or Jack Dragna. Columnist Florabel Muir said a stranger called her office and offered her $10,000 if she could either connect Mickey Cohen to the murder or arrange a private meeting between the caller and Virginia Hill. There were also newspaper stories claiming that a standing $50,000 offer was made, anonymously, to anyone who could prove that Siegel's "little black book" even existed. None of the offers was ever picked up.

Anderson then tried another strategy. He offered immunity to Allen Smiley if he told everything he knew about the murder. Smiley was, by this time, under federal indictment for immigration violations. Smiley refused.

Anderson set his sights on Joe Epstein. He leaked an FBI report that showed that Epstein had flown to New York with Virginia, accompanied her to various nightclubs, and was seen with Hill "at the homes of and in the presence of" unsavory, unnamed underworld characters. He hoped to drive a wedge between Epstein and Hill when he said that Epstein admitted to federal authorities that he had given Virginia great sums of cash, which she had not reported, and that he had also withheld money from her. Epstein said he took more than $8,000 of Virginia's cash while they were in New York.

Word of the swindle got back to Virginia in record time. The thirty-year-old mob Queen phoned Epstein from Paris, and the two had a loud and hostile argument over the phone. When Hill hung up, she made yet another suicide attempt, the latest a sickening routine.

After the incident in Paris, in which Epstein's call roused her back to consciousness, Hill tried again to take her life on July 2 in Monaco. A maid found her unconscious, and she was rushed to the Villa Albert 1 Clinic.

On July 23 she received the bill from the physician who treated her in Monaco. She paid less than half the bill, claiming she was broke, and promised to send him the rest as soon as she received it. He never heard from her again.

She returned to Paris, picked up where she left off with French heir and former paramour Nicholas Fouillette, and quickly went through what little cash she had left. A frantic call to Epstein resulted in an airmail package that replenished her cash reserves. Four days later, she gulped another handful of sleeping pills and was rushed to the American Hospital in Neuilly. Again Hill skipped out on the bill and wanted to return to America.

According to French law, Hill, along with every other tourist, had to declare on her passport exactly how much cash she brought into the country, how much she was taking out, and the value of items she had purchased. Virginia knew there was no way she could account for the cash without arousing suspicion. To get around the problem, she worked a scam she had learned years earlier from Joe Adonis.

Virginia told the American embassy in Paris that she lost her passport and needed to replace it so she could fly home. The new passport, of course, would not have any of the declarations Hill had made when she entered, so the authorities would not be able to calculate the difference between the amount of cash she took in compared with the amount she took out. Hill, of course, claimed she brought in as much money as she was taking out.

The embassy accepted Hill's claim that she had lost her passport and quickly obtained a new one for her. Hill then flew a plane to New York and was off scot-free. Less than an hour after her plane took off, a maid at her Paris hotel found Hill's old passport stuffed behind the sofa cushions. The pages in which the cash declarations had been listed had been torn out. Once again, Hill had beaten the system.

But upon Hill's return she was stopped by a U.S. Customs official in New York and a special investigator for the Los Angeles District Attorney's Office, a man named Tom Slack. Though Virginia's luggage seemed to be in order, the official noticed a rather large diamond ring on Hill's finger. Getting the nod from Slack, the agent questioned Hill as to whether she bought the ring in Europe and its value.

The following is Hill's version of the story, related in a formal complaint to federal authorities.

So the fellow asked me, "Did you buy that ring abroad?" I
told him no. Ben Siegel once gave me a watch in Los Angeles. I didn't like it so I traded it in for this ring at the Lack-
ritz store in Beverly Hills. So the fellow says, "Can I see
it?" I gave him the ring to look at. There was this commo-
tion outside, a plane crashed or something. The next thing
I know I turn back around and ask this guy to give me back
my ring and he says he doesn't know anything about any
ring.

After she filed the complaint, she was asked whether she
intended to press charges.

"No. The stupid thing wasn't worth much, anyway. Couldn't
have cost more than five or six hundred. Benny was a cheap-
skate."

The newspapers refused to let Hill alone and quickly figured
out that the "mysterious Alabama heiress" was hiding in Florida. Chick and his new wife, Jerri, ran interference for Virginia,
but the reporters were determined to crack the Siegel case and
link the Bug's mistress to his murder. Her home had now turned
into an army bunker of sorts, and she could not leave without
being followed. Virginia was never certain if her pursuer was a
reporter or a gangster. The pressure became so intense that
after a short time she never set foot outside.

Hill became a recluse and used the telephone as her only life-
line to the outside world. She called Epstein, who once again
played his elusive dodge with Virginia. Joe Adonis also ignored
Hill but sent her one package that reportedly contained
$4,000. Insiders say Hill flushed the money down the toilet,
screaming, "I don't want your fucking money, you bastard!"
Then she went nearly insane, smashing things, bellowing about
Epstein and Siegel at the top of her lungs.

Chick and Jerri reportedly tried to subdue Virginia, but to no
avail. Each time she calmed down she would read about herself
in the paper and throw a temper tantrum. If Chick or Jerri
denied Hill access to the newspapers, Virginia became even
more hostile, convinced that they were conspiring against her
and that the press was so bad they were afraid to let her see the
stories. Virginia was right on both assumptions. (She also used

her assumptions about the conspiracy as a wedge between her brother and Jerri Mason to break up the marriage she so adamantly opposed.)

Then Virginia tried to end her life yet another time. According to the book *We Only Kill Each Other*, Chick could not rouse Virginia when he knocked on her bedroom door. The door was locked, so he kicked it until the lock shattered. He saw his sister flat on her back. Chick shook and slapped Virginia, trying to bring some color back into her cheeks and get her breathing. When he pried her mouth open, he found a tightly rolled handkerchief stuffed between her teeth. Then he saw an empty pill bottle on the dresser and called an ambulance.

She was rushed to St. Francis Hospital in Miami Beach, where her stomach was pumped. It was at least her fourth alleged suicide attempt in as many months. She later told reporters that she could not get to sleep and had become careless in the number of sleeping pills she took. She later claimed that Jerri tried to kill her. In retaliation, Virginia threatened to kill Jerri, threw her out of the house, and ordered Chick to divorce her. Chick did; he obtained a quick decree in Pensacola, Florida, for fifty dollars. Jerri was not present and received the uncontested decree in the mail.

By late August 1947, the once-sultry, quick-witted, fast-talking mob Queen was in a rapid downward spiral, fast on her way to becoming a sloppy, loudmouth, ill-tempered, drunken paranoid who decided she could not even trust her own brother.

Hill suffered major bouts of depression and crying jags during which she reportedly went off on tangents, accusing Epstein and Adonis of using her and Charlie Fischetti, Jack Dragna, and the others of taking advantage of her innocence and corrupting her. As 1947 headed into the fall season, Virginia Hill was no fun to be around.

Virginia and her younger brother, Chick, left Florida; they sped out of the state in a convertible and toured the country. They went back to Marietta, to Alabama, to some of their old haunts. But they reportedly steered clear of New York and Chicago. Virginia said she did not want to go anywhere near any cities that did not want her.

Then, late in September, Joe Epstein tracked down Virginia. He claimed he had been tied up on business and could not be distracted. The call seemed to boost Virginia's spirits, and she invited him to go hunting in Montana. Epstein, who could not have been a more unlikely candidate for the role of the "great outdoorsman," surprisingly agreed to come along. Associates say Joey E felt remorse for Virginia's ordeal and wanted to make certain that she was all right.

They also say Epstein had another reason for seeing Hill. It had little to do with concern for her or a desire to go hunting. He had known about Virginia's secret diary since she started keeping a record. In fact, he had advised her to keep careful records of all business transactions early in her money-laundering days in Chicago. But now, with all the recent emotional problems Virginia had suffered, he needed to know what she had put in that diary and where she had hidden it.

With many underworld figures still smarting from the allegations in Siegel's diary, word of yet another and possibly more sensational diary could blow the lid off the Mafia. Epstein knew that if Hill had included details of his bookmaking operations in the diary, his days would be numbered. If she had taken notes on other mob dealings, the ramifications would be dire for the underworld.

Federal authorities had been working to find evidence strong enough to jail the mob leaders and, in effect, shut down the underworld. And the diary, if found in the wrong hands, could be the catalyst the government needed to deport, imprison, or execute nearly half the Chicago and New York underworld.

Epstein, who was an old-looking forty-six, overweight and out of shape, had difficulty keeping up with the group on the hiking expedition. Virginia later told friends that Epstein made the last three miles "flat on his big, fat ass. He sat on a log, like a bump, and gave up. Funniest thing I ever saw."

Epstein left Virginia with $2,000 in cash and returned to Chicago without the diary. But he had not given up.

Associates say that he was afraid to press Virginia out of fear she would turn the diary over to the authorities out of spite. He was also concerned that if she did anything rash, Joey Adonis would have to call in his marker on her and put into action the plan that he ordered stopped two years before. Epstein still obviously cared about Hill and had hoped to protect her.

He met Virginia once again in a hotel in Spokane, Washington, early in November. Federal records show that Epstein arrived on or about November 10, 1947. The same file shows that Hill had also checked into the lodge under the alias Ona V. Hill. Hill and Epstein shared a room overnight and then went their separate ways.

Though the federal record sheds no light on what happened in the room, associates of Epstein's have filled in the details.

The two stayed up most of the night talking, secure in the fact that the room had not been bugged and their conversation would not reach federal ears. Virginia drank quite heavily, as she was now prone to do, and Epstein sipped a scotch on the rocks, as he was known to do on occasion. They talked about old times, the old gang, and some of the old scams they pulled in Chicago. After about three hours of reminiscing, Epstein laid the purpose of his visit on the line.

He reportedly never spoke in terms of "I" but rather "we," implying that he was not representing his interests but the interests of the Chicago mob and possibly the New York contingent as well.

"We want your diary. No questions will be asked. We will not use it against you."

Then he spoke in confidence. "If you want, I will keep it and tell the others you destroyed it. I will give them my word on it for you, but that means the issue is dead. No more diary. Ever."

Virginia purportedly laughed in Epstein's face and told him that she never had a diary, that anything she might have said in the past about having one or keeping any records about anything was a joke. Epstein knew Virginia rarely told the truth about anything when pressed, and he knew she was lying then.

"If you need help, let me know. But if you make me look foolish, then there's nothing I can or will do to help you."

They slept in the same bed, their backs to one another. Epstein left in the morning and returned to Chicago, once again empty-handed. He told Fischetti and the others that Virginia could not produce any diary and that he was not entirely convinced that one had existed.

But one certainly did exist. And those connected with the outfit knew it. What no one yet knew was the contents of the ledger.

Virginia had kept careful records of her transactions and those involving Siegel and the New Yorkers. The members of the Chicago mob were also prominent entries. But she stopped keeping records two weeks before Siegel's death. The last entry appeared on June 4, 1947, indicating a $10,000 transaction between Charlie Fischetti and Siegel, then another similar deal between Fischetti and Adonis. The purpose was never indicated.

On November 24, federal records indicate that "Mrs. Norma Hall" and another woman, a Mrs. Sylvia Nettler of Chicago, checked into the Paradise Inn in Phoenix, Arizona. Hall was just one in a string of Hill's aliases. The identity of the other woman was not clear, nor was the purpose of their visit. Hill, as Hall, seemed more relaxed, played some tennis, watched her diet and drinking, and seemed fairly well adjusted. With her wardrobe of expensive clothes, furs, and jewelry she appeared as a society matron who had come to Arizona to enjoy the sun. Though still suspicious of strangers, it seemed that Hill had become confident and carefree again.

That was until December 12, when she was found unconscious in her room. She was hospitalized at Good Samaritan Hospital for more than a week. Chick delivered her convertible and left. Virginia checked out eight days later and disappeared from sight. She turned up in Mexico City four months later.

With the profits from the sale of her home in Miami, Virginia toured South America under a string of aliases. When she settled in Mexico City, she leased three floors of an exclusive apartment building and reestablished the life she left in fear several years before in Los Angeles. Hill was the party queen, the social butterfly, and the center of attention in Mexico City, sought after by nearly every man within sight, available or not.

One of her closest companions was the notorious Mom Chung, who had previously been linked to Hill when Virginia left town for Paris. Chung had close associations with entertainers, businessmen, politicians, and gangsters; all seemed to meld together during Virginia's and Chung's parties. Chung was under federal surveillance for narcotics trafficking. She was also believed to have been part of the drug-running and money-laundering ring that operated through Siegel, Hill, Epstein, and the rest of the Chicago–New York connection. Underworld contacts say that Chung was a key link in international drug trafficking, though authorities could never make a charge stick.

Buoyed by renewed confidence and energy from her social

whirl in Mexico, Virginia decided it was time to head back to Los Angeles. It was her first such venture since she was ordered to beat a hasty retreat to Paris in June 1947, prior to the Siegel assassination. She contacted her old friend and landlord Juan Romero about leasing another home and made it clear that she had no desire to go anywhere near Linden Drive or Beverly Hills. She hoped to find a place in Hollywood or Brentwood or a house by the ocean, if available.

While Romero was securing a place for Hill, word of her desire to return to Los Angeles reached Chicago. Once again, Joe Epstein intervened and showed that he was still in charge of Virginia Hill's life.

Hill received one order over the phone. The order was given so strongly and so directly that she dared not question or tell anyone about it. "Stay out of Los Angeles. For good."

The call was from Epstein. Virginia boarded the first plane to Chicago and checked into the Sheraton Hotel on June 28. Epstein had arranged for her accommodations and saved her life once again. Jack Dragna was about to make his move in Los Angeles, and Virginia Hill could have been caught in the crossfire.

16

Eddie Cannazero described Jack Dragna as "a first-class gentleman with first cabin on everything and [who] took care of his people." Dragna, who hired Cannazero in the Siegel hit, called upon the hit man once again on July 19, 1949. He wanted Mickey Cohen out of the way. Cohen had taken control of the Los Angeles–area bookies after Ben Siegel's murder and had become a roadblock to Dragna's plans. Dragna wanted the major wire, *Consolidated Racing Wire Services,* to control the entire western region bookmaking phone lines and oversee all bookmaking in the six western states. Cohen held out and refused to put his men under Dragna. The Mick actually believed he was invincible and that no one dared make a move against him. He had already survived several assassination attempts and had no reason to think he would not survive others.

In a 1984 KNBC-TV interview, conducted three years before his death, Cannazero, who was dubbed "The Cat Man of Agoura" because of his quirky tendency to take in scores of stray cats, hinted at his personal involvement with the man many called "The Al Capone of the West."

I was glad to be associated with Dragna because I learned things from him, how to conduct yourself as a man in this world, because he was 100 percent man. The cops thought he was a bad apple and all that, but that's baloney. Absolute baloney. What did the guy ever do wrong? Some people it's better that you put them in a gas chamber, not in a gas chamber, but the chamber that they use for animals. It would be nice if you put some people in there and sucked out the air and put them in a casket and buried them.

Dragna, "the bad apple," sent Cannazero out into Hollywood on the night of July 19, 1949, to stalk Cohen and his friends. Cohen was already under guard, assigned by the state of California, as protection because the gangster was to be called to testify in a special state probe into links between organized crime and the police. Cohen had been the target of several death threats, and prosecutors did not want anything to happen to him. Federal files indicate that there were several gunmen sent by Dragna on a shooting spree that left at least three people dead. Syndicated columnist Florabel Muir happened to be in the wrong place at the wrong time but lived to tell about it.

Muir said that as she stepped out onto the street, she got caught in a hail of bullets. She had stopped to buy a newspaper, which delayed her journey by several minutes. Muir said that if she had not stopped, she would have been caught in the middle of the street with no place to hide and probably killed.

Muir had just finished eating at a Sunset Strip café called Sherry's, which was a known hoodlum hangout. At first, Muir reported, she thought she heard firecrackers. Then she saw Cohen's henchman Eddie Herbert fall to the ground, bleeding. Next was actress Dee David, who took two slugs in the neck. Seconds later, Muir felt a sharp pain in her hip. A shot had ricocheted from a stone and hit her. Another whizzed past her head and crashed through the restaurant's glass front door.

Muir said that she ran outside to see if Cohen was all right. Being a popular columnist and one trusted by Hill, Siegel, and Cohen, she knew full well who the gangster was. There is even popular speculation that Muir had been eating with Cohen and his goons at the time of the attempted hit. Cohen told Muir that he had been shot and ordered another one of his bodyguards to bring his car around. Cohen climbed in the back as soon as it stopped by the curb. Cohen told Muir to get in the car. As she did, she saw the bleeding body of Harry Cooper, special investigator for California attorney general Fred Howser. Cooper was a companion of Cohen's.

Three people who were with Cohen had been fatally injured. Muir's wounds were not serious. Cohen suffered only a shoulder wound. He cheated the fates yet another time. The last assassination attempt was only one month before, just one of many since the earlier murder of Cohen's chief bodyguard, Hooky Rothman, in Cohen's Sunset Boulevard money-laundering front–haberdashery.

Cohen said he knew for a fact who was behind the plot. At first, he thought the order came from back East, but Cohen said he recognized one of the gunmen and he was definitely from Los Angeles, hired by a "Hollywood" man.

The newspapers speculated that the hit was orchestrated by someone in the Los Angeles Police Department to try and silence Cohen before he talked about the police department's ties with the underworld. Cohen and seven of his henchmen had recently been indicted for conspiracy in an assault case and also charged with plotting to obstruct justice. When this incident went down, the group was awaiting a trial.

The L.A.P.D. had already been under scrutiny when a known whorehouse madam, Brenda Allen, testified that she had paid members of the police vice squad to protect her prostitutes. She named names. Cohen threatened to be another nail in the force's coffin.

When asked if a member of the force was involved in the shooting, Cohen said only this:

Police are behind everything, don't you know that? Either they're in the way or they're being paid off. When they're in the way, they usually start trouble that wouldn't have been started otherwise. When they're paid off, they're involved. As far as this thing [the shooting], no cop pulled the trigger. But it couldn't have happened if the police weren't involved.

Immediately after the shooting the police seized Cohen's private telephone directory. It listed names of everyone imaginable: sports stars, politicians, gangsters, and Los Angeles cops—from street cops to captains and up. The phone directory was quickly destroyed, or rather "lost," by the Los Angeles Police Department.

Though they could not make the assault or conspiracy charges stick, Cohen was eventually jailed for income-tax evasion. Once behind bars, he was severely beaten, which resulted in his being confined to a wheelchair. He never again returned to the position of power he held in the days of Ben Siegel and Virginia Hill, though Hill claimed she never had much respect for Cohen. When asked by reporters what she thought of the Hollywood bookie, Hill sneered and laughed. "He was just an errand boy. We don't move in the same circles."

Jack Dragna and Johnny Roselli eventually got what they wanted, control of the West.

With Dragna firmly in power in the West, Hill packed her bags and moved to Sun Valley, Idaho. She later told federal investigators that a man she had known for years in Mexico, Major Amezcua, gave her the money for the move. She called it "a love gift," which amounted to something close to $15,000. Amezcua gave her no such money. It was another package from Joey E to get Hill in a so-called safe place, with a little extra to spare if she needed to bribe officials, either in the United States, Mexico, or Europe.

Hill partied it up in Sun Valley in January and February 1950. When out on a bender, she picked up the tab for the entire bar, which some nights ran close to $1,000 in drinks alone. Hill's never-ending money machine seemed to be back in full gear. Virginia had at least two suitcases filled with cash, hordes of hundred-dollar bills, wrapped together in bundles of $5,000 each. Her clothes were tailor-made. No off-the-rack bargains for her. She flashed her diamonds and gold and consumed more alcohol than any five people combined.

She flirted with every man at the resort—some gangsters, some businessmen, some playboys. She went to bed with most, if not all, during her stay. When her name was mentioned in hushed tones and the more respectable would turn away or look down when she entered a room, Virginia said she did not care.

Her flat answer to anyone who questioned her loud and bois-
terous and brazen behavior was: "Fuck 'em!"

Hill said she had returned to the vow she made to herself as a
child, that she would neither trust nor get close to any man ever
again. She told friends that she had been used and been burned
by men she thought were friends, let alone those she considered lovers. She never admitted that she, too, had used nearly
every man with whom she had become associated, nor did she
mention that she still had her secret diary in which the transactions of the Mafia had been neatly laid out in green and red
ink. Hill only saw herself as the victim, never as the aggressor,
always as the abused, never as the abuser.

Then, in February 1950, she met the tall, dark ski instructor
Hans Hauser. Hill found him dashing, independent, cool, and
athletic, a trait that few gangsters shared. He also had a quirky
sense of humor and an illicit past. It was probably the latter that
intrigued Hill the most.

Hill had Hauser's background checked through friends in
Chicago, perhaps because she had fabricated so many tales
about herself, perpetuating the heiress stories and painting a
self-portrait that rarely resembled the truth.

Hauser, an Austrian, immigrated to the United States as a Sun
Valley ski instructor prior to World War II. When the war
began, Hauser had been suspected of being a Nazi sympathizer
and was imprisoned in an enemy-alien camp in California for
three years. He moved back to Sun Valley after the war, was
cleared of all charges, and was rehired as an instructor. Hill was
smitten. She said it was the first time she had ever fallen so hard
for a man. And she was not even ordered to do so.

Finally, after years of taking orders and desperately reaching
out for love, Virginia looked as if she had finally met a man, on
her own terms, who just might be able to love her for herself,
not for what she could do or pay.

Virginia chased after Hauser the only way she knew how,
with money. She took up skiing, in which she previously had no
interest, made a point of being in the lodge when he was there,
and arranged a series of "accidental" meetings. With the ice
broken, she paid a tidy sum and bought up every one of his
bookings for ski lessons.

Hauser's curiosity was piqued. Though he played "dumb,"

those who knew the man insisted he knew all about Virginia Hill and how much money she lavishly spent in Sun Valley. Everyone in the ski resort knew about Virginia Hill.

There are several stories describing how Virginia induced Hauser to remain at her side, on the slopes and off, during her stay. Some claim that she took him back to her room, "accidentally" opened a suitcase filled with hundred-dollar bills, grabbed a handful, then paid for everything he needed or wanted. Others say it was through sex. The experienced Hill was a master at sexual techniques that most women had not even heard about and had no qualms about doing anything in bed or on her knees. Others say they like to think it was just a mutual attraction. However, one can not overlook the fact that Hill spent at least $15,000 during her two-month stay in Sun Valley. And that was only the funds for which she kept records and did not include money spent picking up other guests' bar tabs or on tips.

In March 1950, Hauser and Hill traveled to Glenwood Springs in Colorado, registered as man and wife, then traveled to Aspen under the same cover, and finally made their relationship legal before a justice of the peace in Elko, Nevada. They went back to Sun Valley for their honeymoon.

Hill never paid much attention to what her new husband did in the off-season. She was not used to working men and probably never bothered to think much about Hauser's summer job or the ramifications of their marriage on his employment. Hans and Virginia learned the lesson the hard way. Unfortunately, what bliss they enjoyed in Sun Valley was soon shattered.

Hauser had never become a U.S. citizen. Though he was now married to a citizen, he was still supposed to be employed. When not working at Sun Valley, he was employed as a ticket clerk for the Union Pacific Railroad. The railroad was careful about its image and that of its employees.

After the honeymoon, Virginia, without thinking about the consequences, took a train to Chicago. She was there to see Epstein. She had also transported some "clean" money back to Chicago.

News of Hill's marriage grabbed front-page headlines, and word quickly spread that Hill was on the train. When the train arrived at Union Station, it was greeted by a crush of reporters clamoring for photos, information about her marriage, and the background of her new husband.

"Is he connected to organized crime?"

"What? I don't know anyone connected to organized crime."

"Is he tied with the Chicago gang? Does he work for the mob?"

"No."

"How did you meet him?"

"None of your damn business."

The questions so infuriated Hill that she started to swing her purse and beat the reporters so that she could get out of the station. Then she turned back and shouted, "If ya want something to print, try this!" Her next sentence was never printed, but one can imagine that it was riddled with expletives.

Hauser was immediately fired when the story appeared in the newspapers. He left Sun Valley in disgrace and traveled to Chicago to meet his wife. The incident at Union Station also caused another problem for Hauser. It brought the ever-scrutinizing eye of the Immigration and Naturalization Service (INS) zeroing in on Hauser's background.

It was his imprisonment in the California alien camp as a suspected Nazi sympathizer during the war that caused the INS to take a closer look at Hauser. Though now married to an American, his war record took priority, and it officially labeled him an "undesirable," though he subsequently had been cleared of charges.

Hill pleaded with her Chicago friends for help to no avail. She turned to Mom Chung, who said she had no pull in Washington. Hill handed Hans a fistful of cash and told him to leave Chicago. He took a bus to Spokane, Washington, where he was met by a friend from Sun Valley who said he had some sort of clout on Capitol Hill.

While Hauser waited for his friend to move on Capitol Hill, he insisted to federal authorities that he was unaware of his wife's background, that he had been unjustly accused during the war, and that he had worked as an honest citizen in the United States for more than five years. Nothing helped.

Finally, his friend came through. He explained the situation to Sen. Warren Magnuson, a Democrat from the state of Washington, who introduced a bill to make Hans Hauser an American citizen. Magnuson enlisted the support of the Girl Scouts of America, which claimed that Hauser was a "noble man who had performed a great service in teaching skiing to 200 high school girls." The organization submitted a detailed list of the services Hauser had provided, along with the personal recommendation of the executive director of the group.

The bill was presented as a motion on the floor, accompanied by a rider that also allowed Hauser to remain in America if the actual bill should not pass before the senate subcommittee to which the motions were presented. Both were summarily rejected on February 16. Hill and Hauser went to Chicago for help but received none.

Virginia vowed to get even with those who now turned their back on her. She "let leak" the fact that she had indeed maintained a secret diary.

Reporters called the diary "Virginia Hill's most excellent life insurance plan." Hill said that the diary had been safely tucked away in a safe deposit box in Chicago, with the key and instructions given to a highly trusted source. She said the instructions specified that if anything happened to her or her husband, the safe deposit box and the diary would be opened in public and the diary's contents shown to the press. Hill said that she wanted to publicly display the diary so that "no one could grab it and say it disappeared." She hinted to the press that the diary named gangsters as well as some very highly placed public officials.

As an added bonus, Hill also told reporters that she had served as a messenger for the mob, had carried large sums of money between New York and Chicago, and had received cash in shipments of $1,000 and more while in Paris during the Siegel murder. She insisted, though, that she had no hand in his killing but implied that she knew who did murder the Bug.

She also talked about her husband, saying that she met Hauser at the Sun Valley, Idaho, ski resort, that he was not connected to the mob, and that she stayed there from January 4 through February 25, 1950, at which time she vacationed with Hauser, then married him.

Hill also said that some "pretty high officials are trying to get to her through her husband" and that "they're trying to kick him out of this country when he didn't do a damn thing wrong."

Though several reporters found that part of the story sweet and sentimental, most focused on the diary and barraged her with questions. Hill told the press, "I've said enough. More than I should." She knew her threats would go right to the mob.

Everything backfired. Her pleas failed to free her husband from the ire of the INS. They also brought her to the attention of a U.S. Senate committee formed to investigate organized crime in America.

17

Virginia Hill knew how to handle mobsters, Hollywood stars, and ordinary men. She controlled them through sex, money, or intimidation. But when confronted by Sen. Estes Kefauver and his panel, Hill faced a formidible opponent who was unimpressed by her wealth or sexual prowess. To Kefauver, Virginia was a Mafia tramp who deserved little respect. To Hill, Kefauver was a mean-spirited tyrant.

Estes Kefauver was a flamboyant Tennessee Democrat who championed liberal causes, proposed controversial legislation calling for congressional reform, and survived numerous smear campaigns in which he was labeled everything from a philanderer to a Communist.

Born into a wealthy and politically influential Tennessee family in 1903, Kefauver graduated near the top of his Yale Law School class. His 1935 marriage to socialite Nancy Paterson Pigott was hailed in the newspapers as the "highlight of weddings among Chattanooga society." With a large financial stake and political backing, the Kefauvers' life seemed set.

But marriage and a law career were not enough for the ambitious Kefauver, who successfully ran for a seat in the House of Representatives in 1939. Describing himself as a "New Deal Democrat," Kefauver became a major supporter of Franklin Roosevelt and proved to be one of the Democratic party's chief fund-raisers. He proposed controversial legislation, such as a law abolishing poll taxes and legislation calling for a formal pro-ceedure under which cabinet members could be questioned on the House floor. He stood up against the House Un-American Activities Committee (HUAC) and its blacklisting of those it declared Communists, even voting against citing for contempt sixteen witnesses who refused to cooperate with the commit-tee. For this courageous act he was labeled a Communist. Kefauver then broke ranks with other southerners by pushing for antilynching laws and equal rights.

After serving nearly ten years in the House, Estes Kefauver realized he could further his causes and political ambitions in the Senate. Fearful of his liberal views, Republican opponents compared Kefauver to a raccoon, calling him both deceitful and full of trickery. But Kefauver used the mudslinging to his ben-efit. He donned a coonskin cap, compared himself to other famous Americans who wore the pioneer headgear, and used it and its "pro-American connotations" as his rallying point. Wherever he went, he handed out coonskin caps to the press, supporters, and opponents. The cap became his trademark in a race labeled by the press as "The Coonskin Crusade." Kefauver won a landslide victory in Tennessee and took office in 1949.

While in the Senate, Estes Kefauver grew curious about the financial power base in America—exactly who controlled big business, labor, and the purse strings in the country. His curi-osity ignited a personal crusade, and he conducted a quiet investigation. After examining reports from crime commissions in Michigan, Illinois, and California, the senator became con-vinced of one thing: Big business and the Mafia had formed a powerful and unholy alliance.

In January 1950, Kefauver introduced Senate Resolution 202, which called for a probe into organized crime in America. The resolution propelled the senator into national prominence and made him the figurehead for what was to become the most riveting public probe into the Mafia to date.

Congress asked Kefauver to spearhead the committee formed to conduct the probe. The senator reluctantly agreed, knowing such an undertaking could take years to complete. After considerable debate, the panel was chosen: Republican members of the Judiciary and Commerce committees Alexander Wiley of Wisconsin and Charles Toby of New Hampshire joined Democrats Lester Hunt of Wyoming, Herbert O'Connor of Maryland, and Kefauver of Tennessee. Signed on as chief counsel for the five-member panel was Rudolph Halley, whom Kefauver chose on the recommendation of a New York State supreme court justice. Halley had been chief counsel for the 1933 federal investigation into the Wall Street crash. He was also involved with other legal matters on behalf of the Democratic party and was considered knowledgeable and unwavering in his beliefs.

The panel agreed that the hearings would travel to major cities to avoid extradition proceedings and interrogate anyone suspected of having personal knowledge of the underworld, from politicians to law enforcement to suspected mobsters and their associates. The questioning would take place in fourteen major cities: Washington, Tampa, Miami, New York, Cleveland, St. Louis, Kansas City, New Orleans, Chicago, Detroit, Philadelphia, Las Vegas, Los Angeles, and San Francisco. More than eight hundred witnesses were called to testify.

Before the actual testimony got under way, the panel subpoenaed a number of people that it believed could supply background information on the mob and its business dealings. One of the first subpoenas issued was for Joe Epstein, but the Chicago authorities said they could not locate the elusive financier. Federal investigators turned to Virginia Hill to ask about his whereabouts. Hill told them that the last place she saw Epstein was at the Clover Bar, a mob-owned cocktail lounge at 172 North Clark Street, a block from city offices in Chicago. She also told the investigators to try his home at 25 East Delaware Place. A federal officer phoned the Clover Club and asked for Epstein. He was told that Joey E had not been there for months. A call to the switchboard of his apartment building produced the same result. The Clover Bar was eventually raided as a vice den and shut down by federal agents. They never did find Epstein, who proved slippery and maintained his mysterious air.

The committee then subpoenaed Hill, believing she could tell them all about the Chicago bookmaking operations. Several newspaper reporters organized a betting pool on whether Virginia would say anything at all, lead the committee on a wild-goose chase by lying, or tell everything in exchange for immunity. The pool reportedly went as high as $1,000.

But Hill surprised the reporters, the committee, and even herself. She was taking on a new role in life.

The Hausers rented a small cottage in Bar Harbor, Maine, in June 1950 and kept a low profile, blending in with other summer vacationers and locals. Virginia avoided all contact with her former friends and associates and kept out of view of the press. Hans made sure that the trouble he faced with the INS was never discussed inside the home, nor was Virginia's past life. Virginia was pregnant, and she wanted it kept a secret between herself and Hans. She desperately wanted to keep her new life away from the ever-present press. But, as usual, a stronger force had intervened.

Virginia was ordered to answer questions before the committee in its preliminary investigation in Chicago on September 29, 1950. She was forced to tell the panel about her pregnancy in order to delay her appearance. Virginia was thirty-four years old. She said she could not have been happier about the prospect of becoming a mother and, for the first time in her life, having a real family. She knew the Kefauver interrogation would be stressful, and she wanted to sidestep anything that could pose a risk to the unborn baby.

The committee agreed to delay her interrogation until after she delivered and recovered sufficiently to withstand the ordeal of the hearing. It agreed to forgo the preliminary round of questioning and would face her for the first time, on the stand, on Friday, March 16, 1951, when the committee conducted its New York session.

On November 18, Virginia checked into St. Elizabeth's Hospital in Brighton, Massachusetts, under the alias Mrs. Ona Herman. Two days later, on November 20, 1950, the Hausers became the parents of a healthy baby boy. They named him Peter.

The following month the family leased an apartment in New York, spent the holidays in the city, then traveled by train to Spokane, Washington. They rented a luxurious home at 4206 South Latawah Street and finally purchased a house at 3905 Sky View Avenue. In yet another ironic twist in her already strange life, the home Virginia and her husband purchased stood across the street from Mr. and Mrs. Clifford Rice. Rice served as a special agent for the Intelligence Division of the Internal Revenue Service and was indirectly involved with the Kefauver hearings.

The IRS had been working with the panel, supplying information about the tax returns and income of alleged mobsters. Virginia Hill was one of those targeted by the agency, though she was unaware of the investigation of her taxes.

At first leary because of his connections with the government, Virginia and Hans chatted with the Rices and slowly established a distant, albeit neighborly, relationship. They often talked in front of their homes and waved across driveways. The Rices knew their neighbor's identity because of the secret IRS probe and because Virginia had been targeted as a witness by Kefauver.

With the preliminary questioning wrapped up, the formal Kefauver hearings finally got under way in February 1951. The panel had traveled to Miami, Chicago, and Kansas City. Scores of people had told their version of the truth, or what they hoped the panel would believe was the truth. When the Kefauver Committee moved to New York on March 12, the hearings turned into the television event of the year.

The hearings were carried by television stations in twenty cities on the East Coast and in the Midwest, with newspaper coverage throughout the world. More than 86 percent of all homes in New York were tuned into the hearings, more than had watched the World Series. Literally overnight, millions of television viewers and newspaper readers had become followers of Estes Kefauver and his anticrime crusade. Kefauver played to the crowd, putting on airs of disgust and shock at gruff and colorful testimony offered by underworld figures.

As Kefauver's name became familiar, so did the names of once-obscure gangsters, such as Frank Costello, Meyer Lansky, Lucky Luciano, Charlie Fischetti, Jake Guzik, and Joe Adonis. Few in America believed anything the mobsters said but sat riveted to their black-and-white television sets and hung on every lie and mobster's refusal to answer direct questions about underworld associations. Most knew there was a Mafia and that its members were not "plumbing-supply salesmen," "produce importers," or "clothing salesmen," as they claimed under oath. Most believed the gangsters were killers but vicariously imagined themselves sitting next to them in court or having a few drinks with them in a quiet bar. The hearings made the gangsters American heroes, chief among them Virginia Hill's paramour, Joe Adonis.

The following excerpts from Joe Adonis's testimony are typical of the rude and arrogant answers that many of the mobsters provided Kefauver and his committee. As chief counsel for the committee, Rudolph Halley interrogated Adonis, who was called by his birth name, Doto.

> Halley: Did you know Virginia Hill?
> Doto: I decline to answer.
> Halley: Have you ever heard of the Mafia?
> Doto: I have heard of it.
> Halley: Can you tell the committee what it is?
> Doto: I would not have any idea.
> Halley: In what connection have you heard of it?
> Doto: By reading it in the newspapers.
> Halley: Did you ever have any connection with the Mafia yourself?
> Doto: I don't know what it is.
> Halley: And have you ever known any persons whom you believed to be members of such a secret organization?
> Doto: No, sir.
> Halley: Were you ever a member of any secret organization?
> Doto: No, sir.
> Halley: Do you believe that such a thing as the Mafia exists?
> Doto: I am not a judge of that—I am no judge of that. I wouldn't—I don't qualify to answer that question.
> Halley: Witnesses before this committee have testified, if you don't mind my making a statement . . .
> Doto: . . . go ahead.
> Halley: . . . by way of explanation that in their homes, in various neighborhoods where people of Sicilian descent live, they have heard people talk of the Mafia as an old Sicilian organization. Have you never heard of it?
> Doto: I am not Sicilian, so it would not be spoken in my home.

Adonis's smug answers had newspaper reporters chuckling, but Kefauver was not enjoying the joke. Adonis was slapped with a ten-count indictment for his failure to properly answer questions, under oath, about his knowledge of the Mafia. One of the indictment counts specifically cited his refusal to answer questions about his relationship with Virginia Hill. The indictments were ordered by unanimous vote of the committee on January 23, 1952.

The ten-count contempt-of-court indictment was then expanded to sixteen counts, and Adonis was found guilty by the committee without the benefit of a trial by jury.

But the indictment was a paper tiger. Adonis was arrested on gambling charges shortly after his Kefauver testimony, found guilty, and sentenced to two to three years in the New Jersey state prison in Trenton. An additional three-month sentence for contempt of court was tacked on to that term.

Then, on June 23, 1953, Adonis won a reversal of his conviction for contempt. A federal court of appeals threw out the ruling and ordered Adonis acquitted. Judge John McGohey found that Adonis could not legally claim the privilege of "not answering for fear of possible prosecution or incrimination" because it was not a crime not to know the answers to specific questions or, in the case of questions about the bribing of public officials, to make "political contributions."

Adonis eventually fled the country on January 2, 1956, to avoid another prison sentence for racketeering, leaving his wife and four children in New York. Joe A sailed on the Italian liner *Conte Biancamano*, wearing a $750 suit and a new pair of shoes and carrying no luggage. He was met in Naples by Lucky Luciano, who had returned to Italy from Cuba several years earlier.

While Joe Adonis and other racketeers faced their day in court against the Kefauver group, an anxious American public asked one question: "When will Virginia Hill testify?"

18

The Kefauver committee, the press, and the country eagerly looked forward to the second week in March 1951, when the woman whom the press had now officially dubbed the "Mob Queen" was set to take the stand.

Because she could not appear for the prehearing questioning, Virginia agreed to a closed-door session with several of the investigators prior to the public hearing. She answered the questions in an evasive and flippant fashion.

Virginia told the investigators that the last time she saw any of the "old gang," as she called the boys in the Chicago outfit, was in January 1950, when she stopped in that city. Hill said she attended a big New Year's Eve bash that had politicians rubbing elbows with "the guys you want to ask me about." When asked to name names "off the record," all Hill said was: "You know the usual guys. Charlie Fischetti, his brother Joe. He was my favorite, and I haven't talked with him in a long time."

Virginia said that when she left, she told the group of gangsters exactly how she felt about them, how they had mistreated her in recent years, and called them "a bunch of cheapskates and pikers." Hill said she was especially angry with Charlie Fischetti but refused to say why." She added, "And Adonis hasn't heard the last yet, either."

Hill supposedly gave the investigators details of how and

from whom she received her never-ending flow of cash, but they refused to offer any of the details to the press, saving it for the television cameras. "This promises to be a hot one," Senator Toby of New Hampshire told the reporters. "I'm sure Miss Hill will be filling in some of the details that Frank Costello left out in yesterday's session."

Costello's testimony followed that of Joe Adonis and every other mobster; he did not know there was a Mafia, he was not a member, and he knew nothing about anything. The Kefauver Committee hoped Virginia would be the crack in the Mafia's armor.

One reporter described her entrance into the hearing room in New York as "pure Hollywood pandemonium . . . something like a movie premiere, only here there was only one star—Virginia Hill." When her taxi pulled up to the front of the U.S. courthouse in Foley Square, a mob of reporters popped flashbulbs and stormed the car, jamming microphones and television, movie newsreels, and still cameras in her face. Though her exact words could not be printed, several reporters who were on hand filled in the blanks.

"Get your fucking cameras out of my face, you cheap fucking bastards!" Virginia screamed as she flung open the rear door, harder than necessary, apparently trying not only to clear a path but bruise as many of the reporters as possible.

On her big day of testimony she wore a silver blue mink stole, a big black hat, and a black suit with a scarf around her neck. She was an expert at makeup and seemed to wear more than the usual "street" cosmetics to ensure she looked good on television.

As she entered room 318 at nine-thirty in the morning on March 16, 1951, television-camera floodlights blinded her, and she was swallowed up in the crowd. Several women tried to grab at her; reporters shouted so many questions that all were inaudible. Hill gave them one massive shove, which sent three reporters tumbling back onto one another. "Get out of my fucking way!" She swung her purse and belted a woman, then tried to grab a camera away from another reporter.

"Don't I have fucking police protection? Or you guys too busy harassing innocent citizens and collecting payoffs?" Three courthouse guards took their time making their way forward to help Virginia Hill get through the crowd and into the court-room. It seemed as if they wanted the mob Queen to get her comeuppance before they helped out.

Before she entered the room, she turned back toward the press wolves. "I hope the fucking atom bomb falls on every one of you."

Once Hill was inside the courtroom, the television lights nearly blinded her. The courtroom was packed, and the audience refused to quiet down. Hill pleaded with Kefauver for help. "You don't know the trouble I've had with these bums," she said. The senator saw that Hill was visibly frightened and upset and ordered silence. He also requested that several of the lights either be redirected or switched off as a courtesy.

For the record, Kefauver told the court reporters that he had ordered sealed the testimony that Hill had given to the committee prior to the public hearing. He mentioned that minor details of that conversation had been given to the press, but nothing further would be released, and no questions were to be asked of any member of the committee about that testimony.

With that proviso, the formal testimony of Virginia Hill Hauser of Spokane, Washington, began.

The continual burst of flashbulbs blinded Virginia, who was called Mrs. Hauser by the committee, and she complained to Kefauver.

Halley: Now, Mrs. Hauser, most witnesses have had their pictures taken, and they have stopped as soon as they started to testify.

Virginia: I know, but most of them never went through with those bums what I did.

Halley: I'm sure that they don't intend to upset you.

Virginia: Oh, they do upset me.

Halley: All right, it will stop in a moment. What is your full name?

"Virginia Hill Hauser," she answered.

With that, the spectators and press settled down, and the interrogation began. Virginia seemed nervous at first and leaned forward, on her elbows, against the table, as she spoke into the microphone. But after she answered several questions about her background and her finances, she seemed more confident. Virginia leaned back, flung her right arm over the back of the chair, and adopted a flip and arrogant demeanor. She lied about her income, her friends, and her taxes, and she deluded herself into believing Halley, Kefauver, and the group were accepting her answers as the truth.

> Halley: Do you think you would like to tell the committee the story of your life, insofar as it involved your financial affairs, and the contacts you may have had with known gangsters since that time? Do you think you could just go ahead and tell it best in a narrative fashion?
> Virginia: Well, I worked for a while. Then the men I was around that gave me things were not gangsters or racketeers or whatever you call these other people. The only time I ever got anything from them was going out and having fun and maybe a few presents. But I happened to go with other fellows. And for years I have been going to Mexico. I went with fellows down there. And like a lot of girls that they got [sic]. Giving me things and bought me everything I want. And then when I was with Ben, he bought me everything.

Though her answers were a bit convoluted at first, Virginia tried to portray herself as a fun-loving party girl who was showered with gifts from numerous boyfriends and admirers, among them Bugsy Siegel. Halley sensed that Virginia was going down the same path as many of the other witnesses who lied and deliberately tried to mislead the Kefauver panel with vague and rambling testimony. He was determined to pull enough information from Hill's answers to use as evidence against other mob associates yet to be interrogated. He also hoped to give the IRS sufficient information to build its tax-fraud case against Virginia.

The interrogation quickly turned into a verbal Ping-Pong game. Halley attacked Hill with solid facts and figures about her expenditures at Sun Valley. Virginia fired back with casual and arrogant remarks that she was at the ski resort on someone else's tab, though she would never identify her benefactor.

No ground was gained during the first set of questions, so Halley changed the focus from Hill's Sun Valley expenses to the

mysterious Joe Epstein. Virginia understood she had to protect
her benefactor's privacy and deliberately evaded the questions.

Halley: Now, Mrs. Hauser, returning to Chicago, it was
about 1935 that you began asking Joe Epstein to keep your
money; is that right?

Virginia: Well, when I met him I didn't begin immediately, because I didn't—You just don't start doing something like that fast. I got to know him, and we became
friends, and good friends, and then he told me that I should
take care of my money, and then I told him when I have it,
I always spend it, so he says, well, he'll hold it for me, try,
you know, to keep me from spending all, you know, that I
had to think about tomorrow and all that stuff.

Halley: Have you spoken to him recently?

Virginia: Yes.

Halley: Can you think of any reason why he should be
dodging this committee's subpoenas?

Virginia: I didn't even know he was dodging them,
because I saw him in Chicago and he was out everyplace
with me.

Halley: Well, an attorney even saw me on his behalf but
refused to divulge his whereabouts.

Virginia: Oh, it didn't look like anybody was looking for
him when I was there last week. He was with me.

Halley: Last week you were with him?

Virginia: Yes, I went out to dinner with him.

Halley: Where do you think I can find him? Where did
you see him?

Virginia: I saw him in Chicago.

Halley: In what places?

Virginia: Let me see. We went to the House of Eden for
dinner with some friends of mine.

Halley: Where is his home?

Virginia: Twenty-five East Delaware.

Halley: Was he home during that period, do you know?

Virginia: Well, I wasn't there. I don't know.

Halley: Where is his place of business?

Virginia: I don't know.

Halley: Where did you meet him?

Virginia: I met him at the Clover Bar.

Halley: Would you phone him at his home?

Virginia: No, I never phoned. I always called friends of
mine and asked them to get in touch with him.

Halley: Well, he seems to be a little elusive. Maybe that's why we have trouble finding him. Where would you suggest I find him if I want to reach him?

Virginia: Well, I would call the Clover Bar and ask was he around.

Halley: That is not a very good way for a senate committee to reach a witness, to call the Clover Bar, is it?

Virginia: Well, that's the way I found him.

Halley: I hope all your friends aren't this fly-by-nightish. Doesn't Joe Epstein have a place of business or a home?

Virginia: If he had a place of business, I never heard of it.

Virginia now seemed quite pleased with herself. She believed she had made a mockery of the panel in front of the newspaper and television reporters. The courtroom erupted in laughter several times during her remarks about Epstein and the Clover Bar: each time, Estes Kefauver intervened and demanded silence.

As Halley and the panel regrouped for the next set of questions, Virginia smiled at the reporters and glared at Halley. She convinced herself that she was in complete control of the show. But Halley was not about to let Virginia Hill Hauser win the day.

After a brief pause, he waved off the questions that focused on Epstein and returned to the matter of Hill's expenses. He again bombarded her with details about her expenditures at Sun Valley as well as telephone calls to New York and Chicago, trips to Mexico, investments in clubs in Chicago and New York, and the recent purchase of her Spokane home. It was apparent that the panel had done its homework.

As the committee pressed Virginia for specific answers, her confident demeanor rapidly deteriorated. She spoke slowly and carefully but continued to claim she never earned a dime that had not been accounted to the government. Hill insisted that much of the money she spent came from savings or that the bills had been paid for by friends. She even maintained that the government owed her a tax refund for the years 1947 and 1948 because her income dropped considerably after the murder of Bugsy Siegel. She said the murder affected her income because she no longer received lucrative racetrack tips after his death.

As Halley pressed Virginia about her relationships with Siegel, Adonis, Costello, and Fischetti, she lost her temper and pounded her fist on the table and yelled that the committee had tried to trap her into incriminating herself. It was apparent Halley hit a raw nerve and point-blank asked her about being a mob money carrier.

Halley: Now, I have a note that you once told an agent for the Internal Revenue that you were on occasion asked to carry cash between Chicago and New York.

Virginia: That is not true. And if they told that, they told a lie. The only cash I ever carried is what belonged to me, and I've never carried anything for anybody. And if anyone said that, that's a big lie. And I don't care who said it.

Halley: If anybody said it, you say it isn't so?

Virginia: Yes, because the only cash I ever carried was my own, and I never carried anything for anybody—cash or anything else.

Then the interrogation went back to Siegel and the killing.

Halley: Now, you left the United States shortly before Siegel was killed. Would you tell the circumstances that led to your leaving the United States?

Virginia: I was planning to leave the United States long before that. I had gone to San Francisco. I got my passport, and I knew these people in France, and I was supposed to go there and visit them. But then a friend of mine wrote me a letter and said about all the people we were going to see; and I told her not to do that; that if Ben ever saw the letter, he would get mad. So he got the letter and read it and saw all these things I planned to see in Europe, and these people, and he didn't like this boy I knew in Europe. So then he told me I couldn't go. So then, later on, I had a big fight with him because I hit a girl in the Flamingo and he told me I wasn't a lady. We got in a big fight. I had been drinking, and I left, and I went to Paris when I was mad.

Halley: Before you left, had you heard any rumors that Siegel was having trouble with any of his gangster friends?

Virginia: I never heard any kind—that he was having any trouble. And all I know, he was worried about the hotel. I hated the place, and I told him, why didn't he leave it and get away from it, because it was making him a nervous wreck.

Halley: And your leaving was completely a personal matter?

Virginia: Yes, it was.

Then Halley skipped subjects and finally settled on allegations that Virginia had been involved in drug trafficking.

Halley: Have you ever known anybody who was in the narcotics traffic in Mexico?

Virginia: Well, since it's been in the papers, I don't know anybody in the narcotics traffic; but since I've been going to Mexico, a lot of people have approached me and tried to give me those things. One fellow came up to me and said he had a lot of H. and C.—which I didn't know what it was, and when I asked him what it was, he told me it was heroin and cocaine. I told him to get out of the house. He told me I don't know people. I said they'd break my neck if I mentioned such a thing. I had people who used to come and say, "Don't you want some?" I had an awful time getting rid of people down there that offered it to me.

Estes Kefauver took over after forty-five minutes of banter between Halley and Hill. He changed the line of questioning to Bugsy Siegel, to the assassination and rumors that Bugsy's murder was triggered by problems with the Flamingo or by the racing wire services.

Kefauver: Do you recall the instance where he (Siegel) had trouble with some other people about spending too much money of the Flamingo's?

Virginia: No. The only time I ever saw him, he was pacing the floor up and down, was because the way, I don't know, sometimes at night, he said that he had lost, or I don't know what was the matter. But I told him, why did he want to stay in that thing like that if it was worrying him so, because he seemed to be awful worried about the business. And he couldn't get the kitchen running right, and all that stuff. He said everything was upside down.

Kefauver: Then this chap that came out from New York to take over the Flamingo after Ben Siegel was killed, do you know him?

Virginia: Well, you see, I know nothing about it. I haven't been around, I haven't got in touch with those people, I know nothing about it.

Kefauver: Did Ben have much to say about his wire-service difficulties he was having at that time?

Virginia: I never heard anything about the wire service. One time I was going to read something in the *Time* magazine, I saw his picture, and he took it away from me.

Kefauver: Didn't that arouse your suspicions, that he wanted to keep that a secret from you?

Virginia: Well, he told me I had no business knowing that, don't read that, and everything, so . . .

Kefauver: He didn't usually just jerk things away from you, did he?

Virginia: He did. I was in an airport with him in Las Vegas, and I saw it, but he wouldn't let me read it.

Kefauver: Anyway, he didn't want you to know about his wire-service difficulties?

Virginia: He didn't want me evidently to know about anything.

Kefauver: Well, particularly when he saw that you were reading in a magazine about his difficulty with the wire service, he jerked *Time* magazine out of your hand; is that true?

Virginia: He said, "Don't read that baloney."

Kefauver tried to learn what Virginia might have known about the Siegel murder.

Kefauver: Do you feel like talking about it? Do you have any theory about what happened, who it was had it in for him? I don't want you to mention any name.

Virginia: Mr. Kefauver, if I knew anything about it, believe me, I would be the first one to talk. I don't know anything, and I have asked people, and they say they don't know anything. Nobody seems to know anything . . . nobody ever told me anything about him or anything. And he never told me, outside of, he said he liked to travel, and

that's why I should go with him, because we would go to
Europe and all this stuff, and he knew all the pretty places.
He used to go with me to little resorts, and he liked to ride
horses like I did, and swim, and all that stuff. I never knew
these other things.

Kefauver leaned forward and glared at Hill to make the point
that he knew she had not told everything she could have about
her relationship with Siegel. Hill leaned back in her chair,
flicker her hair in a defiant manner, and smiled.

No new insight into the murder of Siegel had been gained,
but Virginia did offer an unusual glimpse into Bugsy's character: Although domineering and forceful, he seemed to be a good
companion who liked to show his lady love a good time.

Estes Kefauver dismissed Virginia, and the committee
recessed for ten minutes.

As Virginia rose to leave the courtroom, the spectators stood
up and gave her a hearty round of applause and a standing ovation. The blinding light of flashbulbs lit the courtroom, and, as
in her entrance, Hill was mobbed by reporters. But mixed in the
mob now were "Virginia Hill fans," men and women reaching
out to touch and shout out to her.

"Hey, Virginia, ya done good!" "You really gave them what
for." "Hey, Virginia, how about a date?" "Look, the Mob
Queen!"

Virginia stole the show, which did not go unnoticed by the
committee. Gangster Frank Costello was recalled to the stand.
Costello and Hill passed one another in the hall, each looked in
opposite directions and never acknowledged one another's
presence.

Hill believed she had sidestepped every question and would
be free to go. She believed she had bamboozled the senators
and offered nothing that could be used against her or her underworld friends. As she left the courthouse, Hill believed she was
finally able to break free from her criminal past. As she stepped
into an awaiting cab, she offered a triumphant wave to her fans
and the press. She had no idea that she had become ensnared in
a trap set by Kefauver, his panel, and the Internal Revenue Service. Though she provided no concrete testimony about how

she obtained her wealth, she offered nothing to account for her extravagances in Sun Valley and abroad. The IRS had all it needed to bring its tax-fraud case against the mob Queen. Virginia Hill had no inkling that she had played into the government's hands with her vague and conflicting testimony.

19

While Virginia Hill reveled in what she assumed to be a victory over the Kefauver Committee, the panel moved its interrogation to Los Angeles. More than twenty witnesses took their turn at the microphone during the week's session, but the committee learned nothing new about vice in Los Angeles or the country. Though the hearings were still being covered extensively on television and in the newspapers, many well-known mobsters had already given their testimony. With few new underworld celebrities to entice viewers, Kefauver became concerned that the proceedings had lost some of their impact.

Frustrated, Estes Kefauver decided that his group should pursue the Benjamin "Bugsy" Siegel assassination, which was still a hot topic around the country. Though he learned little from Virginia Hill, Kefauver believed there still were many unanswered questions about Siegel, his associates, and his business activities. The senator also believed his political career would soar to even greater heights if he could solve Bugsy's murder.

Beverly Hills police chief Clinton H. Anderson agreed to testify. Hill's Spokane neighbor, Clifford Rice, conducted the session. Kefauver asked Rice to join the committee because of his knowledge of organized crime and Virginia Hill, obtained through his association with the mob Queen. Kefauver was determined to present an ironclad case against Hill and knew Rice would be able to ferret out additional information from Anderson. Rice began with the Siegel murder.

Anderson testified that he believed Siegel was killed in a mob hit, most likely because of his association with the *Trans-America Race Wire Service,* drugs, or the financial problems with the Flamingo Hotel. The police chief portrayed Siegel as a high-rolling gambler who spent money faster than he made it and had no qualms about cheating to get it.

With that, Clifford Rice concentrated on the night Siegel was killed. Though Anderson had interrogated a number of people who had intimate knowledge of Siegel's murder, he only offered information previously published in the newspapers. He also insisted he had no suspects in custody, nor was he actually close to having the case solved. Anderson never mentioned that he had questioned and released triggerman Eddie Cannazero. Rice dropped that line of questioning, then focused on Hill.

Rice: Now, Chief, what did Virginia Hill have to do with all this?

Anderson: Virginia Hill is alleged to have been familiar with the entire operation and the trouble between some of the individuals involved. It is reported that she was aware that the killing was to happen and she was out of the United States at the time.

Rice: Now, Chief, were there any money transactions involving Virginia Hill that came to your attention in connection with the shooting or the Flamingo?

Anderson: Yes. I had a contact in Mexico City. I was informed by him that a letter carrier for the Mexican government had stolen a registered letter containing, if I remember rightly, two thousand dollars in currency and that he had been arrested and the money recovered. Now, the letter was addressed to a friend of Virginia Hill's, but she [Hill] was to receive the money. It came from Chicago, and there were many occurrences like that.

Then Kefauver questioned Anderson about Hill's mysterious diary.

Kefauver: What is there to the story about Virginia Hill supposing to have in a lock box her memoirs and a biographical sketch of what took place, and so forth, that you are going to be the heir to in case something happens to her?

Anderson: I am patiently waiting for that communication, although I haven't seen or heard of it.

Kefauver: Well, you have heard of it, though?

Anderson: I have read it in the newspapers.

Kefauver: Where are these documents being kept, do you know?

Anderson: I don't know.

Kefauver: She has not let you in on the secret, has she?

Anderson: No.

Though the Siegel assassination was no closer to a solution, the committee did gain one valuable bit of information. That was that money had changed hands between Chicago and Mexico, and it went directly to Virginia Hill. The case against Hill gained significant strength.

So did Senator Kefauver's public image. When the hearings finally ended, in September 1951, Kefauver was among the most respected and recognizable personalities in America. He was in constant demand on the lecture circuit, earning upwards of $25,000 for his personal appearances. He lent his name as a coauthor to a book on the investigation, *Crime in America*, which made the *New York Times* bestseller list for three months. CBS-TV aired a Kefauver Committee–type tabloid show called "Crime Syndicated" and paid the committee members to do the weekly narration. Kefauver himself narrated the introduction of the Humphrey Bogart movie *The Enforcer* and the epilogue for *Captive City*.

Unfortunately, Kefauver's popularity and political clout quickly dissipated. Not one of the twenty-two contempt-of-court cases stemming from the crime investigation was upheld. All were dismissed in federal district court or reversed on appeal. The committee submitted 221 crime-related proposals for legislation, few of which were voted into law. Kefauver lost two bids at the presidency. In 1952 he failed to win the party's nomination. In 1956 he won the Democratic nomination for vice president, on the ticket with Adlai Stevenson, who lost to Eisenhower.

Estes Kefauver died on August 10, 1973, from complications after a heart attack, but his name will forever be associated with the organized-crime hearings, the first event to exploit the drama and power of live television and forever alter the public's perception of organized crime and its sinister influence on the nation.

20

The Kefauver hearings had made Virginia Hill a national celebrity, albeit as a gangster's moll and smart-mouthed tramp. She won few friends and made some very powerful enemies in Washington, D.C., and in the underworld. With the help of the Kefauver panel, the Internal Revenue Service cemented its tax case against Hill and prepared to move against her.

Though she revealed little information about her mob associates on the stand, Virginia had become *persona non grata* among the mobsters. Since the murder of Bugsy Siegel and her apparent alliance with him, she was no longer welcome in Los Angeles and Las Vegas by both the police and Jack Dragna's clan. Dragna considered her part of the old guard, the group that had fractured and dissipated since the Kefauver hearings sent many of Hill's friends into hiding in different parts of the country and the world. Epstein kept a low profile; Adonis shipped out to join Luciano in exile in Italy. Dragna no longer needed Hill's services, nor did he care for her personally. And since she made a splash at the hearings, rumors that Virginia narrowly escaped execution at the time of the Siegel hit spread throughout the underworld and in law enforcement circles. In mob law, once a person is marked for death, the assassination can happen at any time. Even if the intended victim has won a reprieve.

If Virginia knew she was not welcome in Los Angeles and had the sense to avoid Las Vegas because of her association with Siegel, she quickly discovered that Chicago offered no safe haven, either.

Anne Fischetti, wife of Chicago mobster Charlie Fischetti, made a point of snubbing Hill. Anne had testified when the Kefauver hearings traveled to Chicago, and she had nothing but contempt for Hill when questioned about the mob Queen's association with the Fischettis. With her husband considered the top-ranking mobster in the Midwest, Anne Fischetti's attitude was echoed in every other underworld household. When Hill tried to register at the more upscale hotels, such as the Sherman House, a notorious gangster retreat, or the Palmer House, they refused to rent her a room, claiming they were booked. The front-desk clerks made it abundantly clear that the establishment of the hotels did not care for her patronage.

When Virginia attempted to see Epstein two weeks after the hearing, he could not be found. Joe E vacated his East Delaware Place apartment and left no forwarding address. Virginia left repeated messages at the Clover Bar that went unanswered. Then someone told Virginia that Joe E did not appreciate her "blabbing his address all over the world." She was frozen out of the city that gave Virginia her start in the underworld.

When Virginia Hill walked out of the courtroom in New York, she believed she had beaten the committee, that her smug and snide remarks gave the senators little information and won the favor of the American public because she outsmarted the politicians. In fact, she had won nothing and was about to lose still more.

Shortly after the hearing, newspaper reporters pressured Kefauver and his men to release the prehearing transcripts of the interview Hill had given privately to investigators James Nellis and Alfred Klein. The reporters were convinced that Hill's claims of innocence on the stand hid the real dirt Hill divulged behind closed doors. But Kefauver refused.

He told the group that the investigators learned little about her underworld dealings but did "receive a good orientation in the love life of Virginia," and "she insisted love and money were the only motivation in her life, and she said, 'And that ain't hay or criminal.'"

Though Kefauver would not say much about Hill's private testimony, he was very open about his reaction to the woman's public comments on the stand.

I found Virginia Hill to be a sad and very mixed up lady. The strain of the life she has led has taken its toll. The fading underworld queen is now a ravaged woman. Her friends are shying away and moving away. She has become a symbol of the past corruption and decadence of the Mafia. That symbol has been crushed. I imagine Miss Hill would think hard about whether the life she led was worth the price she had to pay for having her name nationally famous. I would have preferred to spare her the ordeal. But this was something she brought upon herself. One can not live as she did and not expect to pay for it later down the road. And I am afraid that Miss Hill is not yet finished paying for her ways.

Kefauver had tipped his hand.

Before the hearing, Hill and Hauser had gone to Bar Harbor, where they were dogged by FBI agents. The only bridge in and out of town was heavily guarded by federal men with radios who monitored the couple's every move. Now in Spokane, Washington, the Hausers found themselves under the same federal watch; every time they left their home, an FBI agent was close behind. Hans became a recluse, afraid to venture out for fear of being stopped, harassed, arrested, or deported. He had hoped his loving wife would do the same.

Shortly after she returned from Chicago, Virginia packed her bags again and moved from city to city, leaving Hans and their son, Peter, behind. Virginia claimed she was trying to find Epstein, to get him to intervene on Hans's behalf, to stave off his imminent deportation and secure powerful attorneys who knew where to provide the right amount of cash to get things done in Washington. Those who knew Virginia said she actually began to panic over the pressure from the FBI. She also felt trapped in her marriage to a former ski instructor who was out of place when he was off the slopes. The glamour of their marriage and of her former life no longer had any meaning.

Hill finally found Epstein, who had been "vacationing," as an associate explained it, in San Francisco. Virginia was tipped off to his whereabouts by a friend at the Clover Bar who contacted her after her return to Spokane from Chicago. Hill and Epstein traveled together using aliases, though Hill was invariably recognized even when she hid behind dark glasses and wore scarfs. They went to Seattle, to Reno, and back to Chicago, where Joe supposedly gave her a $10,000 cash payment. He told her it would have to be the last.

Virginia knew she eventually had to move out of her Spokane home, but getting Hans out of the country was the more urgent problem.

Having lost three appeals before the INS, Hauser was ordered to voluntarily leave America by September 1, 1952, or be booted out of the country. Hill decided to use the $10,000 to get Hans out of the country, possibly to Chile, to become a citizen there and work once again as a ski instructor. She believed that once in Chile, Hans could make the immigration "quota" list, return to America, and apply for citizenship, for not that many Chileans sought to emigrate to the United States.

Her problems were not that easily remedied. She decided that she and her infant son, Peter, would remain in Spokane and take the brunt of the harassment from the FBI until Hans was safe in Chile. Hill told Epstein that she would drop all contact with her former underworld friends and try to live "as a normal American citizen." Epstein continued to dodge Kefauver and faced a prison term for contempt of court. Both Joey E and Virginia agreed that it was in their mutual best interest to sever ties permanently.

But Epstein left her with one parting note: "If you really need me, you'll know how to get in touch with me." Both understood that a message left at the Clover Bar would be the key. Both also understood that the Clover Bar had been bugged by the feds and that the front and back entrances were under constant surveillance, so they had to be careful with their choice of words and actions.

By now, Virginia told friends, she had become used to finding bugs in her home and telephone and being followed on the street and stared at in public. But what annoyed her most was that the "shadowing" was unsettling to Hans. With both their nerves frayed over the unwelcome attention, Virginia and her husband quarreled violently and constantly. Any little annoyance became a source of irritation and produced a battle.

If Hill and Hauser tried to ignore the fact they were constantly being followed on the street, they were continually reminded of the Kefauver episode and the IRS investigation into their finances at home. Clifford Rice, the Kefauver interrogator and federal revenue agent, had kept an ongoing surveillence on the Hausers and had reported their every move to the government.

Virginia had to have known what Rice was doing. She knew he was a federal agent when she and Hans first bought their Spokane home. Rice also made the national press as a result of questioning Beverly Hills police chief Clinton Anderson when the Kefauver group held court in Los Angeles. Virginia was clever and shrewd and must have understood that every move was reported by Rice to the government. But Virginia also considered Rice an honest and compassionate man, a friendly neighbor, and the only one in the government she could trust. Virginia telephoned Rice to find out if the government would allow Hans to take their new Cadillac to Chile. She knew that he could get a fair price for the car overseas and could use the money to establish himself in South America.

Rice realized that the FBI had no solid case yet to prosecute her for underworld activities. The Treasury Department had yet to nail down its case against Hill for tax evasion and was not yet prepared to move against her and needed to stall for time to complete its case. Rice knew that the IRS wanted Virginia to hold on to her assets and not liquidate any large merchandise that would have to be traced and its worth revalued.

Rice also felt sorry for Virginia. He looked upon her as a tragic woman desperate to overcome a dark past. Rice also realized that her marriage and attempt at a more mainstream life had caused her misery, for now both the government and the mob were against her. He told Virginia that the government would not allow her to move to Chile or sell the car. He said that doing anything with the car would force the government to file tax-fraud charges in order to legally seize her assets. He explained that the best thing for her to do would be to leave things as they were and let Hans go to Chile alone, without any major financial backing from Hill.

Virginia listened but thought better of taking Rice's advice. That night, she and Hans hooked the Cadillac up to a new trailer, packed their bags, and somehow escaped the watchful eye of their neighbor.

Rice discovered the Hausers' move the next morning. The FBI issued a nationwide dragnet. Customs and Immigration agents joined with the Treasury and FBI in their hunt for the couple. The Mexican and Canadian border patrols were also alerted. Everyone believed Virginia and Hans would be arrested within a matter of hours. But they were wrong.

There were reports that the Hausers' Cadillac and trailer were spotted in Missouri, Nevada, Indiana, and New York. It seemed that the couple had turned up all over the country at the same time.

Three weeks later, the FBI was tipped off that the Cadillac had been located in a storage garage in Palo Alto, California. When authorities seized the car, the odometer had been reset to zero, and the car was completely cleaned out; no dust or dirt and practically no fingerprints. There was absolutely no trace of where Virginia and Hans had gone and nothing to indicate how far they might have driven before dumping the car. The government finally auctioned off the Cadillac and received slightly less that $4,000 for it.

The Hausers were still missing. A thorough search of Palo Alto uncovered absolutely nothing. They had not stayed in any local hotels, nor were they ever seen on the street. Their photo was splashed across the local newspapers, but no one came forward with any information. If the Hausers had been in Palo Alto, they had friends who were hiding them. If they had not been there, then someone had to explain how the car wound up in that town. No one knew anything, and the mystery deepened.

Their vanishing act prompted Treasury agents to accelerate their efforts against the Hausers. The IRS put several task forces on the case; each was assigned to cover different periods of Hill's nefarious life.

One group reconstructed the time she spent in Mexico City and asked local shopkeepers to open their books to see exactly how much money Hill spent south of the border. The team hit pay dirt. On one trip the men learned of purchases of $650 for

ANDY EDMONDS

hats, $3,500 spent at a nightclub, hotel bills of several thousand dollars, $4,000 for liquor, and $1,200 for lingerie.

The same agenda was repeated in each city Hill had been spotted in prior to her testimony; New York, Boston, Bar Harbor, Washington, Chicago, Sun Valley, Denver, El Paso, San Francisco, Los Angeles, Las Vegas, Spokane.

When the agents finished their footwork, the total expenditures were compared against the income reported by Hill for various years.

In 1944, Hill listed her income at $14,500. The government figured it had to be closer to $37,690. In 1945, she claimed $15,500, but the IRS added up numbers amounting to $34,541. The following year, Virginia declared $23,370 in earnings. But the Treasury Department figured her income at $78,079. She gave $15,500 as her total earnings in 1947, but the government believed it was closer to $45,415. The IRS's case against Hill was now firmly in place. It had the numbers to prove she had cheated the government.

On June 20, 1951, Immigration went public with its move against Hans Hauser, hoping to lure him out of hiding by publicly embarrassing him.

The *Chicago Tribune* quoted John P. Boyd, district director of Immigration in a biting article:

Hans Hauser, husband of the former gamblers' playgirl Virginia Hill, again has been ordered to leave the United States. If Hauser, former Sun Valley ski instructor who now lives in Spokane, does not leave by September first he will be deported. Hauser has outstayed the time allotted in his visitor's visa permit. He is a native of Austria and came to the United States from Chile in 1940. Friends reported that the Hausers were planning to fly to Santiago, Chile, within three weeks.

Then the newspaper added a comment of its own: "Mrs. Hauser was a friend of the late Bugsy Siegel, who was slain by gunmen in her Beverly Hills home."

But Virginia and Hans were still nowhere to be found. The IRS said it wanted to question Hill and "know her direction of travel" because it was "always interested in a taxpayer's whereabouts when checking income." When rumors of their plans to fly to Chile were published in the newspaper, federal authorities ran a quick check to see if Hill had reapplied for a passport under her married name of Virginia Hill Hauser. No papers were found.

Virginia finally turned up, alone, on Thursday, July 5, in Denver, Colorado. She had flown in from El Paso, Texas, and planned to catch a connecting flight to Spokane. An airport clerk named Lilymae Ward reported Hill to the authorities. Ward said she spotted Virginia Hill immediately from the newspaper reports and the television hearings. She said that Hill arrived at the gate moments before the plane was to take off for Spokane. Hill could show no proof of having a reservation and was carrying a "great deal of baggage." Ward said that it made her a little suspicious, and she contacted airport authorities, who then detained Hill.

Virginia told authorities that Hans and Peter had already gone ahead to Chile, but she had trouble securing a new passport and could not leave the country.

By the time her plane landed in Denver, word of a scuffle earlier in the day with reporters in El Paso had made the evening papers. Two El Paso reporters tracked Virginia to her hotel. One, Neil McNeil, slipped a note under her hotel door requesting an interview. The note was ignored. As she left the hotel, another reporter, Walt Finley, tried to grab her in the lobby. She cracked him in the head with her shoe.

It took no time for word to spread that Virginia Hill had been found and was being detained at the Denver airport. A crowd formed as two investigators from the Denver district attorney's office, Al Decredico and Lawrence Stone, flashed their badges. They said they had no order to "hold" her, just to return her to Spokane for questioning. But when they approached her, she took a swing at Stone, and he grabbed her arm.

"Oh, I thought you were one of those reporters," Hill said.

"Don't you know I could arrest you for that?" Stone said, still holding her arm.

"Go ahead. Everybody can arrest me and apparently wants to."

One reporter from Seattle suspected that she had not yet been told the full story.

"Hey, Virginia," he shouted, "did you know they slapped a tax lien on your home?"

Hill was stunned. She had only been told that she was being brought back for questioning and assumed that no action had been taken against her property. She became red-faced and ran outside the terminal. The investigators shoved her into a waiting car, and she turned for a minute to talk to reporters.

"I have been cooperative with the government, but I don't know what this is all about. I'll be willing to talk to government agents in Spokane. My husband and child were allowed to go on to Santiago, Chile, and I plan to join them there as soon as I can make arrangements."

She turned and took one step inside the car. She was visibly shaken. She turned back to the crowd. "If I had a gun, I'd shoot you reporters."

She drove off with the investigators with the understanding that no reporters would travel along with them.

The agents asked a few questions, the nature of which can only remain a matter of speculation. Stone only said that she told him she would be "glad to leave this damn country."

She was allowed to return to Spokane the following day. When she did, she received the shock of her life.

Hill was barred from her house. A small card was taped to the front door. "Seized for the account of the United States." Hill peered inside the front window and saw a large black trunk sitting in the middle of the living room, which was nearly bare of furniture. A similar card was taped to the trunk and each item in the room.

For the first time that anyone could recall, Virginia Hill cried. As she turned away from the house, Stanley Fogelquist, head of the IRS office in Spokane, stepped out of his car, which had been parked across the street.

"Miss Hill?"

"Yes."

"Miss Hill, I am authorized by the federal government of the United States of America to serve you with this notice. This is a formal tax lien for the amount of $161,000 for back income taxes for the years 1942 through 1947. We have seized your home, which has been estimated at a value of $35,000." The notice had been filed July 6, when Hill was in Denver.

"I ain't got no money. I don't know where you're going to get
it, because I don't have it. If you're thinking all that jewelry I
told you about during the hearings was worth that much, you're
wrong."

Following Fogelquist was the usual contingent of reporters.
When asked where she planned to stay, Virginia said she had no
idea.

"They'll have to let me take a bath. I don't see how they could
throw anybody right out of their home. All the clothes I got are
in there. They'll have to let me sleep there, won't they? I told
them when I came back they'd have to take care of me."

It is not clear who she meant would take care of her. Some
believed she was implying that when she came back from the
Kefauver hearings, the Mafia would have to take care of her.
Hill never clarified her statement.

To make matters worse, some sort of business convention was
in town. The only hotel in Spokane with a room was the East
End Motel, which was below Hill's usual high-class accommodations. But it was clean, and the front desk agreed to ward off
any reporters and put through no calls unless they were from
her husband. She rented a car and headed out to New York to
see Joe Adonis.

Virginia thought she was up against the worst of it. Then she
bought a newspaper during a one-night stopover in Riverside,
Illinois, a suburb just outside of Chicago. She found out that she
had been slapped with another tax lien, issued from the Chicago
office of the Internal Revenue Service.

The lien was for $48,369 for unpaid taxes for the years 1946
and 1947. It was filed by John T. Jarecki, Chicago-area tax collector, on behalf of the Internal Revenue Service, Tacoma,
Washington, division. Jarecki refused to disclose any specifics
about the lien to the press but said it had something to do with
property Hill had owned in Cook County, Illinois. "A lien
wouldn't be filed here unless we knew she had something in the
county."

Filing of the lien was meant to prevent Hill from transferring
or selling any property. It was generally assumed that she either
owned or fronted property and that the lien was attached
against the Clover Bar, in which Hill had invested a sum of
money, though she lied to the Kefauver Committee about

exactly how much she had invested. If the lien was filed against the Clover Bar, as most assumed, it certainly would have ignited the further wrath of the underworld, which did not need any additional harassment from the law.

But the pressure against Hill did not stop with the tax lien on the property. The IRS flooded Loop-area banks in downtown Chicago with letters detailing the nature of Hill's omissions and a priority request for any banks with accounts or safe deposit boxes in Virginia Hill Hauser's name to be immediately seized and reported to the government. The government hoped to uncover boxes filled with cash or documents revealing where she may have had hidden the money.

One box in a bank on North LaSalle Street was reported to have been owned by Hill. When federal agents unlocked it, the safe deposit box was empty. If she had cash or documents stored in it, the box had been cleaned out. There was no signed card to indicate that Hill had even gone into the box once she rented it, though the rental payments had been made on a regularly and timely basis. Exactly who paid the rent each quarter was unclear.

When Hill arrived in New York in mid-July of 1951, she left word that she wanted to see Joe Adonis. He refused to see her. He was fighting his own battle, trying to avoid a jail term for contempt-of-court charges resulting from his Kefauver testimony, and attempting to block Immigration's move to deport him. He did not need any further problems from the woman who dumped him for Ben Siegel.

Virginia returned to Spokane, knowing that she had absolutely no friends left in the underworld and no place that would welcome her. She adopted a "who cares" attitude and returned to her motel room in Spokane.

She told one reporter:

I can't worry about it. If I did, I'd go nuts. The government already decided that it wants to clean me out. So let 'em. They can have it all. I'm fed up with them, and I'm fed up with this country. I'm fed up with everything. When this is all over, I'm getting out of here to go live with my husband and son. I just have to wait until Uncle Sam decides he's through bothering me and finds someone else to pick

on. They can have my furs, my pearls, everything. I just
want to get out of here.

The IRS set August 2 as the date for the formal auction of
Hill's house and possessions. Virginia received one final notice
claiming that if she came up with the money due, the sale would
be canceled.

I don't own that kind of money, and I never did. They're
just pushing this thing and pushing me around because of
all the publicity I've had. If I was a nobody, they'd leave
me alone. I just got stuck being the example, that's all.

An inventory notice of sale was tacked up in the post office
and the police department in Spokane and was printed in the
local newspapers. It listed some of the items that would go on
the block:

Two American ranch mink coats, a white mink stole, a
royal mink stole, a silver blue mink stole, a natural sable
mink stole, a short black Persian lamb coat, three strings of
pearls, ten trunks—contents unknown, seven suitcases
and fifteen boxes of soap flakes.

It indicated that the sale would begin on August 2 and continue for at least one more day if merchandise remained. All
money raised would go toward paying off Hill's debt to the federal government. Surplus funds, if any, would be returned to
Virginia Hill Hauser. The federal revenue agents knew that the
government would be lucky if it raised anything close to the
debt owed by the former mob Queen.

Virginia Hill was allowed to enter her house one final time to
go over the contents, shed any light on its value, and help take
inventory for the government. She was not allowed to remove
anything from the house, not even toiletries or such family
mementos as pictures or personal letters. As she combed
through her possessions, she was followed and closely guarded
by two agents.

Hill's neighbor Clifford Rice was believed to be one of those
ordered to guard Virginia. Rice felt deep compassion for the

plight of his neighbor. He believed that a familiar face would diminish Virginia's fears of the ordeal. Apparently there was no animosity or resentment on Virginia's part; she understood that Rice was doing his job and had no choice in the matter. She also appreciated his help, for she reportedly offered to give Rice some sort of trinket when she got back on her feet. Rice refused the offer. Virginia and Clifford Rice parted friends. He was probably the last friend Virginia would make in the United States.

21

Adonis was struggling to stay one step ahead of the government. Jack Dragna and Johnny Roselli had been called to testify before the Kefauver Committee and wound up at the same end of Estes Kefauver's wrath. Dragna faced deportation to Italy, and Roselli would eventually wind up in pieces in an oil drum off Key Biscane, Florida, in the 1970s. Joe Epstein was in hiding, Bugsy Siegel was dead, and Virginia Hill had absolutely nowhere to turn. But the government was not yet finished with her.

On July 10, 1951, Mickey Cohen was sentenced to five years in prison and a $10,000 fine for income-tax evasion, falsifying documents, and lying to the IRS. Cohen was found guilty of three counts of tax evasion, but the judge ordered his sentences to run concurrently. The fine was levied for four counts of falsifying documents. Cohen was found to be more than $156,123 behind in his tax payments and was also charged $100,000 for the cost of the trial to convict him.

Cohen claimed he was broke and took a "pauper's oath" in which he agreed to serve an extra thirty days in prison to avoid paying a $10,000 interest penalty on the amount owed.

As Cohen was led away in handcuffs, one reporter asked how he felt. Cohen had only one thing to say. "See my attorney."

It was Cohen's first conviction on anything other than bookmaking, and it was clearly the end of the old guard in Los Angeles; the last of Siegel's cronies was headed into oblivion.

It was clear that no one in the Mafia had any sympathy for Virginia Hill. They all had their own demons to battle, and no one was safely out of the clutches of the Internal Revenue Service. Hill's problems were no greater than any one else's in the underworld. Moreover, many of her old friends believed that she had enjoyed an easy ride for the twenty or so years that she had been associated with the Chicago outfit.

Hill was never involved in murder or extortion. Nor did she have to face the barrel of a gun to achieve or maintain her position. The only real intrigue she ever had to deal with consisted of placing orchestrated bets on sporting events or transporting cash or stolen property from one point to another. She was paid handsomely for her services and enjoyed the good life, mixing with the wealthy, the famous, and the politically powerful for years. If anything, her friends in the underworld believed Hill's problems were nothing more than a minor nuisance that would be solved when her house was sold.

As far as her separation from Hauser, few in the Mafia cared for him and felt she was better off without him. He was an outsider, and many in the outfit believed he was causing many of Virginia's current problems. His battle with Immigration, they believed, just brought down more heat around Hill. While she was being pursued by the IRS, the less problems with the government, the better. Many people who knew Hill claimed that if she had rid herself of Hans Hauser in Sun Valley instead of marrying him, she probably would have fared better with the feds. But with Hauser in tow, Hill had become a troublemaker who not only harbored an alien but tried to smuggle him back into the country to skirt immigration laws.

On August 2, 1951, thirty-five-year-old Virginia Hill was thrown to the wolves, left to face a hungry and greedy crowd of bargain hunters and curiosity seekers who swarmed down upon the front lawn of her Spokane home.

More than two thousand people showed up for the auction, which quickly deteriorated into a free-for-all carnival sideshow. People grabbed up anything and everything, hoping to own a cheap souvenir of the woman who was once the darling of the underworld. One by one Virginia's private life was paraded out and put on public display. Everything, from her shoes to her cosmetics to her underwear, was waved about and hyped before the mob.

More than a hundred pairs of shoes were paraded before the hungry shoppers. Tables of expensive silverware, lamps, and dresses were set up and pawed over by the shoppers, who acted as if they were at a "Day After Christmas" sale. Even garbage cans were displayed and put on the auction block. Fortunately, Virginia thought far enough ahead to smuggle her expensive jewelry out of the country when she first heard about the IRS seizure. Some went with Hauser and Peter; others, with another friend. So the crowd never did get its hands on the diamonds and gold jewelry it expected to see in the collection of the mob Queen.

A 250-pound man named G. T. Gregson, who asked reporters to refer to him as "Greg Himself," pounded the gavel at ten A.M., and the auction began.

A man named Smith bought a leather belt for ten dollars. Another man, who refused to be identified, purchased Hill's .25-caliber pistol and two boxes of shells for thirty-six dollars. A silver blue mink coat went for the highest price. The coat was valued at $5,000 and sold for $1,550, purchased by Michael Feudersinger, who said he bought it for his wife, who was "just about Miss Hill's size." A brown ranch mink went for $925. A white mink cape valued at $3,500 sold for $750. A man who gave his name as Dr. Roger Anderson of Seattle bought them both. A woman who refused to give her name bought a brown sable for $750. It had been appraised at $5,000. The two garbage cans sold for four dollars; a laundry basket, for a dollar-fifty.

A man named Gehrig got swept up in the excitement and found himself the owner of a pair of cheap plastic earrings and a ring for ten dollars. The ring was covered with flour. When he washed it off, it turned out to be a diamond. It was Virginia's wedding ring.

Hill's attorney, Anthony Felice, came to the auction to watch the bidding and make sure the government kept accurate records of the sales. When he told his client about the odd ring, she immediately recognized it as her wedding ring, which she claimed Bugsy Siegel had given her, and they contacted the government agents supervising the auction. She asked them to find the man who bought it, explaining that it was her wedding ring and that she had taken it off to bake a cake and was kicked out of her home before she could retrieve it.

The agents agreed that it was the very least they could do to help her get her wedding ring back. Fortunately, Gehrig returned to the auction the following day. He told agents the ring was appraised at $450, and he refused to return it to Hill. He apparently recognized a collector's item when he saw one.

The first day of the auction had turned into a madhouse. It took more than six hours to sell off all the items displayed on the front lawn and in the living room. The temperature soared past the ninety-degree mark, but the bidding was quick, though the items sold for far below their worth. More than $3,000 was raised in the first three hours. At the end of the first day, the government collected more than $10,000. The house itself went on the auction block the second day.

Virginia hid in her motel room. She took the phone off the hook, closed the drapes, locked the door, and drank herself into oblivion.

The next day, August 3, Hill's house went on the block. It had been appraised at more than $35,000. Two hundred people showed up. Most wanted nothing more than a chance to tour the home and had no intention of purchasing it. Only one man offered a bid, Jack Vertrees, the man selling the home. He offered $30,237, and his bid was accepted by the government. He also assumed the unpaid mortgage of $15,487, which was the balance left on Hill's loan.

In all, the sale raised only $41,000 against the unpaid balance of $161,000. If the government had tried to get top dollar for the house and Hill's clothes, it could not have raised more than $60,000. There was no way Virginia Hill would ever be able to pay off the bill. And there was no way, she vowed, she was going to jail on what she believed was a trumped-up charge.

She fled Spokane with nothing more than the clothes on her back and a small amount of cash in her purse.

On September 25, 1951, Hill applied for, and received, an Austrian passport under her real name, Onie Virginia Hauser. She traveled to Florida, then to Texas. All the time she was being watched by federal agents. She sent word, through an emissary, to the Clover Bar. Epstein was to meet her in Houston.

He was also followed by the authorities, who made one mistake. They sensed that Epstein planned to rendezvous with Hill and assumed they could arrest Hill and Epstein together in a quiet raid on their hotel room. When Epstein arrived under an alias, he was greeted by Hill's longtime Mexican friend, Maj. Luis Amezcua, who had crossed the border into the United States under diplomatic immunity. His status also prevented the American authorities from taking any action against him or his companions. Epstein and Hill were both safe from federal hands as long as they were with Amezcua. They beat the U.S. government.

The trio checked out of their hotel on October 12 and quickly dashed across the Mexican border by way of Laredo. The three checked into a hotel in Mexico City, and Epstein went his own way. Many people assume that Hill had set the escape up as a way of helping Epstein. He was able to roam free, out of the reach of American authorities, and unwind for a while. He eventually returned to the United States. After seven years of legal battles, he finally won his fight against Kefauver and the authorities.

As for Hill, once safely across the border, she stood on the side of the road, faced the United States, and spat on the ground. "I will never return. Those rats in Washington can do what they want now. They've got everything I ever had, but they ain't gonna get me. They hurt me, and I can't forgive any of them."

Then, with one last yell, she shouted at the top of her lungs, "Fuck you, America. And all those fucking jerks who ruined the country." Whether she meant the government or the Mafia is not clear.

Virginia claimed she intended to forget about America and the government agents who had ruined her life. She was quickly forgotten by most of the American public as well. When she was mentioned, it was in small blurbs, relegated to the middle or back pages of newspapers. The woman who once captivated and titillated the country had become yesterday's news.

One July 14, 1952, a small article appeared showing that some of the old Virginia was still alive and kicking. Virginia was in Vienna with her husband, Hans and sixteen-month-old son Peter, relaxing at an unnamed, "fashionable" resort. According to the article, she hit a cameraman with her tennis racket when he tried to take her picture. Apparently she had found some money somewhere, recovered her jewelry and sold some of it for quick cash, or had a secret financier. Either way, she was not struggling financially. She was back in the high life, hobnobbing with the wealthy, relaxing, playing tennis, and still commanding center court in the foreign press.

But the U.S. government was not finished with Hill. Though she was out of the country, the IRS wanted to make sure that she either stayed out or wound up in jail if she ever returned. It indicted her for income-tax evasion for the money still owed to the government after the Spokane auction. And the federal authorities also took an unprecedented step that seemed unduly cruel and unjustified. The government was hell-bent on destroying what was left of the Queen of the mob.

22

Up until this time Hill had only faced a civil suit from the government for back taxes. Her assets were attached and sold. But now the government was seeking a criminal prosecution of Virginia Hill. U.S. Attorney Norman Neukom said he would take his charges to the Los Angeles grand jury and push for a so-called net-worth indictment, the same rap that nailed Mickey Cohen and other gangsters. The net-worth indictment was basically the amount of the outstanding debt, plus a fine and a jail term if Hill ever returned to the United States.

The tone of the process seemed rather harsh on the surface. But according to witnesses, Hill owed the government more than $131,000. A hearing was set for February 24, 1953, in Los Angeles.

Before the hearing, the tax agents laid out their facts and figures in a press conference so that everyone could get a clear picture of what Hill actually owed and how the government arrived at its conclusions. It wanted to make sure that absolutely no one sided with Hill in believing that she had been railroaded, persecuted, or victimized by the government. The agents began their meeting with a simple statement:

We would like all good citizens and taxpayers of the United States to understand how Mrs. Virginia Hauser became the subject of intense federal scrutiny. Through her own admission, on the stand, in front of the senate committee and the nation, Mrs. Hauser gave a set of numbers she stated as to be her expenses. In a meeting before the hearings she also was specific as to how much money she had spent during several given years. The Internal Revenue Service has conducted a thorough investigation into these expenditures and has found these numbers do not correlate with those given by Mrs. Hauser on her income-tax returns.

Then the federal authorities unveiled the chart. It showed that Hill spent $242,826.79 during the six years in question. She paid federal income taxes of $27,488.54, which would have left her a net income of $102,381.46 to spend. The Internal Revenue Service added this sum to her declared income and found a tax liability of $85,954.99, plus penalties of $45,085.98. That left the total owed $131,040.97.

The IRS took the position that Hill "falsely and intentionally omitted" the correct figures from her returns.

The IRS agents informed the press that Hill did offer a formal reply through her attorney, Joe Ross, of Beverly Hills, who had been Bugsy Siegel's lawyer. The letter was received and filed by the IRS on November 26, 1951. In the letter, Ross "admits that petitioner Hill had available for expenditure during the years 1942 to 1951, inclusive, amounts in excess of the amounts of her taxable income for the years 1942 to 1948."

The letter, which wove through assorted legal mumbo jumbo, also stated that Hill:

alleged that said excess amounts available for expenditure was [sic] derived in part from amounts on hand prior to the commencement of the period of years from receipts during said period not constituting taxable income under the Internal Revenue code.

In short, Hill admitted, sort of, that she probably earned more than she declared. But she did not believe that the additional amount was taxable according to what the IRS considered taxable income. Neither side really believed any of it. While Ross stalled for time, the IRS put pressure on Hill as it prepared its indictment.

While the Treasury Department scrambled to nail down its case against Hill, the FBI placed her under surveillance. Agents were ready to move in the moment she moved from Vienna. Somehow Virginia had obtained a passport, but it was issued for her as an Austrian, not American, citizen. In effect, Hill had given up her citizenship. By doing so, the U.S. government could make it difficult, if not impossible, for her to return to America. It also could label her an "undesirable alien," much as it had done with her husband, Hans. The FBI also was ready to grab her if she requested a visa or clearance to return to the United States.

Then the government did an about-face in its attitude toward Hill. The Treasury Department and the FBI joined forces and agreed that their mutual interests could best be served if they allowed Virginia back to the United States. Both agencies wanted to use Hill for information against the Mafia.

Hoping to lure her back to America, the government decided to keep her old U.S. passport active and did not move to revoke it, though she had, in effect, given up her American citizenship when she took an Austrian passport. It hoped she might be forced to use the U.S. passport if she ran into trouble on foreign soil, as had happened in Paris and Mexico. It also believed that if it made no attempt to extradite her, Hill might believe she was even welcome back to the United States. Income-tax evasion was not an extraditable offense, and the government could not move in that direction, anyway, but it reportedly hoped Hill would not be aware of the law and mistake the inaction for a sign of a change in its attitude toward Virginia.

But Hill was no innocent and naive girl. She knew that the moment she set foot on America soil she would be arrested and what little cash or personal articles she had left would be confiscated. Hill, Hauser, and Peter reportedly drifted from one European resort to another. Hauser taught skiing while Virginia socialized; both were apparently too busy to spend much time with their two-year-old boy. Peter played with the local children and was raised and educated by the most expensive nannies money could buy.

Virginia was receiving money from somewhere. But no one

knew where. Foreign newspapers carried stories that Hill and Hauser met with architects and bankers to "lay plans to build the most expensive ski resort in the world." Echoes of Ben Siegel and his Las Vegas resort. The resort never materialized.

There were reports that Virginia and Hans traveled in two Mercedes-Benzes, paid cash for everything, and never seemed to want for jewelry, tailor-made clothes, or furs. On a mountain-climbing expedition, which was strictly a gathering of the social elite on the French Riviera, Hill and Hauser wore custom-made outfits; Hill wore tailor-made hiking shorts, a halter top, and, observers said, way too much makeup. Though she was only thirty-six, Virginia looked well into her forties. She obviously tried to hide the wear that by now showed in her face.

If Hill seemed unaffected by her situation, Hauser had dramatically changed. The once stoic "ski bum" now doted on his wife, comforting and defending her to anyone who dared make an unkind remark or reference to her past.

Actually neither had realized that they were not at all accepted by Europe's rich and famous. They were invited only as social oddities and objects of curiosity. They called him "Herr Hill" and her "Frau Gangster" behind their backs.

Bored, restless, and still on edge from the long-distance pressure they must have felt from U.S. authorities, Virginia and Hans maintained their now-normal routine of hopping from one city and one country to another. They traveled to Hong Kong, Paris, Italy, and finally to Switzerland, where they stayed for a time in the ski resort town of Klosters, the European getaway for the very rich trying to avoid the limelight.

Hans spent most of his time on the slopes, while Virginia drank more than ever, hoping to wash away any memories of her past life. The couple was not aware that the U.S. government had prepared to stage another fight against Virginia. This time it would go further than seizing her assets. Now the government was ready to indict her for fraud and play upon the motions of the press and the public to unite against Virginia and her husband. The first step in the plan against the Hausers took place in Los Angeles.

Treasury authorities in Los Angeles had planned on going before the grand jury to win its tax-fraud indictment in late February 1953. But for some reason they delayed their plans for seven months. Several people familiar with the case offered varying opinions for the delay.

One woman who had worked in the Los Angeles office of the IRS—she is now retired—believes the case was delayed because the prosecutors did not have strong enough evidence to bring before the grand jury, especially since Virginia Hill was out of the country and therefore inaccessible for questioning on the stand. She also believes that the Treasury Department had not yet presented Virginia in a bad enough light and that public sympathy for her, as a "victim of the mob and the heartless American government," could work against it.

The government had portrayed Virginia Hill as a mob moll, the Queen of the mob, a woman of corrupt morals, and a rich underworld socialite who had diamonds, furs, and expensive cars at her disposal. But many in America who had followed Virginia's life during and after her Kefauver appearance seemed to have a much different view.

Those who offered opinions or shared in gossip seemed to believe Hill was a victim not only of the Mafia but of a desperate attempt by the government to deport or imprison anyone connected with the underworld. Hill appeared smug and confident on the witness stand during the Kefauver hearings, but somehow she had endeared herself to the public. The highly publicized auction of her house and personal items in Spokane only solidified the average citizen's sympathy for her. Most people felt that Virginia had tried to put her years with the mob behind and start a new life as a wife and mother, which was a very American "up from the bootstraps" thing to do. Many believed that by attacking Virginia, a married woman and an independent, self-made lady who overcame a poor background, the government had attempted to destroy a person who epitomized the very best in American values. The Treasury Department's move against Virginia had backfired and had made Hill a heroine in the public's view.

The Treasury Department had no choice but to postpone its indictment of Virginia on tax charges. It had hoped that the public would forget about Hill if she faded from the newspaper headlines and front pages. Federal prosecutors also needed to taint any positive opinion of Virginia, so they set about to depict Hill as anti-American. It made certain the public knew she "cheated" the IRS out of tax payments while "honest, hard-working citizens" paid their fair share. Moreover, the government portrayed her Austrian husband Hans as a Nazi. Though World War II had been over for nearly a decade, anti-German feelings still ran high. For most Americans, that hatred included Austrians and anyone or anything connected with Germany.

The opportunity for the Treasury Department to turn the tide against Hill presented itself in the spring of 1953. A special House of Representatives committee had been established in 1938 to investigate any activity it deemed "un-American." Just before World War II, Congress passed several laws forbidding Communists to hold certain jobs in the government or defense industries, and employers forced workers to take "loyalty oaths."

On October 20, 1947, the House Un-American Activities Committee (HUAC) opened hearings in Washington, D.C., targeting the Writers, Directors, and Screen Actors guilds, which the committee had seen as the root of communism through so-called subversive movies and their influence over the country. Scores of studio executives, writers, directors, and stars were called to offer testimony about the "red influence" in Hollywood. Workers were fired, executives demoted, and movies shelved as one witness after another pointed a finger of guilt at another or flat out refused to participate in the proceedings. The hearings ended a year later. Ten writers and actors who had refused to answer the committee's questions were convicted of contempt of court and blacklisted. By the early 1950s, the number accused of Communist alliances swelled to four hundred, and the nation seemed immersed in anti-Communist fervor.

In February 1953, Wisconsin Republican senator Joe McCarthy picked up where HUAC left off. With "pro-American" zeal he hoped to establish a public image as the "defender of American values and virtues." As chairman of the Senate's Committee on Government Operations and head of the Permanent Subcommittee on Investigations, McCarthy began a prolonged investigation into subversion in the Voice of America, the State Department's international radio station. Interrogation of workers was carried intermittently on television, though often the hearings escalated into courtroom drama as riveting as the Kefauver hearings as employees accused one another of Com-

munist activities in an effort to save their own jobs. Soon
McCarthy expanded his witch hunt to include the entire government and the country.

The McCarthy anti-Communist hearings went public on February 16, 1953, in Washington after a series of closed-door
hearings in New York. On February 18, the Voice of America's
director resigned, and McCarthy's panel subsequently voted to
ban the works of 418 authors it considered subversive.

The ban produced public outrage and polarization about the
McCarthy committee and the Communist threat, which quickly
became the country's favorite topics of discussion. In March,
the McCarthy panel traveled across the country in its quest to
weed out Communism in America, much as Kefauver had done
to seek out racketeers. The proceedings were first televised on
February 19, 1953, for two hours each day. Within two weeks,
the program became the number-one show in the country.

In a political climate where it was attack anyone who seemed
to be against traditional American, conservative, middle-class,
and patriotic values, the Treasury Department seized the
opportunity to move against Hill. This time it would not incur
the wrath of anyone who may have sympathized, or at least
empathized, with her plight. The department approached
McCarthy about a possible deal to extradite Virginia Hill as a
witness for the committee.

The government's purpose was twofold. Tax fraud was still
not an extraditable offense, so Senator McCarthy might be able
to force Hill back to the United States. Once here, she immediately would be arrested on tax-fraud charges. McCarthy
could then get "star" value for his hearings and publicly interrogate Hill about her "Nazi" husband and her tax problems and
allude to Communist connections among her friends in Europe
and Mexico. The government could offer her leniency in the tax
case in exchange for her testimony, or vice versa. As the IRS saw
it, both sides would win.

McCarthy turned down the request. The senator believed
that Virginia Hill was "old news." She could offer nothing
new to his proceedings; nor could she shed any real light on
the "Communist problem" or bolster his already high public
profile.

Treasury Department internal reports recorded on March 5,

1953, and April 9 of the same year show that IRS authorities took their cause to HUAC, which was still conducting its own anti-Communist investigations. HUAC was not interested. The IRS would have to find another means to bring Virginia Hill home.

The federal government went to work and sorted through Hill's finances. Virginia left no formal records of expenditures and income outside of her diary and the receipts from her Sun Valley stay. She had kept few receipts of her track winnings, and the IRS already suspected that there was a vast discrepancy between her winnings and what she had declared on her tax forms. The treasury agents began their investigation with the paperwork compiled during the previous probe, which had resulted in the seizure and auction of Hill's Spokane home and possessions.

The new investigation lasted approximately one year. Agents retraced Virginia's steps. They went to the racetracks she frequented in Illinois, New York, and California, combed through her investments, and interviewed neighbors, nightclub operators, and resort owners. The government finally had enough additional evidence of fraud to file charges.

The Treasury Department pleaded its case before a federal grand jury in Los Angeles in May 1954. A tax-fraud indictment against Hill was returned on Wednesday, June 23, 1954.

The jury found evidence that Hill had skipped the country still owing $80,180 in back income taxes. It also uncovered other discrepancies on her back tax reports, among them allegedly deducting travel between Chicago and New York as a business expense. The IRS also disallowed many deductions.

The prosecutors detailed expenses for each year in question by resurrecting the records of the initial probe. The grand jury ruled in the government's favor. U.S. judge Ben Harrison issued a bench warrant for Hill's arrest, with bail set at $10,000.

Assistant U.S. attorney Norman Neukom had summoned a long list of witnesses who testified that Hill spent massive amounts of money at resorts, hotels, and stores, specifically stores in Beverly Hills. The witnesses produced evidence in the form of receipts and bills to verify the outlay of cash on what Hill claimed to be a meager income.

To paint a clear picture of Hill both for the benefit of the jury and the reporters who had packed the courtroom, Neukom reiterated Hill's lusty love life with Bugsy Siegel, her involvement as a money runner and launderer with the mob, her ties to Las Vegas, and her all-too-sudden rise from Alabama poverty to Beverly Hills wealth.

He put on a grand display. He played on the nation's anti-Communist sentiment by describing Hill as a criminal who refused to pay her fair share of taxes and consorted with undesirables in the Mafia who were bent on destroying the country with drugs, crime, and corruption. He said that Hans Hauser was an alien, a Nazi who never bothered to become an American citizen. He explained that Hauser fled to Chile rather than face deportation or become an American legally. Neukom said that once Hauser had gotten all he could out of America, he took off for greener pastures. He called Hauser an unfit father who took his baby son out of the country, away from his mother. Neukom made certain that Virginia and Hans Hauser would be presented to the court and the public as criminals with anti-American beliefs.

Neukom stated the facts with just enough embellishment to turn sentiment against Virginia Hill. He had also managed to pin a pro-Communist label on Virginia.

After he painted a not-so-rosy family portrait, Neukom restated the government's previous action against the woman he had labeled the government's number-one "pro-Communist tax evader." He made it clear that Hill could not be prosecuted as long as she remained outside the United States because she could not be extradited for tax evasion.

"But if she so much as steps foot on American soil," Neukom vowed,

the Treasury Department, federal agents and the U.S. government will grab her so fast that Mrs. Hauser will never know what hit her. The United States government cannot and will not abide by any citizen who believed he or she can flaunt the laws of this country while honest, hardworking citizens pay their fair share and do their duty as citizens. This country will not and can not stand for anyone who defies the laws.

The Treasury Department had won the day. With the four-count indictment standing against Hill and the news media portraying her as a brazen hussy who cheated the government and "partied it up while the rest of America paid the bill," any positive feelings toward Virginia had severely eroded in the public's eyes.

Then the government landed its final blow.

The Treasury Department issued a "Wanted" poster against Virginia Hill Hauser. It was the first time the government had issued such a poster against a woman for tax evasion. Hill was now not only pictured as a whore and a cheat in the public's estimation; she had become a desperate fugitive and criminal.

More than a thousand posters were printed and distributed to major post offices in every town from Maine to California. In some towns around Chicago and Detroit, "Mob fans" ripped them off post office bulletin boards to keep as souvenirs. In other places, postal workers had to keep replacing them because of the graffiti that continually cropped up on Hill's photo. The poster turned up in magazines and on television. Virginia Hill Hauser was back in the public eye, but it was a sorry and sad vehicle for her return to fame.

The Treasury Department made no move to contact Virginia and inform her of the indictment or the poster. It knew it did not need to. Hill got the message. Some of her acquaintences in the United States mailed copies of the poster to her along with newspaper articles about the indictment and the vow to prosecute her if she ever returned to America.

In Klosters, Switzerland, where Hill and Hauser now had taken up residence, word about the trouble spread. Virginia was gawked at, pointed to, and spoken about in foreign tongues or whispers. Some locals found it intriguing that a "gangster" resided in their midst. Others found it appalling and moved to ostracize her from the more elite social circles.

Virginia reacted by drinking herself into an unconscious stupor nearly every night. The alcohol was beginning to take its toll both physically and mentally.

Virginia became bloated; her face and eyes grew puffy. She developed the very hard appearance of an alcoholic who had endured a great deal of stress. She spoke with a slight slur whether or not she had something to drink. It seemed that she had an alcoholic buzz all hours of the day or night, and most nights she could not sleep. She also appeared to have a constant hangover, for she exploded into a violent, screaming rage at the least provocation. And she also began to imagine things. Her recurrent paranoia about being followed had developed into an obsession, so that she began to double-lock doors and look in closets and under beds for intruders. She also accused Hans of cheating on her and Chick, who had remarried and come to Switzerland for a visit, of taking drugs when they had not.

On several occasions, she physically attacked Chick and his new wife. They had enough of Virginia's abuse and left. Hans grew tired of the verbal and physical abuse and took off on skiing and hiking expeditions without her. She called Hauser every foul name she could think of and told him to get out of her life for good.

The once-fast-talking, quick-thinking glamour girl was now a stress-ravaged, foul-mouthed drunken outcast with few friends, a dwindling supply of cash, and nowhere to go. There are reports that she attempted suicide yet another time but was found by "an attendant" of a local bar who rushed her to the hospital.

Hill once again cried out for help, and one more time someone was there to hear her. But it was never the person or people she wanted to intervene, never Hans or Epstein or Joey A, but usually a stranger.

Virginia was forty years old and desperate and now believed she had only one choice: to try and return to America and face whatever punishment the government would mete out to her. She made a long-distance call to her old Spokane neighbor Clifford Rice, who still worked as a federal agent and had some pull with the Treasury Department. Rice promised Virginia that he would do what he could to convince the government to give her a fair hearing and possibly negotiate some sort of financial settlement. He also made her understand that the federal authorities believed they did not need to bargain with her.

Then she tracked down Joey Adonis, who had fled the United States for Naples in January 1956. Though he was out of the country, he was still connected to scores of gambling parlors, nightclubs, and mob-owned businesses across the United States. Adonis still wielded as nearly as much power in the underworld as he had when he controlled the gambling rackets in New York. Virginia hoped that one phone call or visit with

Adonis would convince her former lover to use his clout with the Mafia to influence corrupt government officials.

Virginia had to convince both the government and the mob that she was serious about wanting to get back into the United States. She knew she needed leverage to negotiate her position. To do that, she was finally going to play her trump card. Virginia Hill was ready to pull out her diary.

23

The underworld had fallen apart. Joe Adonis and Lucky Luciano had been deported and were living in Italy. Jack Dragna was the next to go. Frank Costello was in jail, Mickey Cohen was in prison, Charlie Fischetti was in trouble with both the mob and the government. It seemed everyone from Hill's "old gang" was either behind bars, deported, or running scared. The only one who escaped the law was Joe Epstein, who still forged ahead, making book and laundering money out of Chicago. Epstein laid low.

Hill sent a plea for help and advice to Epstein through the Clover Club in Chicago and received only a brief reply. She was told that the Clover Club had been raided and closed by the FBI. The bar had been a known front for bookmaking and prostitution. The Chicago police commissioner had acted on pressure from the local press and requested that Mayor Richard Daley revoke the bar's license and shut the place down. Daley capitulated and ordered the raid for Friday night, along with an edict to seize the books and arrest anyone unfortunate enough to be there that evening.

Daley and the police were beaten to the punch. Not surprisingly, word got out, and the owners shut the club down on Thursday, removed every scrap of incriminating paperwork, and relocated the bar's prostitutes to other mob-owned establishments in Chicago. In what was supposed to be "the raid of the decade," with a massive sweep of the underworld, only three uniformed officers showed up. They arrested six people, four of them bartenders, a twenty-three-year-old prostitute, and one man named Jerry Kaufman, who told police he had bought a 50 percent stake in the bar three years before.

The only solid evidence of wrongdoing was offered by the prostitute, who said that as many as thirty hookers regularly worked the bar until it was closed the previous night.

The bartenders said they took a "commission" from the girls, marked a slip showing the girl's name and the amount taken in tricks, and placed it in a special box behind the bar. Kaufman, they claimed, collected the slips every night when he tallied the cash-register totals. Then he allegedly gave a cut to the mob.

They were each booked, then released on $2,000 bond. The one question that the FBI and the press wanted answered remained a mystery: "Where was Joe Epstein?" If his name was mentioned by anyone arrested in the not-so-spectacular raid, it was kept from the press. Hill's name was also conspicuous by its absence. If she had been an owner, as alleged, her name did not appear in the records after the raid. Kaufman later claimed that she sold him her stake in the bar.

Epstein still kept a low profile. Although Hill knew that he was her only ally in America, she was hesitant to call upon him for help. She realized that any contact she made back home would immediately be intercepted by the government, the FBI, and the Treasury Department and used against her and anyone she had tried to contact. She still did not know whether the government had located Epstein, was still trying to question him, or had a warrant out for his arrest for his defiance of the Kefauver Committee. She played it safe and called Cliff Rice.

Hill had hoped to work out some sort of deal with the government, with Rice serving as the intermediary. She said she would come home, turn herself in, and serve her jail term on the condition that it would be brief and, when served, her debts would be erased.

Rice laid it on the line. With the strong sentiment in the country against anyone who defied the government and the fact that many of the old-time mobsters had been run out of the country or imprisoned, the Treasury Department believed it had no reason to negotiate any sort of deal with Hill, who was in no position to bargain. Moreover, to do so would set a bad example: that it pays to cheat because the government will, in the end, not punish tax evaders.

Rice told Virginia that the government would not negotiate any deal without an incentive to do so. She would have to face a judge and jury. With good attorneys, she could explain her side: how she was abused by the mob and forced to work as a courier for the Mafia and that she personally had never harmed anyone. She could also claim that the government had already seized everything she owned and had literally driven her from the country. Rice believed she might have a good case if she presented a strong and emotional enough defense.

Apparently, Virginia agreed. She sent word to attorney Joe Ross and asked him to move forward with arrangements so she could turn herself in and stand trial. The one major stipulation was that no one know when she would arrive back in America except for the government. All bets would be off if word leaked out to the press. She told Ross, "If I see one fucking reporter bastard anywhere, it's off. Fuck 'em all if they go back on their deal. I don't need it that bad."

Though Virginia did need the government's cooperation "that bad," she still tried to put up a tough front. She was determined not to let anyone know how far she had deteriorated mentally, physically, and emotionally. She understood that if she showed the slightest weakness during those delicate negotiations, the government would realize just how desperately she wanted to come home. Sadly, Virginia failed to understand that she really had no one left to come home to.

Ross worked quickly from his Beverly Hills office and sent word of his client's interest to federal agents in Washington, D.C., Los Angeles, Spokane, and Seattle. Because she still considered Spokane her home, he also contacted associates in the state of Washington to work on her behalf. They met with Treasury agents and the FBI and slowly started hammering out a workable agreement.

The government offered several conditions upon which it would allow Hill's return to the United States:

1. She must revoke her Austrian citizenship and reinstate herself as an American citizen. The government claimed it would expedite the paperwork so that the change could be

made quickly. Once her citizenship was reinstated, the government could then move forward with its case against her.

2. The government would seek a three-year prison term, with time off for good behavior. That would allow Hill, if convicted, a jail term possibly as short as one year. If Virginia Hill caused no problems in prison, the government would intervene with the parole board and "encourage" a favorable parole.

3. All financial claims against Hill would be dropped and the tax debt considered erased once she served her prison term.

4. She would cooperate with the government in giving evidence and testimony against any members of the Mafia with whom she had had personal dealings, including Joe Epstein.

Virginia agreed to the first three conditions but exploded into a fit of hysterical rage when she was handed the fourth condition. She told Ross, "How the hell can I turn in the one fellah who's always played square with me?" Ross advised her to go along with the deal, but Virginia refused. She asked Ross to move in another direction, to try and find a lenient judge who could rule in her favor without all the compromises the government demanded.

Ross found one, Samuel Driver, a federal judge in Spokane. Driver was not a mob associate; he was an honest judge but tended to favor tax evaders who offered to work off their debts. Driver believed that it was far better to collect some of the debt, whether it meant settling for a dime on the dollar or paying off the debt with work trade-offs, than to put the evader behind bars, where he or she would cost the taxpayers even more money. Driver agreed to meet with the Spokane and Seattle attorneys on Hill's behalf.

A meeting was called for March 1958. Driver, representatives from the Internal Revenue Service, and legal representatives from Ross's office and Spokane met in Seattle to work out the arrangement.

The IRS said it would not prosecute if all partners in the situation agreed to a deal. It restated its four conditions that it hoped Hill would be convinced to accept. Ross's office told the group that Hill said she would refuse to turn in any information on Epstein, who still apparently had been a thorn in the government's side. The government men threatened to abruptly end the negotiation and all future talks unless Hill agreed to all four conditions. Judge Driver intervened.

According to government documents, Driver told the IRS that justice would best be served if it backed off on its insistence that Hill help the government locate Joe Epstein. Instead, Driver suggested that the case against Epstein remain independent from the Hill-Hauser case. He told the government agents to reopen the file against Hill and base any involvement with Epstein on testimony she had already offered during the Kefauver hearings and in other interrogations. The attorneys from Ross's office agreed, further stipulating that the government could not now try to force Hill to reveal additional information about Epstein. If it was not already on record, it could not be broached.

The IRS agreed to withdraw the stipulation that it directly interrogate Hill on Epstein's whereabouts but then added several other conditions to its list. It wanted Hill to provide, to the best of her knowledge, a detailed list of how much money she had received from Epstein and how and where she had spent it. The government also demanded that Hill provide a list of contacts, including, but not limited to, bookmakers, betting agents at racetracks and other sporting events, and people who may have been involved, either directly or indirectly, with money laundering or fencing of stolen property, with the understanding that Hill would not be implicated or prosecuted for her involvement in the illegal activity.

Finally, the government insisted that Hill provide any information she had, or any documented evidence she might obtain, on the activities of so-called underworld associates—those already deported or those still not apprehended.

To Hill's attorney, Joe Ross, this new round of stipulations seemed even more outrageous than the previous requirements. Ross refused to even approach his client with the government's demands. The IRS stood firm.

Virginia became increasingly impatient. And she was running out of money. She had repeatedly borrowed from Hans's family. Whether Virginia finally felt uncomfortable asking for more or the family refused to give her more money is unclear, but after several "loans," the Hausers turned Hill away.

Hans's participation in this whole ordeal is also unclear. He was frequently off on skiing expeditions and usually brought seven-year-old Peter along on the tours. It seems that Peter bounced from parent to parent but stayed with his father more often than with his mother. Those who knew Virginia at this time say she loved Peter and cared deeply for him, as did Hans, but because of her personal crises and drinking she was not always able to deal with the basic problems of raising a young boy. Virginia had to worry about herself as she frantically tried to find a solution to her problems.

When word reached her that the IRS was stalling and had piled on even more conditions to her return, Hill realized she had no alternative. Afraid that her telephone was bugged, even in Switzerland, and suspicious that she was still being followed, Hill sent a cryptic note to her attorneys in Seattle. The note stated that she had "some pretty good leverage that the IRS boys would be interested in." What she was referring to as "good leverage" was her diary.

Though the people mentioned in the diary, with the exception of Joe Epstein, were either deported, in jail, or dead, Hill knew that her ledger was still filled with enough incriminating evidence against the New York and Chicago mobs that the government might pay a handsome price to get its hands on it. Many of the mob-owned businesses detailed in the diary were still active, and the diary gave a clear picture of what businesses were fronted by the mob, how much money was laundered through the operations, and who took part in the payoffs. The diary also incriminated several politicians and law enforcement officials. Hill knew she had the key to her freedom.

The government was interested, and Judge Driver was about to move forward and make the arrangements for Virginia to come home. What was supposed to be the final journey was apparently going to begin.

Then a tragedy abruptly derailed the deal. On September 12, 1958, assured that his participation in the deal was over and the matter was now in the hands of attorneys and the IRS, Judge Samuel Driver and his wife began their vacation by driving to California. Along the way they stopped in the town of Woodland, near Sacramento. As Judge Driver stepped out of his car near a corn field, he walked directly into the path of an oncoming car. Driver was rushed to Woodland Clinic Hospital, where he died, never regaining consciousness. The driving force behind Hill's homecoming plan had passed away. Questions remain as to whether or not the death was a tragic accident or murder.

Driver had acted more as an intermediary between the IRS and Hill's attorneys than a courtroom judge. Now the wheeling and dealing rested solely between the two factions. Joe Ross knew that a new judge would not be as lenient as Driver, would not encourage the Treasury Department to agree to a deal, and would probably grab the case as a surefire shot at publicity and fame. Without any outside legal support, Ross knew that only one bargaining chip remained. That was the diary. But he was not willing to release it unconditionally and advised Virginia to sit tight.

Though Ross was Hill's attorney, he had not actually seen the diary; he had to take Virginia's word that it did exist and accept her explanation of its contents. Confident that Hill was telling the truth, he informed the government about the diary and its possible ramifications in respect to the Mafia still operating in Chicago and New York. He also spelled out its far-reaching effects on the politicians named in the document. The federal authorities seemed impressed and agreed to wave the conditions that had focused on Hill's turning evidence against her mob friends in exchange for the document, which the government claimed achieved the purpose of the conditions. In effect, the government was making no concessions whatsoever. It was trading Hill's verbal account for a written history that was perceived as being the more accurate of the two.

Realizing the government had conceded nothing, Hill's attorney insisted that all charges against her be dropped in exchange for the diary. He explained that there had to be some incentive for Virginia's turning the document over and, by doing so, putting her life in jeopardy. The IRS refused to budge. No deal.

Ross gave Virginia the ultimatum presented by the government: a three-year sentence with a parole review after one year, with the promise that the government would intervene on her behalf in exchange for her diary or verbal account of the dealings of the Mafia. The attorneys offered no recommendation to their client to either accept or reject the deal. Virginia told him that she "smelled a rat" and accused the lawyers of selling her out. She said she did not need their help and fired them. It was the last time she communicated with Ross or tried to work a deal with the U.S. government. From this point on, she was on her own.

Believing that she had no friends left in America, Hill tried to seek financial support and help from old friends in Cuba. Before Castro took over the country, the New York, Los Angeles, and Chicago mobs had invested heavily in nightclubs and hotels on the island. Cuba had become a popular tourist town and a weekend vacation spot for the wealthy because of its close proximity to Florida. Cuban mambo music was the rage in the 1950s; bandleaders such as Xavier Cugat and Desi Arnaz were at the height of their popularity. Americans wore "Cuban" heels on their shoes and played the bongos. Cuba was a wild country where gambling, prostitution, and hot night spots were plentiful. Even American movie stars invested in the country, including George Raft, who lost nearly everything when Castro seized all American assets.

Hill had traveled to Cuba frequently when she lived with Ben Siegel. They had invested tens of thousands of dollars in hotels and casinos and reaped even more in profits for themselves and the mob. Virginia believed she still had friends on the island, though by the early 1960s Cuba was considered a hostile country and Castro and Kennedy were nearing a missile crisis that threatened to blow up the Western Hemisphere. Twenty years had passed since she was the mob Queen traveling with the handsome Ben Siegel, but she had convinced herself that she was welcome and would be as warmly received as she had been in the old days.

Virginia landed in Cuba but never got out of the airport. As she stepped off the plane, army guards grabbed her, spirited her off to a holding area, interrogated her, took what little money she had, and ordered her out of the country. Though she carried an Austrian passport, she was still an American, and a notorious one at that. Virginia was convinced that someone in the U.S. government had tipped off Cuban authorities that she was about to enter their country. She vowed never to trust anyone in the U.S. government again.

Hill then tried to enter Mexico. At the airport in Mexico City, she tried to contact her old friends. They were either unreachable or insisted they only "vaguely" remembered her. All were aloof and cold. There was no mistaking that Virginia Hill was not welcome. She could no longer do anything for the Mexican officials or society crowd. She was a wanted woman with no money to flash around town. They certainly did not need her.

Depressed and dejected, Hill headed back to Switzerland and skidded into a week-long manic-depressive drunken stupor. She did not answer the phone or contact her husband or son. Her life was slipping away, and she could not have cared less.

What finally drew her out of her stupor is not known, but shortly after the beginning of the New Year in 1966, Virginia pulled herself together and plotted what would be her last attempt to get back on her feet. She wired two men, played one off the other, and used her diary as a weapon against them both.

24

All previous accounts of Hill's last days either gloss over or completely ignore the final months of her life. The accounts offer no involvement between Hill and her former gangland associates Joe Epstein and Joe Adonis. Most historians or crime buffs incorrectly assume that because Adonis had been deported, he was no longer involved in New York crime and had no contact with Virginia Hill. In fact, most people believe that their relationship had ended when she ran off with Ben Siegel.

Quite the opposite is true, especially during the last months of Hill's life. Virginia Hill had kept in contact with Adonis sporadically through her occasional money laundering and various fencing scams. Adonis had also kept tabs on Hill since he had spared her from the fate that had befallen her lover Siegel. From that moment on, Adonis was considered responsible for Hill's life, in the eyes of the underworld, and her actions. Now that Virginia was in serious trouble, both financial and legal, Adonis shouldered the responsibility.

Adonis's underworld associates, still active in New York's crime families, were well aware of Hill's diary. Though the bulk of the information was old and focused on "old-timers," such as Luciano, Siegel, Costello and Adonis, they knew of the possible incriminating link between the underworld and legitimate businesses the diary could expose. Most mobsters, such as Costello and Lansky, hoped Virginia would merely fade away and remain out of sight in Switzerland or Austria. However, they knew there was little chance of Hill's remaining silent when she suddenly went public about her diary.

Newspapers across America and Europe published stories that Hill had first mentioned the day before her testimony at Kefauver. She had told newspaper reporters that she was going to write a book, naming names and letting "everybody know just who these people are and what they really are doing." She also said that she had kept detailed records of everything she saw or did and that these records would serve as the main source of information for her book.

The story did not create much of a sensation at the time, and Hill never mentioned anything about her diary or book again. But fifteen years later, in 1966, forty-nine-year-old Virginia Hill believed it was her last chance to return to her old life of high society and lavish parties.

When the U.S. government seemed unimpressed by the diary and held firm to its demands that she return to America, Virginia sent a telegram to "Mr. J. Epstein, 162 East Ontario Street, Chicago, Illinois, U.S.A." It set the last turbulent episode in her life in motion.

The complete story of Epstein's involvement with Hill toward the end of her life has never before been made public. But by piecing together information obtained through federal files, newspaper accounts, and extensive interviews with former associates of Joe Epstein, we now have a clear indication that Epstein had been loyal to Hill right to the very end; in fact, he made every effort to save her life.

According to gangland associates, sometime in January 1966, Epstein received a telegram from Hill, who had now separated from Hans Hauser. Hill had moved into a mid-priced hotel in Salzburg with Peter, who was fifteen years old. Peter had taken a job at the hotel as an apprentice waiter. Hans offered no financial support and was working full-time as a ski instructor, traveling across Europe. Hill said that she was in dire straits and needed money in a hurry.

The contents of the telegram were recalled from memory by two of Epstein's friends. Hill wrote that she needed "a package" to carry her through the next few weeks and that Epstein should make "the usual arrangements." The telegram seemed normal. There would have been no problem as far as Joe E was concerned except for a line at the bottom: "Unless prompt—notes public." Epstein fully understood what she meant by that last line. Unless he sent the money she needed promptly, she would go public with the diary.

Epstein had been a loyal friend to Virginia, though he had put some distance between himself and his lady friend since the Kefauver hearings. He always considered Virginia a friend and always viewed her fondly. Epstein was shocked that a woman whom he believed he had done so much to help and promote would now assume such a tough and threatening posture. Joe E was appalled. He sent Hill $10,000 in cash with a short note: "Accept medicine . . . return or packages stopped."

It was now Virginia's turn to be outraged. She had long considered Epstein an insignificant, bookwormish clod who hid behind layers of fat and thick black glasses. Hill told friends and newspaper reporters that Epstein "was no man," implying his homosexuality without a direct accusation, and that his only value was in his ability to invest money.

If Virginia despised Epstein because of the type of man she believed him to be, she now hated him for dragging her into a life of crime. By the end of her life Virginia had even convinced herself that if it were not for Epstein she would have been happily married and had a "normal" life, two children, a house in the suburbs, a station wagon, and a doting husband who played golf every weekend with his friends. The more Hill drank, the more her hostility toward Epstein intensified.

She believed the funds that Epstein had sent her were due her as a return on the money she had asked Epstein to invest for her. Though it seems highly unlikely that Hill could ever had accumulated enough money to earn a sizable return on her investment, both she and Epstein insisted that every dime he sent to her was legitimate. Both claimed that no money she received or spent was a bribe, payoff, or money earned through performing a job for the mob. Everyone, from Hill and Epstein to the underworld and federal officials, knew that the real source of the money had nothing to do with investments. Everyone understood that the money was initially earned by Hill for her work for the mob and later came as gifts given by Epstein.

When Virginia received the telegram demanding she return to America, she was outraged and spiraled into a massive depression. She drank herself into oblivion once again, and when she emerged, she downed a handful of sleeping pills.

Those who knew of the incident claim that, one more time, Virginia did not intend to commit suicide. When she drank, she often lost track of how many barbiturates she was taking, and when a few did not have an immediate effect, she absentmindedly took more until she overdosed and went into a coma.

Once again, she was rescued by a hotel maid, who phoned for help and saved Hill's life. The incident was later reported as another suicide attempt.

Word reached Epstein, who became greatly concerned that Virginia might have attempted to actually take her life out of despair. Epstein believed that the latest attempt was triggered by his order to return to America and quickly sent Virginia another bundle of cash, this time believed to be nearly $20,000. Associates suspect the cash was intercepted somewhere in transit, because Epstein never received confirmation that it had been received. They suspect that someone in the hotel had caught on to the scheme and had opened the package and stole the money.

Neither Epstein's demand that Virginia return home nor his subsequent telegram inquiring about the whereabouts of the latest package were ever acknowledged. He assumed that Hill had chosen to discontinue all forms of communication, which caused him a great deal of anxiety, for he continued to believe that he had overstepped his bounds and forced Virginia into suicide.

When several weeks went by without word from Hill, Epstein sank into a deep depression himself. Though he felt more comfortable in public, since the government had years ago abandoned its attempts to ferret him out for questioning after he dodged the Kefauver Committee, he rarely socialized and grew weary of strangers and the ever-present reporters who still considered Epstein "good copy" because of his notorious past. He limited his social engagements to his relatives and close friends, who understood that most questions about Virginia Hill were taboo.

Hill had been one of Epstein's last links to the "glory days" of the Capone mob. His old cronies were no longer in power, and while he still ran the Chicago downtown Loop bookmaking operations, he was considered one of the old-timers and out of step with the new wave of the Mafia, which had no qualms about dope dealing and even going so far as to murder Mafia wives if they got in the way.

Sam Giancana and Tony Accardo now shared control of the Chicago outfit, and neither thought much of Joe Epstein, though Epstein and Accardo had a history together that went back to the old days of Al Capone. Epstein was an outsider who saw himself becoming a relic. He needed Virginia Hill now more than she needed him. Both were desperate people trying to recapture the past.

While Epstein lamented Hill's absence from his penthouse in Chicago, Virginia turned toward Joe Adonis in Italy for help. Though Adonis's power had somewhat been undercut by his deportation, he still had strong, solid connections with the underworld in New York. His primary ally was a man named Gaetano Ricci, better known in the underworld as Tony Ricci or Tony Goebels.

Goebels lived in Brooklyn and conducted business throughout the United States and in South American and Europe. Anywhere the Mafia was operating in the world, Goebels had a hand in the till. No major decisions were made without his knowledge or approval, and he was kept abreast of everything involving the Mafia. He was considered its "chief expediter."

Goebels melded the factions of the Mafia into one megaorganization, turning it from a collection of underworld gangs that operated solely within its geographic boundaries into one national corporation, with selected bosses calling the shots at various levels. Bosses were assigned to handle territories and specific business operations much as vice presidents of a major conglomerate.

The Mafia still answered to people like Costello, Lansky, and Giancana and a Kansas City, Missouri, racketeer named Joseph "Little Joe" Guerera, who controlled the rackets in Wisconsin and had connections with the Chicago outfit.

When Adonis received a telegram from Hill asking for a "settlement" in exchange for "silence," he apparently understood exactly what she meant. Adonis sent word from Naples back to New York informing the leaders of the Luciano mob that Virginia might be trouble. Adonis then chose to remain silent and ignore her telegram.

In late February, Adonis received a second telegram from Austria, far more explicit than the first. Sources say the telegram spelled out Hill's intentions to the letter. In effect, she told Adonis that unless he started to send her regular cash payments, on the scale of those previously provided by Epstein, she would reveal the contents of her diary to the U.S. government. She also made it clear that she had gathered enough information about the Luciano mob to put those still active in jail for murder and extortion and close down scores of mob-fronted businesses.

Then Hill made what many consider the most dangerous move of her final days. She went public with her plans and believed that the press, which she had always despised, could help protect her from any adversity by publicizing the fact that she had a diary. Hill thought that if she was killed, the press would immediately print a story that would cast suspicion on Adonis, the New York crime cartel, or even Joe Epstein because they were the apparent focus of her ledger.

Once again, Virginia misjudged the press. A small item appeared in late February in an Austrian newspaper, which was picked up by UPI and repeated in various small publications in the United States. It said that "former mob queen Virginia Hill is in the process of compiling her memoirs" and "the story should prove intriguing if Miss Hill names names as she promises to do." It alluded to the fact that no manuscript had as yet been prepared, nor had any publisher expressed interest in making an offer for it.

With the release of the story, the IRS made one last offer to strike a deal. The government said it was now willing to compromise to get its hands on the diary, provided that prior to any agreement it could review the diary to make sure it actually existed and delivered what Hill had promised.

Virginia rejected the offer through attorney Joe Ross's office in Beverly Hills. She said that once the authorities got ahold of the diary, they would photocopy it, and the IRS would have the information it wanted for nothing. Virginia gave Ross, whom she briefly rehired, an abrupt reply to the government's offer. "Fuck 'em." It was the last time she ever communicated with

Ross and the U.S. government. She knew she would never return to America.

Her hope now was to either get money out of Adonis or reestablish communication with Epstein. Both seemed unlikely.

Hill sent yet another telegram to Adonis on the assumption he had either seen or heard the story about her writing her memoirs. Whether he had heard the story or even took her threat seriously, Adonis still played possum for several weeks in Italy.

Then, the last week in February 1966, Virginia received a small manila envelope in the mail. It contained $3,000 in cash. It came from Adonis. There was no note or any indication of why he seemed to change his mind and gave in to Hill's demands.

Those connected with the underworld have offered several explanations for this seemingly odd turn of behavior.

Some believe that word came from New York ordering Adonis to comply, for a time, so that he could learn whether Hill indeed possessed a diary or whether she had been bluffing. If she did have such a diary, then he would have to force her to turn it over to him.

Others claim that because Adonis intervened on Hill's behalf during the Bugsy Siegel execution, he was responsible for any action, adverse or otherwise, Hill might take. Moreover, if that was the case, Hill's exposure of mob rackets, while informing on her old friends, would become Adonis's responsibility. Any negative consequences that resulted from Hill's diary would also befall Adonis.

Both explanations have some validity. The underworld certainly needed to know exactly what information Hill possessed, and Adonis was indeed responsible for anything Virginia might do that could endanger Mafia operations.

If Adonis assumed that a mere $3,000 was sufficient to silence Hill, he was wrong. Once she received the money, she assumed that Adonis was a willing pigeon ready and eager to pony up for her silence.

Hill sent Joey A a short letter to his villa in Naples, Italy. It said that since the $3,000 was such a small pittance compared with what the diary could buy on the open market, Adonis should make another cash payment of $3,000–$5,000 and send it to Hill's hotel in Austria. The package should arrive on a Wednesday so that she would know to watch for it to make certain it would not be stolen.

The second cash payment of $3,000 supposedly arrived on March 1, 1966. Joey A told associates in New York that he regretted sparing Hill's life and was now paying for his one act of kindness. He vowed that never again would he help anyone unless it directly benefited him. He would keep that promise.

25

Time was running out on Virginia Hill. Chances are she probably knew it. She had successfully shaken down one of the world's most notorious gangsters and made it clear she would tell all unless he continued to meet her cash demands. A woman with Hill's knowledge of the Mafia and background of toughing it out on the streets certainly must have known that no gangster would sit still for a double cross or shakedown. Adonis had submitted to both, and from a woman. He had to make a move or his reputation would be sullied. At worst, he would present himself as a has-been who had become vulnerable. Virginia had forced his hand.

Adonis had given Hill at least two payments of three thousand dollars. What she had done with the money and why she craved still more from her former paramour are unknown.

Crime sociologist Dr. Lorraine Blakeman, an expert on underworld psychology and criminal behavior, suggests that Hill was mentally near the end of her rope and paints a portrait of a broken and desperate woman.

> From what I've heard about Virginia Hill at this time, and from what I've read, it seems clear that she was hitting her bottom, bottoming out. To put it in layman's terms, she was desperate to recapture what she thought was her glo-

rious past and saw that it had completely slipped away. In her mind she had convinced herself that she held an even greater position in the mob than she once had, and with that, convinced herself that she could control these men. Hill was obviously a paranoid woman with delusions of grandeur. I'd go so far as to say she was on the verge of a complete breakdown, if she wasn't already in the midst of one.

There's just a very sad desperation there. She was reaching out in the only way she knew how. She wanted attention, not money. She probably had it stockpiled somewhere. The money was not at all the issue, I believe. It was attention. She wanted these guys, the government, whoever, to take notice again, to respect her and to look up to her. She believed that as long as she had the evidence to destroy them, she could force that attention and respect.

It also seems clear to me that it was all a delusion. If they were at all intimidated by her, they would not have kissed her off like they did. Joe Epstein cut her off for a while, didn't he? I'm sure that to Adonis the money was a pittance, nothing. Just to appease her. I think it was more of a brush-off or an insult than a real fear of her. And I think she must have known it. Adonis must have seen what was happening, too.

I think Hill herself was dangerous, not because she had any power but because she was a loose cannon. That's always dangerous to any type of organized criminal society.

Hill was definitely a loose cannon. Convincing herself that she actually had Adonis on the run, she tracked him down at his villa in Naples and telephoned him on March 20, 1966, at 4:48 P.M., something that she had been solemnly warned against doing because Adonis suspected both his lines and Hill's were bugged. They were.

The following partial transcript was provided by sources in the FBI who had obtained a copy of the conversation from law enforcement authorities in Italy. The transcript appears to be edited, and parts of the phone conversation were inaudible and therefore not detailed in the document. Nor is it indicated exactly who was speaking, but it can be assumed that at least two of the participants were Adonis and Hill. It is suspected that

Adonis had picked up the phone but refused to identify himself at first. The transcript shows that Hill had incorrectly assumed she had bargaining power with Joey A:

> Four double telephone rings.
> "Hello?"
> "Yes."
> "Joe?"
> "No."
> "I want to speak to Joe Doto."
> "Who?"
> "Joe. Joe Doto."
> Silence; no reply.
> "This is you, I know. You know who this is, too. Stop playing games, damn it."
> "What do you want?"
> "Joe."
> "What do you want?"
> "I need to see you."

There are three or four sentences that were inaudible and therefore not transcribed.

> "There. I can see you there."
> "No."
> "Listen you son of a bitch. I need twenty thousand more. If you [inaudible] believe you can just walk away you're wrong. [inaudible]."
> "You have what you wanted; didn't you get it?"
> "Some. Not all."
> "No more."
> "I have to turn it over."
> "You do that."
> "Joe, listen to me. Remember back in New York? C'mon. Let's get together. Old times."
> "I don't know what you are talking about."
> "Don't pull that act with me. You [inaudible]. You're not going to leave me like this. I have the final word, not you. I can always go back and give them what they want."

The conversation ended. Duration: four minutes, thirty-two seconds.

The phone conversation was obviously strained. Many of the sections that were "inaudible" were apparently Hill's expletives, which were deleted from the transcript.

Though Virginia's threats were seemingly vague in wording, their intent was clear. She was ready to release her diary. As a result of the conversation, Adonis became convinced that Virginia Hill had lost all rational sense and was ready to give in to the demands of the Internal Revenue Service; that she would tell all she knew about the money-laundering scams and mob operations in exchange for leniency.

Virginia's information was old, but there was no way of knowing what she would or would not fabricate under oath out of hatred and revenge. Adonis had to intervene. He already had received the approval to kill her from the Mafia hierarchy.

As word of Hill's explosive diary had spread throughout the ranks of the underworld, so had rumors that Hill had to be silenced, that she was out of control. Joe Epstein had definitely heard the talk in Chicago but did nothing to intervene. He later told an associate, "Virginia made her bed. She had to lie in it. There was nothing I could do to help. I tried. She pushed me off. You can only go so far with someone. Then it's up to them. Virginia knew the score. She knew the consequences."

Epstein realized it was now only a matter of time before he received the news that he did not want to hear.

Two days after her phone conversation with Adonis, Virginia Hill literally vanished from her Salzburg hotel. Peter, though a teenager, could handle himself well enough to be left alone, and Hill was probably not concerned about leaving him. It was not the first time she had wandered off for days at a time, and Peter had no reason to believe that foul play was at hand, nor was his curiosity aroused as to her whereabouts. She left no word as to where she was going, nor did she take any large amounts of cash with her.

The last two days of Virginia's life has never been accounted for before, but underworld sources have all independently provided a similar story, given to them directly by Joe Adonis or friends of his who had heard the same tale. True or not, there is no way to confirm this account.

According to these sources, Hill flew to Naples to see Adonis. The date was Tuesday, March 22, 1966, two days after their phone conversation. She did not send word ahead of time and planned on surprising Adonis at his villa. As she stepped off the plane, two of Adonis's men grabbed her, one on each arm, and ushered her into a waiting Mercedes-Benz. The car belonged to Adonis. How he had known of her arrival ahead of time remains a mystery. Adonis never offered an explanation.

Hill was taken to a well-furnished private home outside Naples where she was locked in a back room that had been used as a den. She was made comfortable, offered a drink and food. The two men who had "greeted" her at the airport then left.

One half hour later, Adonis entered and quietly closed the door behind him. He poured drinks and tried to make Virginia as comfortable as possible. Adonis was as stoic as ever but tried to put Hill at ease by talking about their days together in New York and what had happened to their lives. The two reminisced for several hours. A meal was brought in, and the two ate. The time was approximately five-thirty P.M.

Adonis had always maintained to friends that Hill had made a pass at him and that he accepted it. He claimed the two spent the night together and made love most of the night. But Adonis was a self-inflated egotist and braggart. It seems highly implausible that Virginia would bother with Adonis, considering the way he had treated her, unless she assumed she could get something out of him, such as money or some assurance that he would "fix" things for her if she returned to the United States. Adonis initially offered neither.

The following morning, Wednesday, March 23, Hill and Adonis shared breakfast and got down to business. Adonis claimed that he tried to talk Virginia out of the diary, but it was to no avail. He then claimed that he tried to reason with her, to convince her to calm down and learn to live life as a European, as he had. Again, Virginia refused to listen to him.

Hill allegedly demanded money; this time she wanted $10,000. It was more than her previous $3,000 demands but enough, she claimed, to get her back on her feet and buy a house for herself and Peter. Adonis reportedly gave her the money: $10,000 in cash; hundred-dollar bills in American money. Hill agreed to cool down. She also agreed never to contact Adonis again.

She left his home early that morning, with the intention of

catching a train back to Salzburg. Adonis ordered his two friends to accompany Virginia to make sure she "arrived safely."

Adonis kissed Virginia Hill on the cheek and said good-bye. Virginia gave Adonis a puzzled look, as if she suspected there was more to his good-bye than he made it appear. They looked into one another's eyes for several moments; then Adonis walked out of the house, away from Hill. She climbed into the Mercedes with the two men, and they drove off.

26

Forty-nine-year-old Virginia Hill was found dead on Thursday, March 24, 1966, near a brook in Koppl, Austria, a small town near Salzburg. Her body was discovered by two hikers who had been walking down a small path near the water and reported the discovery to the local authorities. Initial reports said there was no apparent sign of violence, and it seemed there was no struggle or fight for life. An autopsy was ordered.

The following day, the coroner's court ruled Hill's death a suicide by an overdose of poison. The local police then claimed they found a suicide note confirming the coroner's finding. In the note Hill allegedly claimed that she was "tired of living" and "fed up with life."

The medical examiner who performed the autopsy and later fielded reporters' questions only said that she "apparently had taken her own life with an overdose of poison, most likely barbiturates," and that there was "no reason to believe-otherwise."

Obituaries reported her frequent suicide attempts as if they were a confirmation of the conclusion drawn by the Austrian authorities. It all seemed to add up.

Hans Hauser engaged in only limited conversations with reporters, playing down the fact he and Hill had been separated and that the former mob Queen was living in what some newspapers now described as "a low-rent rooming house on a small side street in Salzburg supported by her 15-year-old apprentice waiter son." The press even tried to imply that the breakup of the marriage had triggered her suicide.

Later, Peter only said that he doubted his mother committed suicide, that she was not at all tired of life, as the reports had claimed. He insisted that she was probably murdered but could not generate a response from the authorities when he prodded them to open an investigation.

As far as the U.S. government, the Austrian authorities, the press, and the underworld were concerned, Virginia Hill had killed herself after a two-day drunk, during which time she wandered off, felt sorry for herself, wrote a suicide note, and downed too many pills. The conclusion was accepted as fact for more than twenty five years.

But the official story could not have been further from the truth. Virginia Hill did not kill herself. She was murdered.

Approximately three days before her death, Joe Epstein received a letter in the mail. Inside the letter was a key. It belonged to a safe deposit box in a bank on North LaSalle Street in downtown Chicago. There was no note, nor were there any instructions. Epstein knew it was from Virginia because of the return address, but he made no move to open the box. He must have known what was inside.

The day of Hill's death, on March 24, Epstein and a friend went to the bank and opened the box. Only one thing was inside: Hill's diary. It was wrapped in plain brown butcher paper and tied with string. The only writing was on the outside, and it was in Virginia's hand. "Open in case of emergency . . . or my death. Virginia Hill." Virginia had tried to make a joke, but she must have sensed something sinister would befall her. Just how the diary got into the box is not clear, but one can assume that she either had a secret confederate in Chicago, other than Epstein, or had slipped the diary into the vault during her wanderings around the time of the Spokane auction.

That the diary had turned up in Chicago and that Hill mailed Epstein the key shortly before her death would indicate that she sensed something was about to happen. If she had killed herself, she would have sent more explicit instructions to Epstein, and chances are, if she thought enough of Joe E to tell him the whereabouts of the diary, she would have sent him a farewell note.

Also, the timing of Epstein's retrieving the document is curious. Why did he wait until Thursday morning to open the box, for which he received a key on Monday? And why did he remove the diary almost at the exact same time that Hill was dying? Had he known the details of her death down to the minute? Epstein's actions leave too much to chance and coincidence. He must have had prior knowledge of Hill's fate.

A written inquiry by a third party to the Salzburg medical examiner's office has turned up two reports: one prior to the autopsy; another written immediately after. The first report indicates lateral bruises around Hill's neck. But the bruises were never mentioned in the second report, nor was it ever indicated exactly what type of "poison" Hill had consumed. The reports would seem to indicate that Hill had probably been forced to take the poison, the pills or liquid crammed down her throat. But the second report deleted mention of the bruises to ensure a finding of suicide.

In any event, the reports do cast at least a shadow of a doubt over the ruling that there were "no signs of violence" in Hill's death.

Perhaps the most convincing of all are reports of Adonis's actions during the mysterious last days of Hill's life.

The meeting at his villa was bizarre and implicated Joey A in some sort of conspiracy against Hill. When questioned about the two "mystery men" who approached Virginia at the airport, then escorted her out of town, five people independently confirmed the same story and identified one or both men involved. Four of these sources are connected to the underworld, one to the FBI. All but one have asked that their names be kept confidential.

The two men who approached Virginia in Italy were thugs who worked for Adonis. One, identified by all who had been questioned as Jackie "Two Black Shoes" Tiadori, had allegedly carried out several hits in Italy and Europe ordered by Adonis and others connected with the Luciano mob. As far as anyone knows, Tiadori never worked outside of Europe, nor did he ever come to America. He earned his nickname because of his penchant for shiny black Italian leather shoes.

Tiadori and his partner, whose name was offered by only two of those questioned and was not known as one of Adonis's regular assassins, intercepted Virginia at the airport, supposedly with prior orders from Adonis to carry out her execution. Those with inside information about the case insist that Adonis had planned to have Virginia killed shortly after the second "ransom" payment, approximately three weeks before her actual execution.

The scenario they provide seems plausible. Tiadori and his partner left Adonis's hideaway and drove to Koppl, where they got out of the car and walked with Hill down an isolated footpath. It is assumed that at this time Virginia must have known that she was about to die, if she had not suspected it when she bade her final farewell to Adonis. Tiadori, who was approximately six feet one and weighted more than 250 pounds, held Hill from behind, wrapping the fingers of his right hand around her throat while pulling her arms back in an arm lock. The bruises indicated in the initial report would conform to the marks made by a large man's hands.

While Hill was pinned, Tiadori's partner allegedly pumped a large dose of the sleeping pill Mogadon, also known as Nitrazapam, down Virginia's throat. Tiadori held her mouth shut until she swallowed. Though not a barbiturate, Mogadon, which was widely prescribed in Europe, would cause drowsiness, dizziness, and eventually a coma. Death usually occurs within an hour or so, three hours at the most, enough time for the men to get away before Hill died but strong enough to ensure that Hill could not get medical help in time to save her life. Adonis had reportedly used the drug in several other executions, and it was also the trademark of Tiadori's assassinations.

If Virginia had committed suicide, she broke the pattern of her previous attempts in many ways. The drug taken was different from the ones she had used during the other episodes. She reportedly had been using chloral hydrate as a prescription, and later, Valium or Librium.

In other so-called attempts she took only enough to pass out and timed her pill taking so that she would be found by a maid, her brother, or a friend. Psychologists always maintain there is no such thing as an "attempted suicide." If one wants to take one's life, he or she will do it when assured of succeeding. Hill only took pills when she was certain of being discovered. There was nothing typical about this final attempt, if it was indeed an attempt.

Tiadori never spoke of the incident. He died in Italy in 1976. He was never charged with the crime or with other murders of which he had been suspected.

Joe Epstein died on October 18, 1976, in Chicago, of a heart attack at the age of seventy-five. He died a bachelor and said very little about his affiliation with Hill to the press. He never released Hill's diary, nor did he even publicly announce that he had obtained it. When asked by a close friend why he did not sell it to the press or Hollywood, Epstein only replied, "It would be more trouble than it's worth." He never explained his remark.

Shortly before his death, he turned over the diary to a close friend who is losely connected with the Chicago underworld and who holds the diary today.

Joe Adonis disappeared from sight after 1975. Whether he is alive or dead today is uncertain. There is no record of his death in America, nor has any inquiry turned up any death record in Italy. There has been no mention of him in the press since the mid-1970s. If he were alive, he would be in his nineties.

Hans Hauser died of unknown causes in Austria in the 1970s. Details of his death could not be found in any records.

Peter Hauser is currently living in Europe. His exact where-abouts are not known.

As for Virginia Hill, her life will never be equaled. She was the only woman who associated with and was trusted by the inner circle of the Mafia, a position no woman has attained either before or since. Her life ended in tragedy, but she remained an independent and strong woman to the very end. Her only mistake was believing that she could capitalize on a sense of loyalty in men who had none.

The final and saddest irony in her life was that as a child she vowed never to trust a man or let herself be used by any man. Yet as an adult she trusted the wrong men and let herself be used by every one of them.

Jack Pignataro, a businessman loosely connected with the underworld, knew Virginia Hill in her "glory days." He also knew intimate details of her later years and subsequent death. He summed her up this way:

> Hill ran hot and cold depending on her mood and who you were and what you stood for. She had a sense of right and wrong, and more importantly, she had a sense of who she was. She was one tough cookie and one hell of a great lady. Virginia Hill was fire, and she was ice. I hope she finds peace wherever she is.

Index